MW00965184

Stephanie Alexander

Stephanie's Menus for Food Lovers

ALSO BY STEPHANIE ALEXANDER

Stephanie Alexander

Stephanie's Menus for Food Lovers

Photography by Simon Griffiths

VIKING
an imprint of
PENGUIN BOOKS

Viking

Published by the Penguin Group
Penguin Books Australia Ltd
250 Camberwell Road, Camberwell, Victoria 3124, Australia
Penguin Books Ltd
80 Strand, London, WC2R 0RL, England
Penguin Putnam Inc.
375 Hudson Street, New York, New York 10014, USA
Penguin Books Canada Limited
10 Alcorn Avenue, Toronto, Ontario, Canada M4V 3B2
Penguin Books (NZ) Ltd
Cnr Rosedale and Airborne Roads, Albany, Auckland, New Zealand
Penguin Books (South Africa) (Pty) Ltd
24 Sturdee Avenue, Rosebank, Johannesburg 2196, South Africa
Penguin Books India (P) Ltd
11, Community Centre, Panchsheel Park, New Delhi 110 017, India

First published by Methuen Haynes 1985
This revised edition published by Penguin Books Australia Ltd 2003

1 3 5 7 9 10 8 6 4 2

Text copyright © Stephanie Alexander 2003
Food photography © Simon Griffiths 2003

The moral right of the author has been asserted

Designed by Debra Billson, Penguin Design Studio
Food photography by Simon Griffiths
Author photograph by Mark Chew for *delicious* magazine
Other photographs by *Vogue Entertaining & Travel* (page xii), David Tolley (page 3),
The Age (page 5) and Mike Rayner (page 9)
Typeset in 11.5/14.5 pt Bembo by Post Pre-press Group, Brisbane, Queensland
Printed in Singapore by Imago Productions

National Library of Australia
Cataloguing-in-Publication data:

Alexander, Stephanie, 1940– .
Stephanie's menus for food lovers.
Rev. ed.
Bibliography.
Includes index.
ISBN 0 670 91185 2.
1. Cookery. 2. Cookery, International. I. Title.
641.5

www.penguin.com.au

Cover: Watermelon in rosewater syrup (page 26)

For my mother and father

Contents

ACKNOWLEDGEMENTS

It was a pleasure to work on the original edition of *Menus for Food Lovers* with Susan Haynes, who was wonderfully encouraging right from the dubious beginning of the book. The late Tony Hitchin was a most understanding and courteous editor who was instrumental in encouraging the book, as he persuaded me to write an initial series in *Home Beautiful* in 1980 and later to continue with my 'Bouquet garni' page in *The Epicurean*.

This book became the responsibility of several editors after Susan Haynes left Australia for London and as its imprint shifted and changed due to the publishing reshuffles that happened during the intervening years. I am happy that it has now come back to sit alongside most of my other titles at Penguin Books, under the caring and watchful eye of the Executive Publisher, my friend Julie Gibbs. Julie deserves a special thank-you for convincing me that *Menus for Food Lovers* should not be allowed to go out of print, as it documents an important phase in Australian culinary history. I would also like to thank the hardworking team at Penguin, especially senior editor Katie Purvis and senior designer Debra Billson, who have slaved over this book; Simon Griffiths for his wonderful photography; and Natalie Paull, who helped with the testing and styling of the dishes.

Thank you to all my staff, past and present, both kitchen and front of house, who are special and who make me feel special. Thank you, too, to all the thousands of food lovers who have spent an evening with us.

Preface to revised edition

It is nearly two decades since I wrote *Stephanie's Menus for Food Lovers*. I decided to revisit this piece of work after completing a book on the cookery and traditions of the south-west of France. Everything I read, everything I experienced and almost everything I tasted there reinforced the value of traditional knowledge. It seems that too often traditions are only seen as valuable once they are fading or have faded. Many of the dishes I have prepared over the years have been influenced by traditional knowledge handed on to me by my mother and grandmother and by their friends – women who enjoyed a sort of intimacy that was socially encouraged through the sharing of recipes.

This new edition is offered as a piece of Australian cultural and culinary history. As far as I know it was the first 'chef's book' published in Australia. In it I described my own work and my own world, and detailed my efforts to express myself through the world of food. Sometimes I think that nothing has changed in that world and then I read what I wrote in 1985 and realise that a great deal has changed. Our lives have changed, too. There is less time, less food, less meat and above all there is less skill. The dinner party has almost disappeared, although friends still enjoy simple meals together.

In revisiting the text I have sometimes squirmed, but I knew that once I allowed myself to doctor the menus I would have been writing a new book. So it has been left largely untouched. The original introduction has undergone a few minor changes and is still the most accurate and complete biography of me ever published. A few inaccuracies have been removed, a few phrases altered, and some text added to explain, expand or update. The design has been changed to make the work more accessible, and the dishes have been rephotographed to allow them to be seen in their best light. Here and there I sound very severe. I have mellowed since that time and these days would acknowledge that there is always more than one way to proceed.

Stephanie's Restaurant opened in 1976. After the initial excitement and euphoria came the reality of unrelenting hard work, which was fortunately leavened by my passion for that work and by the pleasure of sharing it with like-minded enthusiasts. By the time we had moved to Hawthorn in 1981, all eyes were upon us. I started to feel that an important part of my work was to pass on to others not just whatever manual skills I had, but, more importantly, my enthusiasm for, delight in and understanding of the potential of a wide range of ingredients, both those that were readily available and those that required more effort to find. This interest in 'product' was a new phenomenon when I wrote the book. In response to being frequently asked how I came up with the restaurant dishes, I also wanted to explain the thinking behind the construction and design of my menus.

With the benefit of hindsight, I can see the first glimmerings of *The Cook's Companion* in the text. The way I have insisted on explaining things reveals the mind of the former librarian, the researcher, the stickler for detail.

There was one fundamentally important event in the food world that took place in 1976. Two French journalists, Henri Gault and Christian Millau, coined the phrase 'nouvelle cuisine' to describe what they saw as a revolutionary and exciting new movement in several pivotal French restaurants. Not long after this I would visit most of those establishments: Michel Guérard's Les Prés d'Eugénie at Eugénie-les-Bains, Alain Chapel at Mionnay, and the Restaurant Troisgros at Roanne near Lyon, where I was to spend a fascinating week in 1982. It was impossible not to be influenced by what I saw and tasted. However, I was always uneasy at any attempt to label *my* work as nouvelle cuisine. I just saw it as an expression of personal style: always a mix of old and new, involving colours and scents, flavours and textures that I enjoyed.

The whole world seemed suddenly to have become interested in food. Food was the new fashion. Dinner parties were a favourite recreation, new food and lifestyle magazines appeared, cooking schools and gastronomic travel flourished, both within Australia and abroad, and chefs were the new stars. The movement was widely misunderstood, and many jokes were circulated about large plates and tiny portions. The dinners people cooked became more and more elaborate. It was in this environment that *Stephanie's Menus for Food Lovers* first appeared. It was aimed at those who wanted to cook for lovely dinner parties, wanted to emulate restaurant cooking and were prepared to spend hours, days even, creating masterpieces. It was also aimed at the new consumers, those who could be influenced to seek out the best and support the few struggling specialist suppliers. It was from these modest beginnings that we have evolved into the sophisticated food country we now are.

For a new generation of cooks at home, in our training colleges and in our restaurants and hotels, I hope this reflection of how we were may prove interesting and enlightening – and that the dishes will still taste delicious.

'*What does cooking mean?*'

'*It means the knowledge of Medea, and of Circe, and of Calypso, and of Helen, and of Rebekah, and the Queen of Sheba. It means the knowledge of all herbs and fruits, and balms, and spices; and all that is healing and sweet in fields and groves, and savoury in meats; it means carefulness, and inventiveness, and watchfulness, and willingness and readiness of appliance; it means the economy of your great-grandmothers, and the science of modern chemists; it means much tasting, and no wasting; it means English thoroughness, and French art, and Arabian hospitality.*'

JOHN RUSKIN, Ethics of the Dust

Introduction

About me. I was born on 13 November 1940, the eldest in a family of four children.

I am descended from Anglo-Saxon stock. My maternal grandmother had some Scottish blood, but she came from the north of England. My paternal grandfather's family hailed originally from Kent. No hint of hot sun, blue Mediterranean, olive trees, goat's milk cheese, garlic or any of the staples I love so much.

My father's world was divided between his love of books and learning and his practical skills of building and organising. My mother's world was cooking, painting, gardening and a thousand other enthusiasms.

She was enraptured with food. It was certainly not just the love of cooking and eating. It was a way to experience another culture. A trip to Sri Lanka was made more vivid by her re-creation of splendid curries with bunches of bananas, special hot sambals and raw cashew nuts cooked in squeezed coconut milk. Another holiday, in Japan, had her making sushi rolls – this was in 1955, long before Japanese food was appreciated as it is now. German friends taught her to make cake from ground poppyseeds and to assemble a Dobos torte. The Kugelhopf became our family birthday cake. These same friends often lunched with us and I remember being entranced by the sophistication of the cold buffet that the adults joyfully assembled. The blood sausage with cubes of fat and pink tongue in it, the crumbling white pudding, the caraway-seed bread (oh, how I hated the taste of caraway, but I couldn't have spoilt their pleasure by saying so), the soured cabbage and the pickles. And the amazing liqueur that Herbert drank with *real* flakes of gold fluttering in it.

From my grandmother, via my mother, I can say that I 'absorbed' (I hesitate to say inherited) a love of starchy foods – in my case mainly bread, rather than the

Opposite: In front of Stephanie's in Hawthorn, c. 1983 – the first Iceberg roses have bloomed.

baked and boiled roly-poly, dumplings and currant griddlecakes that Grandma used to make. I hardly knew my other grandmother, although family folklore declared that her baked apple sago was a masterpiece. My mother used to attempt it, and I always admired its clear, golden, rather leathery skin. Father always said sadly, 'It's delicious, Mary, but still not quite like Mother's.'

I did very well at school, and the automatic assumption was that I would go on to university and do something in 'the professions'. While still at school I read a lot, became interested in painting and cooked at my mother's side. Mum made wonderful Austrian doughnuts filled with sugar and rhubarb (I suspect she substituted the backyard rhubarb for the more traditional plums), she baked bread, she donned overalls and a netted hat to take up beekeeping and she pulled on thick gloves to prepare nettle soup. I cannot overemphasise the depth and extent of my mother's influence on my life and its subsequent directions. I went to university and returned home every weekend for another stomachful of Mother's food. I believe that nobody could have had such a passionate cook for a mother.

I spent my leisure time in Lygon Street, Carlton, and at the Victoria Market. To a whole generation of students Lygon Street was LIFE. It was certainly Europe. We discovered cheese and wine (albeit in coffee cups), and I remember my first taste of fresh stracchino – a real farm-made cheese. In the market Italians stacked the artichokes high, one started to buy baby zucchini, and raw fennel was tasted for the first time. Then there were lots of Greeks in the markets, and the olives were blacker and fatter. South of the Yarra one could find Dutch and German food – north of the Yarra was the Mediterranean and even the supermarkets stocked the enamel-bright olive oil cans. In romanticised biographical novels I read about the Impressionist painters, and the novels seemed to carry as many images of olive oil, crusty bread, garlic and hearty broths as they did of love, paint and tragedy.

After my degree I undertook studies in librarianship, and after graduating worked for ten years in a series of libraries, ranging from the BBC-TV library in London to municipal libraries and finally to school libraries, which I think I enjoyed most of all.

Whilst working in London in 1962, I noticed the poverty of eating in urban London – the beans and mash, the tearooms with trays of stodgy cakes and buns, Devon splits with fake cream, the yellow doughnuts with artificial colouring. It was a devastating contrast to cross the channel and find that the ordinary French family ate so well and with such enjoyment. I wanted to eat like this, every day of my life – a beginning, a middle and an end to every meal.

I was able to satisfy my dream of living in France. I was a confirmed francophile before I set foot on French soil, with my head full of Toulouse-Lautrec, Van Gogh, Carême, Escoffier and other evocative names. Firstly, from May to August 1962, I took a position as an au pair in the lovely town of Versailles. I had total

A busy service at Stephanie's Restaurant. What may seem chaotic is, in fact, highly controlled. Everyone had specific responsibilities to ensure that one hundred diners had their expectations fulfilled.

charge of a beautiful little French girl, aged six. One of the most important things I learnt during this time was the essential differences in the way a French family ate compared with what I had experienced in families up to that time. Meat was eaten only two or three times a week. Many meals were multi-coursed, often with simple soups, and always with delicious vegetable dishes and carefully dressed soft-leafed salads. Always a perfectly ripe cheese and, of course, always the bread bought fresh for each meal. On Sundays, a special piece of meat was prepared. This would have been the subject for serious discussion from at least the day before. The actual slow cooking was accompanied by lots of anticipatory smacking of lips and sniffs of the aromas. The dish was discussed in detail before it finally appeared.

I was usually in a state of greedy salivation by the time of the actual meal. The next major difference was that one slice only would be carved. I was observing at first hand what so many Australian diners still do not accept. Special meals have their ceremony, small courses are more satisfying than one enormous plate and, most important of all, the presence of an interested audience means that success is practically assured for the cook, barring some culinary disaster.

Next, from October 1963 to June 1964, I spent a year as a language assistant at the École Normale des Filles (a teacher training college) in Tours, in the Loire Valley. My duties were to conduct small classes in English conversation. The bonus of this job was that my social life was shared with the young French staff at the school. Furthermore, not only did I learn to speak fluent French, but I spent all of my salary eating at excellent small country restaurants throughout the Loire Valley. I developed a love and an appreciation of quality French regional food that I will have forever.

I learnt so much that year. I had the humbling experience of lunching every day with the students (120 of them) and staff, and there was a proper chef in the kitchen and each lunch was of an extraordinary standard. I was fresh from University Women's College and its appalling food – the staples of which were processed cheese slices, white and coloured cottonwool bread, tinned red jam and lunch-eon meat. Here I lunched on poached fish with real mayonnaise, followed by a pork cutlet, sauce Robert, some local Sainte-Maure cheese and fruit, or braised endives with a ragoût of rabbit and prunes and perhaps a crème caramel. I put on a lot of weight as I couldn't pass up any promising culinary experience.

Amongst all this eating and drinking I met and married my first husband, a tall, delightful Jamaican. I met Rupert Montague (known as Monty) on one of my many trips back to London and we were married in January 1964. Our daughter, Lisa, was born in May 1966. We decided to return to Australia and to attempt to sell West Indian produce to a population having no interest in or knowledge of such exotics as ackees, tamarind, guava, breadfruit and so on. I persuaded Monty that the venture would have more hope of success if we demonstrated how the dishes could be used.

Preparing the stuffed tripe voted the most creative dish at the third Great Chefs dinner, the Rothbury Estate, Pokolbin, 1981. The series of Great Chefs dinners was the interesting idea of wine authority Len Evans. Starting in 1979, they were amongst the first such occasions where equal attention was given to the food and the wine. They were held in the cask hall at the Rothbury Estate in the Hunter Valley and were memorable evenings. Chefs cooked in makeshift kitchens for one hundred invited guests and had a great deal of fun, as well as the odd crisis.

So started the first Jamaica House, sited in Lygon Street, Carlton. Three weeks prior to its opening Lisa was born. They were hectic, exhausting and terrible days to recall. We were absolute amateurs, we had no money, my baby shrieked and screamed hungrily, and we toiled on. It was probably the most harrowing period of my life. Jamaica House continued through three changes of venue (all in Lygon Street) until Monty's death eighteen years later. The marriage ended after three years and I was two stone lighter.

I resolutely turned my back on restaurants and went back to libraries. In the next five years I cooked passionately for myself and my friends. Preparing and serving a lovely meal meant a lot more than just good tastes. Through cooking I felt that I was able to embrace the world, show loving and caring. I felt that I operated in this craft with a sure touch and a confidence in my own judgement that I lacked in so many other areas of my life.

It was inevitable that I would come back to restaurants. It now seems a long gestation. When I met my second husband, Maurice Alexander, he was a barrister not very excited with the law and fresh from a long wander around the world after several years spent working in the excitement of Hong Kong as a Crown prosecutor. I have always been a persuasive orator (my grandfather won a public-speaking event at the famous Ballarat South Street Competition), and Maurice was persuaded. Once again I set up a restaurant.

The first Stephanie's Restaurant was established in 1976 in a single-fronted shop in Brunswick Street, Fitzroy, a few doors south of Johnston Street, long before Brunswick Street became the 'scene' it is today. It was successful, and many of its characteristics disturbed and changed the style of restaurants in Melbourne. The first Stephanie's was small, simple but serious. We served lovely food as carefully as we knew how. Our success threatened to be our undoing. We were too small, the toilets were hopeless, bookings were impossible. We continued there until May 1980, but we had to make a change – I wanted to find my perfect restaurant.

I found it in a National Trust house in Hawthorn. By now I had a second daughter, Holly, born in 1974, and she started her schooling just up the road at Auburn South Primary School. With the generous support of my parents, we were able to purchase the building, turn the first floor into a comfortable home for the two girls and ourselves, and set about creating something that I hoped would continually evolve into a very special place to delight thousands of people.

Stephanie's was the first restaurant in Victoria to offer a totally fixed-price structure. I believe that a meal should have a beginning, a middle and an end. We described our dishes rather than giving them fancy names. Our garnishes were meaningful. If we served a scented geranium leaf alongside the cream, that flavour had been incorporated into the cream. Working within our fixed-price structure, we have been able to offer beautifully balanced meals. We commenced making

Stephanie's at night. The Italianate mansion has a National Trust classification. The restaurant was on the ground floor and upstairs was the family home. This photograph was taken soon after the restaurant opened in Hawthorn, possibly in 1981 or 1982. Certainly it was before our beautiful garden was established.

our own bread and have long since made it known that all pastries, garnishing biscuits, ice-creams and stocks are made in our own kitchens. No booster or artificial flavour has ever been used at Stephanie's. Herbs from my garden and from my friends' gardens are used liberally. I used the contents of my store cupboard and my mother's pantry shelves – recipes for the spiced crab-apples and flavoured vinegars are included in this book. For those who noticed, the tiny posies in the first Stephanie's and the grander flower arrangements in the present Stephanie's are full of special messages. There are the first catkins from our espaliered *Garrya elliptica*, perhaps the incredibly scented native frangipani blooms or, in autumn, the drama of a branch of pomegranate.

I believe in encouraging personal style, be it in cookery, painting, writing, or any other craft or art. A recognisable personal style seems to me to be far more stimulating and exciting than attempting to tack onto some 'school' or 'movement' or fashionably identifiable trend. My own personal style is continually evolving and it is based on the totality of my experience, not merely culinary experience.

It is because of experiences I have had and tastes I have experienced that I push onward. To discover the special taste of grilled sweetbreads or to investigate and understand why the French and the Chinese prize cartilage in foods, or to create one's own boiling sausage, are wonderful discoveries, which lead to new thoughts and new dishes. The sizzle of boiling oil on the skin of a steamed fish is well known to the Chinese. Most French cooks automatically remove the skin of all fish fillets, so they have never experienced this. However, around about 1982 I was served at Girardet's restaurant, at Crissier in Switzerland, a tiny fillet of red mullet with a blistered skin. Did he derive the idea from the Chinese?

It has always been central to my style of cooking that the food be properly displayed. I say this instead of speaking of 'presentation'. This word has been used so much in connection with nouvelle cuisine that it is hard to remove from the mind's eye an instant picture of a lattice-edged plate with three variously coloured blobs. I care about an embroidered cloth, a hand-blown glass cup for the flakes of sea salt, the soft patina on a dinner fork dating from at least one generation ago, the delicate rose of a frilled glass Victorian lampshade. I also enjoy the extra shiver of excitement that comes from serving the caviar, or indeed the watermelon, in a chilled silver bowl, which mists with the cold.

I can see no farther than that I like to produce food that I like to eat myself. My cooking is usually based on French classical methods. Sometimes I have modified the methods, either as a result of my own tastes and experiments, or arising from my reading or speaking with someone as interested in cooking as I am. I try to cast my net as widely as possible, and I enjoy letting my personal life leave impressions on my cooking. My interest in Asian food is definitely enhanced by having friends who

Maurice and me dwarfed by one of the original and still-splendid
stained-glass and hand-painted windows at the restaurant.

are not only Asian or part-Asian themselves, but who are passionate about eating well. I try to use 'foreign' ingredients with subtlety and good taste, rather than to shock or distort a dish.[+]

Time passes. Imperceptibly I have become more critical. Every French meal is not wonderful. Some French restaurant food is overworked. Some French food is more concerned with fashion than with either taste or craft. One notices the strong tastes that shine from the dishes of northern Italy and the delicacy and freshness which are so central to South-East Asian dishes.

The unusual vegetables now easily available from the Asian markets are a timely reminder that while it is exciting to use a new product, standards of quality must always be present. In 1982, in Fauchon in Paris, I saw the most withered specimens of passionfruit being sold for a very high price. With superiority I was appalled that such spent, wrinkled shells should be offered for sale so far from their native West Africa, and yet I have been tempted by canned goods, which can do nothing but fleetingly remind me of the impossibility of transplanting or capturing some of nature's elusive flavours and textures.

And, at the end of it all, when I sit down and eat my favourite dishes, I do see again and again the evidence of a personal style. There is clarity and strength, the broths sparkle and the taste is deep, satisfying and real. The joy in home and hearth is never far away – many of the dishes have been enjoyed for a long time – so tradition, family, love, comfort and warmth all seem to be part of my personal style.

Interestingly enough, these qualities are important to me not just in relation to food but in all things.

[+] These days I would say that my inspiration is drawn from a broader repertoire. French regional cooking and most styles of Italian cooking are still my first loves, but I am also tantalised by the flavours of the Middle East and North Africa. Then there are the spicy flavours of Malaysia and the clean tang of dishes from Thailand, and on and on it goes. And only one lifetime to experiment.

How to use this book

These specific suggestions and general thoughts are intended to help cooks maximise the pleasure in their cooking. Each menu in this book has three main parts: a beginning, a middle and an end. Frequently, as I wrote each section, related dishes or alternative combinations suggested themselves. The result is that there are many extra recipes tucked away in each section. I hope that the index will help you locate these without effort. Most recipes are intended to serve six people; here and there, there may be leftovers, or a biscuit or batter recipe may yield more.✝

MENU PLANNING Be realistic in what you attempt. If your partner or a friend is an enthusiastic and efficient helper, you can be more daring with last-minute operations than if you are cooking on your own. Even for a special occasion one should not attempt two last-minute sautés in one meal, or anything similar.

Do not overload any meal with cream or butter. Rich food dulls the palate. Keep helpings small and avoid very long gaps between courses; 20 minutes between the first and second course is the maximum one should allow. Any longer, and your guests will have demolished the special bottle of wine you had planned to accompany the dish.

If the party is on the Monday of a long weekend and you have the inclination to cook all weekend, obviously your menu will be much more elaborate than if you left your office at 6 p.m. and the guests were due at 8 p.m.

✝ There is a regrettable hectoring tone to this section, as if the reader may be examined at the end of the exercise. I apologise. The temptation to rewrite was very great. Nowadays I believe that the most important things are to enjoy cooking a meal, to choose dishes that fit your mood and the available time, and to substitute ingredients whenever necessary. Too few people cook at all, and few of us are about to worry if we haven't got hot water ready for the serving spoons! But the advice is still sound if – and it is a big if – you want to cook like a professional and present a multi-course dinner.

BE ORGANISED   Professional kitchens are very organised. Ignoring for the moment whether the food from this organised place is any good or not, the food is possible because of organised procedures. A home cook, particularly a man or woman who is also involved in some other profession, needs streamlined organisation in order to make it possible to cook a meal after having done a day's work.

Make a list. Divide it into shopping for ingredients and things to do. I believe that this procedure is essential for every day, not just for a special occasion. For special occasions it is imperative, and should be done at least 3 days in advance. It is often not possible to obtain some unusual ingredients without asking your supplier 2 days in advance. Stocks and sauces will take up very little of your time, as they simmer while you watch television, but they must be started 2 days in advance. *Read recipes right through* and visualise the finished dish.

RESPECT FOR INGREDIENTS   When you have something special, serve it in a way that underlines its special character, and never let it be lost in a jumble of flavours. For example, heavy, green virgin olive oil deserves to be partnered with the very best tomatoes or raw fish or exquisite salad leaves.

RESPECT FOR EQUIPMENT   Provide yourself with strong, sharp knives and a sharpening steel or stone. Use solid, non-buckling pans. Ruthlessly throw out anything that wobbles, is cracked or is inefficient. Buy good kitchen scales.

USE GOOD BASIC STOCKS   It is possible to cook many dishes without using a stock. But no good cook should be fooled into thinking that a can of heavily salted consommé will achieve anything like the same result, and a stock cube will be even less successful. I have included at the end of this book a recipe for an excellent veal stock that will reduce to a quality demi-glace (pages 241–4). If you cannot manage this procedure or you have exhausted your reserves, concentrate your menu planning on dishes that build their sauce in the pan, deglazing with vinegars and spirits, using small quantities of wine and any juices exuded by the resting birds or meat, and perhaps finishing with a little cream or a knob of butter, either plain or any of the compound butters mentioned in this book.

EXPLOIT USEFUL TECHNIQUES

Use steam heat. You do not need fancy equipment. An enamelled colander placed over a saucepan and topped with a lid is a very effective vegetable steamer, and is perhaps the best way of reheating a small amount of pasta. To steam a fish, however, requires a flat surface, such as the perforated tray of a fish kettle raised on 2 upturned bowls, to permit an adequate level of liquid, or a baking tray supported by upturned bowls in an electric frying pan.

Steam is very fast. Vegetable purées and thick coulis sauces will steam to boiling point in 3–4 minutes with no worry about scorching or sticking. Steam also reduces waste. You heat only what you need.✝

Use a bain-marie. This term means to cook or to keep hot in a water bath. No special equipment is needed. A normal-sized baking dish can hold 2 or 3 jugs with different sauces. If the jugs fit neatly in one side of the dish, you can place a small scone tray on 1 or 2 upturned bowls in the other half and keep your foil-wrapped pork or beef comfortably hot and relaxed for 30 minutes at least.

Rest roasted meats. Because I have usually suggested cooking in the professional way, i.e. at high temperature, you must let the pigeon or porterhouse recover from the oven's blast. The meat will relax and stay quite hot. The technique greatly helps your organisation. Time the meat to be cooked just before your guests arrive. Take it from the oven, wrap it, keep it warm as mentioned above, finish your sauce using the pan juices, strain the sauce into the jug, keep it hot also as mentioned above, wash up and relax!

MISE-EN-PLACE   This is the cornerstone of kitchen organisation. It means to put in place. A wide variety of operations are completed either hours or minutes before any guests arrive. You can and should develop great *mise-en-place* skill.

- Vegetables are all peeled and cut and, if appropriate, blanch-cooked.
- Purées are finished and fully buttered and seasoned: they are waiting in the bowl to go directly into the steamer.
- Sauces are mostly completed and are in jugs standing in a bain–marie, in this case probably a baking dish half full of water on the lowest flame or the lowest point on the hotplate.
- Parsley, garlic, toasted nuts, baked croutons are all ready.
- Salads are washed, dried and crisping in clean cloths in the refrigerator.
- Spoons, whisks, fish lifters are all assembled, standing near the serving area in a deep jug or saucepan half full of hot water for instant rinsing.
- Plates are all counted and hot, and resting trays for meat are ready, lined with foil in warming ovens or over water on a low flame or the lowest hotplate.
- Dressings are mixed, coffee makers are clean and complete with measured coffee, cups are ready etc.
- The steamer is steaming.
- Cream is whipped, and cheese is at room temperature.
- All preparation tools have been washed, dried and stored so that the working areas are spotlessly clean.

✝ My preference for steam over a microwave is eccentric and old-fashioned. By all means use a microwave oven for reheating vegetable purées or sauces.

NOTE ON GELATINE[+] Different brands of *powdered gelatine* are available, with slightly different setting powers. The differences are minimal and not enough to worry about. The jelly will be cloudy.

> *1 metric teaspoon of powdered gelatine weighs 3.3 g*
> *1 sachet of powdered gelatine weighs 10 g*
> *2 teaspoons (6.6 g) of powdered gelatine will set 250 ml of liquid to a very firm jelly*
> *1 sachet or 10 g or 3 teaspoons of powdered gelatine will set 500 ml of liquid to an extremely firm jelly*

The *leaf gelatine* recommended and referred to throughout this book is 'Dr Oetker' brand, sold in packets of 6 leaves (a total weight of 10 g). It is widely available in supermarkets. Three Dr Oetker leaves weigh 5 g and will set 250 ml of liquid to a very firm, clear jelly.

Professional cookware shops stock a different brand of leaf gelatine, sometimes labelled 'titanium gelatine'. The leaves are much thicker and stronger than Dr Oetker. Each leaf weighs 5 g and will set 250 ml of liquid to a clear, slightly softer jelly than the same weight of Dr Oetker.

To dissolve gelatine leaves: Soak the leaves in cold water for 5 minutes, then remove them and squeeze well. If the dish you are preparing is hot (such as custard), drop the squeezed leaves into a little of the mixture, then stir this into the larger mass. If you are setting something cold (fruit syrup, for example), bring 2 tablespoons of the cold product to the boil and drop the leaves into it, then stir a little more of the cold product into this mixture before combining it all.

NOTE ON MEASUREMENTS Unless otherwise stated, all recipes in this book will generously serve 6 people. I prefer to weigh flour rather than use cups as I believe there is a greater margin for error in the case of flour. The weight of a cup of flour can vary, depending on how firmly the flour is tamped down.

THE FINAL WORD OF ADVICE Relax and enjoy it, whatever you cook. A bowl of freshly boiled eggs with good bread and butter and fruit with a dear friend is still a special dinner if you have only 10 minutes for preparation.

[+] I thought I understood gelatine, but the products in the marketplace have now made it very confusing. I cannot stress enough that before launching into *any* recipe that uses gelatine you must know what sort of gelatine you are dealing with. I still strongly recommend using leaf gelatine, as the leaves dissolve instantly without cloudiness or lumps, BUT you must know what leaves you are using. A recipe that specifies 3 leaves of gelatine could mean 5 g or 15 g. If there is no other guide (such as weight), you must look at the volume of liquid to be set and make a decision.

Simply perfect

MENU

~

STEAMED OYSTERS WITH
SEA–LETTUCE

JAMBONNEAU OF CHICKEN,
SPINACH NOODLES

WATERMELON IN ROSEWATER SYRUP

~

A lot is said about simplicity in modern French-influenced cookery. In my experience, it is very difficult to find a suitable definition of a simple dish. Certainly the communication between the diner and the dish is instant and direct. To produce a successful simple dish is perhaps the height of artistry, but 'successful' usually means that a great deal of thought, technique and care have been lavished on the dish without being apparent. Is a line drawing by a master draughtsman a simple work? I think it is. I remember the story in a primary-school reader about Giotto, who was asked to submit a work in order to demonstrate his ability to decorate the Upper Church at Assisi. He dipped a brush and drew a perfect circle. The inference was clear – to achieve so easily such perfect form implied great talent and artistry. I was very impressed with this story when I was nine years old.

Simplicity will succeed because of quality. A soft-boiled egg in a perfect tarragon-infused jelly is a simple dish. If the egg has been boiled one minute too long so that the yolk does not spill when the fork touches it, then the dish is unsuccessful. If the jelly is imperfectly clarified, it is unsuccessful. If there are specks of fat left on the surface of the jelly, it is unsuccessful. If the jelly is without sufficient flavour, it is unsuccessful.

Too stringent? I don't think so. To take short cuts that compromise quality or to misunderstand basic technique or the spirit of a dish are not acceptable reasons for producing sloppily executed, so-called 'simple' dishes.

This entrée of steamed oysters with sea-lettuce is a simple dish. In France it is common knowledge that one eats oysters only when there is an R in the month – this rules out summer (*juin, juillet, août*). There is a good reason for this. The oysters are in their reproductive season during the summer months, and the flesh becomes milky and soft. The sharp tang of the sea is diminished and the sensations are altogether different and less pleasant. A traditional Christmas Eve supper in France will include oysters. Of course there is an R in December (*décembre*) but, more importantly, it is cold. In the southern hemisphere we seem to be oblivious to the reason for this rule. So we still eat most of our oysters in the summer months, ignoring the fact that they taste better in autumn, winter and early spring. This dish, then, is intended as part of an autumn menu.

One must go to considerable trouble to obtain oysters still swimming in their liquor. You must either gather your own or buy them not only unopened but, as they say in the trade, 'unrumbled'. When oysters are harvested, they come complete with quite a lot of weed, mud, sand and minute crustaceans attached, the quantity and type depending on the habitat. The oyster distributor puts these oysters on a machine that turns them over and over and sluices them with water. In this way the weed and mud are removed, and the oysters are handed over to the splitters or professional openers. But not only sand and weed are removed during rumbling. One oyster rumbled against another means that the fragile and flaky lips of the oyster shells are smashed, and the precious juices start to seep out immediately. Therefore, oysters bought technically unopened but 'rumbled' are frequently a great disappointment. All one has is the extra effort of opening the oysters without the reward of the briny liquid.

So, when you decide to serve this lovely entrée, first hunt out a supply of unrumbled oysters. Oysters in this condition go on living for quite a few days, so they can be purchased two or three days ahead of time. Tip them gently into a plastic tub and lay over them a soaked cloth or piece of soaked hessian. Keep them in a cool place.[+]

The next ingredient you must locate is sea-lettuce. This is a clear green sea weed that grows in small clumps. It is found in clean water by divers who collect sea-urchin, periwinkles and other shellfish. The name, sea-lettuce, describes it perfectly. It is lettuce-green and delicate in texture, quite unlike kelp or many other seaweeds. It is perfectly edible and has more of a texture than a pronounced flavour. It is crisp, with a fresh bracing aroma that will make you remember the smell of your favourite ocean beach in winter. This entrée was once described by an ecstatic customer as being like eating oysters at the bottom of the sea.

If you cannot obtain this seaweed, there are dried seaweeds from Japan on the market. Both kombu and wakame need to be briefly soaked before use.[+] The outside leaves of an iceberg lettuce are surprisingly good also.

The name of the chicken dish, *jambonneau*, translates as 'little ham of chicken' and instantly transmits a picture of the plump little cushioned 'ham' that results from stuffing and roasting a boned chicken leg. It is an interesting technique, and a great variety of stuffings can be used. The basic pork and veal *farce* mentioned on page 190 can be used, either enriched with pistachio nuts or else mixed with the blanched and chopped leaves of silver beet, or with the addition of a few fine gratings of orange zest. Elsewhere in this book (page 116) I have given the recipe for one of the best-known specialities of Stephanie's – stuffed tripe. The stuffing for the tripe would be another possibility for the chicken leg. All of these stuffings, once sewn and cooked, are wonderful picnic food – they slice very well when cool and are like miniature terrines. Do not stop at chicken legs. Duck legs are also very good, but be careful to remove the heavy tendon as it is very tough. I have given a separate recipe for duck leg on page 24.

With the little ham I have suggested serving homemade pasta. It has become enormously fashionable to make one's own pasta, and I think that freshly made egg noodles swollen with cream or in a rich stock are absolutely delectable. Once the technique is mastered, and you have become comfortable with your small Italian pasta machine, your life will be changed as far as simple meals are concerned. Anyway, I have returned to pasta elsewhere – it is just worth a little warning that where noodles are served in a moat of sauce, as here, one should not serve too many.[*]

The balance of this meal, which may have started to seem perilously rich to

---

[+] More food lovers recognise the superiority of unopened, unrumbled oysters these days, and one expects to receive them in any good restaurant, but it is still difficult to buy oysters of this kind in a suburban fish shop. You will need to order them.

[*] Wakame seaweed, originating in Japan, now grows in the south-east and north-east of Tasmania. It can be found, dried, in health-food stores. Instructions for soaking and using this sea vegetable are on the packet. It swells to enormous proportions.

your guests, is rescued by a magnificent finale. You must search out the ripest, sweetest watermelon, chill it well and serve balls of this exotic fruit in a syrup made from the crushed watermelon seeds and a few drops of rosewater. If you also have a ripe pomegranate, scatter some of its ruby tears over the watermelon. If not, use some velvety petals of a dark red rose.

With this menu, you have flirted with danger. So many people and restaurants do not realise that after a dish combining cream, butter and wine – not to mention pasta – one must minister to the palate, so that your meal ends on an up-note.[+] It is not accident or lack of effort that dictates that many of my meals end with simply but carefully prepared fruit. 'Simple' again. Perfectly peeled orange segments bathed in a burnt sugar syrup, or the peaches mentioned in another meal (page 86), each one chosen perfectly ripe, or sweet golden pineapple tossed with stem ginger. I could go on and on.

[*] I would buy dried pasta for this dish nowadays. Pappardelle would be my choice, either plain or spinach-flavoured. The wide strips soak up a small amount of sauce most beautifully.

[+] Nearly twenty years on, I would happily serve this menu.

Steamed oysters with sea-lettuce

6 oysters per person, 'unrumbled' (see page 16)
1 or 2 large trays big enough to hold all the oysters in a single layer without
crowding them
rock salt (sufficient to spread a 1 cm layer on the tray or trays)
2–3 clusters of sea-lettuce per person or 50 g dried wakame seaweed or outside
leaves of lettuce
1 oyster-opening knife per person
1 large Chinese steaming-basket (or 2 smaller ones) – such as are used for yum
cha meals (when selecting your bamboo steaming-baskets, have in mind the
diameter of the saucepans in your kitchen, on which they need to fit snugly)
60 g softened unsalted butter per person + 60 g extra
few drops lemon juice per person

TO PREPARE THE OYSTERS   In the morning, clean the oysters. With a stiff nail brush, scrub each shell under running water to remove all sand and mud. Don't worry about the barnacles or minute shellfish attached. Do not leave the oysters soaking, as they may open a little and lose their precious juice.

Using an oyster opener, and with your non-opening hand wrapped in a thick cloth, proceed to half-open the oysters. Insert the sharp, pointed end of the opener where the oyster shell is hinged and work it deeply into the join with a twisting, levering action. You will need to exert quite a bit of force and you MUST BE CARE-FUL. When you feel that the muscle is released, carefully place the oyster on the salt-lined tray beside you and proceed to the next oyster. The salt provides a stable bed for the oysters, so that they don't tip over and waste their juices.

Place the tray of oysters in the refrigerator until serving time.

TO PREPARE THE SEA-LETTUCE   Rinse the sea-lettuce to ensure that there is no sand lurking. If you are using dried seaweed, soak it in a large pot of warm water for about 30 minutes, then cut into appropriate pieces with scissors. If using lettuce leaves, select unbruised ones and wash them well.

Have preheated dinner plates ready, as the cooking of this dish is minimal. Set out oyster knives as well as forks and teaspoons and finger bowls.

10 MINUTES BEFORE DINNER   Have ready your saucepan or saucepans half-full of boiling water. Set up each basket with the clusters of seaweed or lettuce leaves, and carefully place your cracked-open oysters on the greenery, hopefully without

too many being piggy-backed on others as you wish to maximise the gush of steam and minimise the time spent over the heat. Don't stand the baskets over the heat just yet.

In another saucepan of approximately 16 cm diameter, bring about 1 cm of water to a fast boil. Remove from the heat and whisk in the butter, about 60 g at a time. When all the butter has been incorporated, return the pan to the heat, whisk for a few minutes so that the butter is warm, and season with a few drops of lemon juice and perhaps a grind of pepper. Move sauce to one side.

Your sauce is, of course, melted butter at its simplest. By whisking it into very hot water the butter emulsifies to a creamy consistency that is great drizzled over these oysters or used for dipping artichoke leaves or asparagus on another occasion. Any finely chopped herbs can be added to the butter.

Divide the sauce into individual containers (previously warmed, but not hot). I find white porcelain egg dishes are suitable, or even plain eggcups. Send the butter out to each diner.

Lastly, place the baskets on top of the boiling water with the lids on tightly and the steam at full pressure for 2–3 minutes, until you can see that the oysters have plumped and just started to frill around the edges. DO NOT OVERSTEAM. The oysters will be warm – not hot – and the sauce tepid.

Each guest now tucks in, ladling a little butter onto each oyster, slipping it down, drinking the juice and nibbling at the greenery. Absolutely delicious – the essence of oyster.

Jambonneau of chicken, Spinach noodles

1 whole chicken and 4 portions Maryland
60 g chopped ham
salt, white pepper
pinch grated nutmeg
1 cup raw, finely shredded spinach, packed tight (known as chiffonnade)
melted butter
1 egg white
60 g ricotta cheese
300 ml cream

coarse linen thread

300 g plain flour
2 teaspoons salt
2 tablespoons cooked, dry spinach purée (about ½ an average bunch)
2 teaspoons olive oil
2 eggs
1 egg yolk

SAUCE

100 ml Noilly Prat or other dry vermouth
500 ml well-reduced poultry stock made with the chicken carcass (see page 23)
salt, pepper
60 g softened unsalted butter

ZUCCHINI

6 small zucchini, shredded with the coarse disc in a food processor

GARNISH

2 tablespoons pine nuts, fried golden
*1 tablespoon chervil leaves, nipped from the stem but not chopped, so they still
    retain their daintiness (known as pluches)*

Remove the legs from the whole bird, leaving the maximum skin on the leg portion. The breast meat will be used for the stuffing, and the carcass, wings etc. will be used to make the poultry stock.

TO MAKE THE STUFFING   Remove the skin and sinew from the chicken breasts and mince with the ham in the food processor. Add salt, pepper and nutmeg. Scrape this mixture into a Mouli and press through the coarse disc to extract all the membrane and fragments that would spoil the texture. Alternatively, press the purée through a drum sieve.

Meanwhile, wilt the spinach *chiffonnade* in a little butter. Return the chicken and ham purée to the food processor and blend in the egg white. Run the food processor for a full minute to thoroughly blend. Add the ricotta and blend again. Briefly run the machine to incorporate the spinach. Scrape the mixture into a spacious bowl and chill for at least 1 hour.

This stuffing is a variation of the classic *mousseline*, which I have described on page 139 in the recipe for the prawn quenelle. The ricotta, ham and spinach add interest to the stuffing of the chicken leg. The chilling step is important, and ensures that before the delicate step of incorporating the cream is commenced, the basic mix is very cold. The more 'working' the mixture can stand, the more cream it can absorb and therefore the lighter will be the finished *mousseline*.

After thorough chilling, work in the cream with a metal spoon, folding thoroughly but lightly. Bring a pan of lightly salted water to the boil, and poach a ball of the mix to check the seasoning. Make any adjustments necessary. Return to the refrigerator until needed.

BONING AND COOKING THE CHICKEN LEGS   Use a small, sharp knife and keep the blade always angled in towards the bone and not towards your fingers. Loosen the flesh around the bone at the top of each leg. Scrape and ease the thigh bone free, then twist it to free the bone completely at the ball joint where it joins the drumstick. Continue to free the bone until you have the about 2 cm of bone left and the rounded knobby piece where the foot was attached. Cut straight through the bone either with sharp poultry scissors or with a sharp bang of a large cook's knife. The foot joint should also be knocked off. In the cooking process the flesh will shrink from this part, and you can finish the dish with a cutlet frill. As this is often done to a baked ham, it seems entirely appropriate to so decorate this 'little ham of chicken'.[†]

Season the inside of each chicken leg with salt and pepper and proceed to half-sew it up. It is infinitely easier to stuff if already partially sewn. Use a darning or tapestry needle and a *long* thread. Leave a long end dangling, as it is much quicker to pull out one long thread than to search for knots when holding a scalding-hot, stuffed *jambonneau*. Start stitching a long seam across the widest opening where the thigh bone joined the carcass, stopping when you have a gap of about 2 cm.

Fix a piping bag with a plain nozzle. Put the piping bag in a narrow jug, fold the top 5 cm over the jug like a cuff and proceed to spoon in the chilled stuffing. Stuff each leg quite full, although not to bursting point as this mixture will swell. Complete your stitching. Remove the needle, leaving a long thread dangling. Wipe the outside of the stuffed legs and roll each one in melted butter.

Preheat oven to 220°C. Cook for 25 minutes, turning once. The legs should look puffed and golden and feel firm. The flesh of the chicken will look rather pink due to the presence of the ham in the stuffing. Allow to rest for 5 minutes while the sauce is made and the noodles and zucchini are steamed.

SPINACH NOODLES   On page 213 I describe the technique of making pasta using a small Italian pasta machine and a food processor. The spinach technique is the same. The puréed spinach will make the dough a little moister than usual, and it is for

[†] This mention of cutlet frills is surprising. I haven't used one for twenty years and I think we can all now cope with the sight of a neatened bone protruding from a chicken leg – although, given the still-common request to remove the head of a fish, I am not quite so sure!

that reason that in the list of ingredients I have used 2 whole eggs and 1 yolk instead of the more usual 3 eggs for 300 g of flour.

Make the noodles as instructed on page 213. Drop the cut noodles into rapidly boiling, salted water with a spoonful of oil and cook for 2 minutes. Drain and run under a cold tap. Sprinkle over a few drops of oil to stop them sticking and set aside until needed.

TO MAKE THE SAUCE AND SERVE   Having removed the *jambonneaux* to a warm dish, tip off any butter in the baking dish and place it on your fastest hotplate. Pour in the vermouth. Scrape and stir to loosen all baked-on particles, stirring them constantly to help them float free and dissolve in the bubbling wine. When the wine has reduced to a syrupy consistency (1–2 minutes), pour in the stock. Once again stir until all is boiling fiercely, and allow to reduce further. Taste for strength of flavour and seasoning. If you are not happy with the flavour, reduce further.

Strain the sauce into a small saucepan and reduce the flame so that the sauce is simmering. Whisk the softened butter into the sauce. Drop your noodles and zucchini into the sauce and simmer for 2–3 minutes longer.

Take your preheated dinner plates. Place noodles and zucchini around the edge of each plate or in a heap in the middle of the plate. Place a *jambonneau* either on top of the heap or in the centre of the plate. Ladle any remaining sauce over and around and liberally scatter the pine nuts and the *pluches* of chervil over everything.

Basic poultry stock

1 chicken carcass
giblets and heart, if included
chicken neck and feet, if included
1 onion
1 carrot
1 leek
1 stalk celery
6 mushrooms
1 tomato, seeded
1 spring onion
1 tablespoon olive oil
1 slice lemon
1 bay leaf, 1 sprig of thyme, 1 sprig of parsley

Roast the chicken carcass, neck, feet, wing-tips etc. until well browned. Chop and fry the vegetables in the oil until well coloured. Put the bones, vegetables and seasonings into a pot and cover with cold water. Bring to a boil slowly, skimming off any scum and fat. Simmer for 4 hours. Strain. Let stand and skim off any fat that rises to the top. Reduce by rapid boiling to the strength required depending on final use.[†]

To make a sauce as in the *jambonneau* recipe (page 23), the stock should reduce by two-thirds or maybe more. The roasting of the carcass adds colour to the stock. If you wanted a very light stock – for example, to make a vegetable soup or a pale velouté sauce – there would be no need to roast the bones.

Duck leg with pork and orange stuffing

1 × 2 kg duck
500 g minced pork fat
2 fresh bay leaves (optional)
2 cloves garlic, unpeeled

STUFFING

300 g minced duck breast (from the bird above), skin off
300 g coarsely minced fat belly pork
1 teaspoon salt
½ teaspoon ground pepper
1 tablespoon cognac
½ teaspoon ground cloves
½ teaspoon ground allspice
2 cloves garlic, finely chopped
grated zest of ½ orange

Mix all the ingredients for the stuffing. Leave overnight for the flavours to mellow and blend.

Remove the legs from the bird, leaving the maximum skin on the leg portion. The breast meat will be used for the stuffing, and the extra fat and skin will be rendered as described below. Chop, bag, label and freeze the bones for a future duck or game stock. Season the legs and sew them up loosely, following the same method as for the chicken *jambonneau* recipe (page 22).

Put the minced pork fat, chopped duck fat and duck skin, bay leaf and cloves

[†] A more complex and deeper-flavoured stock will result if lightly roasted duck bones are then simmered in this basic poultry stock.

of garlic in a heavy saucepan with 2 cm of water. Over gentle heat render all this fat, stirring from time to time to prevent particles sticking to the bottom of the pan. After about 2 hours, strain through a conical sieve into a basin and leave to cool. ✢

Fry a tiny hamburger of the stuffing mix to test seasoning. Adjust the seasoning and pack the mix into the boned duck legs quite firmly, as it will pack down as it cooks. Complete the stitching. Put the filled legs into an ovenproof dish and cover with the rendered fat. Add a fresh bay leaf if you have one. Cook at 180°C for 45 minutes, turning once.

The legs can be removed from the fat when cooked if they are needed the same day or the next day. Do not slice until cold or at least tepid. If, however, you wish them to keep for a week or more, let the legs cool down still covered with the pork and duck fat. This is the method used to preserve pieces of duck, goose and pork in the south-west of France, and you have just created a stuffed *confit* of duck.

This stuffing can be used to fill a duck neck cooked in exactly the same way, or it could be cooked in a terrine, perhaps with any extra strips of duck breast added, which you could have marinated separately in a little extra cognac and fresh thyme. Yet another possibility, if any mince is left over after stuffing the legs, would be to form little flat patties, encase them in a thin wrapping of caul fat and fry them as crépinettes. ✦

If you decided on a little terrine, it should be weighted lightly while cooling to ensure more compact slices.

✢ The skin from the duck breast should be cut into small pieces and added to the pork fat and loose duck fat. It will render its fat and the skin fragments will become crispy at the end of the process. Skimmed from the clear fat, these crunchy morsels are a fantastic garnish for a lettuce and orange salad that might accompany this dish. Add these *grattons*, as they are called in France, just before serving the salad.

✦ Since completing my book on south-west France, I have realised that this stuffed duck leg, or the stuffed duck neck suggested as an option, would both be crisped in the fat clinging to them over a gentle heat before serving, even when being eaten cold. The special charm of any *confit* is its crisp skin. Where *confit* is being used to flavour a stuffing, or in a casserole, the skin would be removed first. It would not be thrown away, however, but crisped on a paper-lined tray in a moderate oven until crunchy, and then used as described above for *grattons*.

Watermelon in rosewater syrup

Hardly a recipe, more an idea. Use a melon-baller (known as a parisienne spoon) to cut up the flesh of a melon. When you have gouged out the maximum number of perfect balls, scrape all remaining bits of pink flesh and all seeds and pass them all through a juice extractor. Add a little castor sugar and rosewater to taste. Cover this liquid and place it in the refrigerator until the sugar has dissolved. Taste for sweetening. A little white rum could be added, if you like, and as mentioned in the introduction some pomegranate seeds would look wonderful combined with the melon. Any extra pomegranate seeds should be fed into the juicer with the watermelon seeds and scrapings to boost the flavour.

If you do not have pomegranate seeds, scatter rose petals over the melon balls and syrup at the last minute.

Autumn

Menu

⌐

Petals of Raw Fish

Rare-roasted Saddle of Hare,
Sauce Poivrade
Semolina and Potato Gnocchi
Roasted Red Pepper Salad

Hot Pear Tart with Sabayon Sauce

⌐

Japanese cooks work gracefully and sublimely well with raw fish. Slivered and paper-thin, cubed or chunky, skin on or skin off, rolled with vinegared rice and nori seaweed, sauced or left plain, it is always recognisable as a Japanese dish. It is therefore a bit like plagiarism to move in with western eyes and attempt to create a dish using raw fish. However, I am about to do it!

There are many young Japanese cooks deployed throughout France's starred restaurants (often paying the restaurateur for the privilege, the rumour goes), collecting skills and techniques to use in restaurants elsewhere. The Japanese are increasingly to be found in restaurants in New York and the US West Coast, creating a sort of culturally blended cuisine – steamed fish with abalone mushrooms on seaweed with sea-urchin *beurrre blanc* sort of thing.

The Troisgros brothers started something big when they sliced their salmon in escalope fashion, flipped it in their new Teflon pans, rediscovered sauce vin blanc and added a handful of sorrel. It was a refreshing dish and a new look at a much-loved ingredient. The fish was *just* cooked, which was a very important detail. *Saumon à l'oseille* now appears on practically every restaurant menu in France, and I have seen the menu of a restaurant in Brazil where it featured after the young chef did a *stage* at Roanne. I confess that I have been asked to cook it myself, and have acceded to the request.

So what about raw fish? Perhaps the Troisgros new look started its popularity in France. Perhaps the Japanese influence started it, but raw fish is being enjoyed by more and more diners outside traditional Japanese restaurants.

Raw salmon was a frequently encountered starter when I was in France in 1983. It was usually served sliced very thin and sprinkled with chives, chervil, parsley, coarsely ground white peppercorns and/or crushed coriander seeds. It was dressed with fruity olive oil, sometimes with lemon or lime juice added; on other occasions the halved citrus was presented to allow for personal taste in acidity. Almost invariably, alongside came a large oval slice of grilled, crusty, country-style bread. It was always delicious. It had that quality I associate with the very finest Scottish smoked salmon, which I have tasted only three or four times in my life – at the same time stimulating the palate so that one is ready for more tastes, and filling the mouth with an almost unbelievable softness and richness. Both dishes really lead into a meal and are the perfect preface where the main dish of the evening will be rich and sauced with a complex blend of flavours. The mouth is left tingling and clean.

Very recently, airfreighted fresh smoked salmon from both Scotland and Canada has become available to good restaurants, but unsmoked salmon only arrives in this country frozen, so it is better to use our large Australian trout. At the time of writing the first farmed Chinook salmon is just becoming available in Australia.[+]

The entrée I have devised uses petals of trout and another white-fleshed fish, such as snapper, blue eye or bream, and overlaps them in the form of a flower. Delicacy linked with a certain amount of fantasy is wonderful when it succeeds,

---

[+] It is difficult to remember back to when we had no salmon industry of our own. This is a timely reminder of the distance we have come in twenty years. The first Tasmanian Atlantic salmon appeared in 1985, just after this book had gone to the printer's. What excitement there was. The industry has gone from strength to strength and, according to figures provided by the Tasmanian Salmonid Growers' Association, total Australian production is in the region of 12 000 tonnes of fish per year. Eighty per cent of Tasmanian export salmon goes to the discriminating Japanese market. Value-adding includes hot and cold smoking, the production of salmon roe and other products, such as pâté.

but it must be handled with restraint. A painted garden can be suggested by using shredded daikon and carrot, both lightly dampened with rice vinegar. Curls of pickled ginger, which are a delicate pale pink, can be used as smaller petals. The centre and stamens of the flower can be red salmon roe, with a final sparse scattering of beluga caviar to represent the starry centre of an anemone or a full-blown poppy.✝

There are a few absolutes to remember when dealing with raw fish:

- The fish must be fresh, fresh, fresh.
- Chill the fillet, but do not freeze it.
- Sharpen your knife.

Clean your knife with a scrupulously clean cloth between slices, and study a good Japanese book for the techniques of tackling differently shaped fillets (for example, Shizuo Tsuji's *Japanese Cooking: A Simple Art*). The plates must be cold, quite plain, and perfectly free of any smudges.

Don't attempt this dish for twenty people. It can be prepared up to two hours beforehand. Cover the plates with plastic film and add oil and lemon at the last minute or, even better, place glass jugs containing the superb green–gold oil on the table to increase the visual pleasure. Of course, the grilled bread should be very hot and of a crusty variety.

Following on from this delicate, cleansing but stimulating beginning, I have chosen a dish to highlight one of our very few real game animals – the hare. An average-sized hare (about 2 kg) roasted as here will serve four people. Only the saddle is used for the recipe. The extra bits of carcass, belly and forelegs guarantee the richness of the sauce. The hind-leg meat could be minced and added to a pork, pork fat and veal terrine, or it could be simmered and braised as a separate dish.

I normally have no sympathy for the squeamish in culinary matters, and am quite intolerant of those who squeal and insist that the head on a grilled fish be removed or who prefer to forget that a pigeon ever had a head or feet, but I must say it is a disgusting job preparing a hare. For maximum enjoyment of the dish, get the preparation over at least the day before, and I prefer to do it alone – certainly a long way away from children with their 'yuk'-type remarks!

However, many of us who were not born yesterday know that chooks used to come from the back garden, and we remember the smell of entrails and the damp

---

✝ Whimsy again. I would be very nervous about offering a 'painted garden of raw fish' these days, although one is immediately reminded of the poetic dish Four Dances of the Sea, which is a signature dish of Cheong Liew, the master chef in charge of the dining room at The Grange at the Hilton International in Adelaide. I am delighted by the poetic and evocative names given to many Asian dishes and ingredients. They are usually translated very prosaically. Compare 'Nine-towered pagoda vegetable' with 'Thai basil', for example. Or 'Happy birds singing together' versus 'Pigeons baked in salt'!

newspaper used to collect the feathers. So don't be put off. It is a magnificent dish, and the technique of making the luscious sauce can be modified and used with other dishes.

With the hare, fried semolina and potato gnocchi are served. Some sort of starchy accompaniment is a good idea as a vehicle for sopping up the sauce. Plain pasta would be equally good, or a very silky purée of potatoes, where the mashed potatoes are whisked with lots of boiling milk. This sort of purée is much thinner than ordinary mashed potato.

As a separate dish I have given a recipe for a roasted red pepper salad. Hares are plentiful in the autumn, so it is a good time to enjoy the last of the sweet red peppers. If you are planning this menu at another time of the year, another sort of salad based on a rather strong-tasting ingredient would follow well after the lush sauce; perhaps radicchio with a few frills of curly endive and some sliced beetroot.

One of our best and most-copied desserts is the finale to this splendid meal. This hot pear tart in puff pastry is magnificent. Once you have mastered the technique of puff pastry, it is simplicity itself. The sabayon sauce does require a strong arm as it needs to be whisked hard. In a professional kitchen the whisking of the sabayon would be done over a direct flame, which certainly speeds up the process but must be done at great speed and with a sensitive appreciation of the right moment to lift the basin high or off the heat. Failure to do either of these things will result in a basin full of rather exotic, sweetened, red-wine scrambled eggs. At a recent dinner for a gastronomic society we made the sabayon with a wonderful matured tokay instead of the red wine, and it was pronounced a highlight.

Petals of raw fish

500 g fillet of trout or *salmon, with a good pink colour*⁺

500 g fillet of blue eye, snapper or *other fine-grained white-fleshed fish*

1 medium carrot

1 daikon (Japanese radish)

white rice vinegar

1 teaspoon cracked coriander seeds

sliced pickled ginger (benishoga; see page 32)

1 tablespoon red salmon roe

15 g beluga or *sevruga caviar*✦

a few whole chives

country-style bread

200 ml virgin olive oil

3 limes, halved

TO PREPARE THE FISH   Chill the fillets well. With a very sharp knife, cut 'petals' of wafer-thin fish following the grain of the fillet. You will probably have some odd scraps of fish left over, which you could turn into a mousse, make into an omelette for the children or pickle in lime juice for a *ceviche* appetiser the next evening. In other words, use the choicest, plumpest part of the fillet and be prepared to use up excess.

On the shredding disc of your food processor, or using the grating disc of a Mouli-julienne grater, grate the carrot and then the daikon into shreds. Squeeze the daikon in a cloth to extract the liquid. Mix a spoonful of rice vinegar through both vegetables.

Crack the coriander grains in a clean tea towel using a strong rolling pin or a meat mallet. Do not use a coffee grinder, as the aim is to crack them, not to pulverise them.

⁺ Tasmanian salmon would be essential for this dish today.

✦ The Convention on International Trade in Endangered Species of Wild Fauna and Flora (CITES) lists all species of sturgeon in its appendices. As such, importing the parts and products of sturgeon (including caviar) requires a permit from Environment Australia. However, obtaining a permit is complicated and nobody is currently importing the products. Babek Hadi, a most knowledgeable importer of speciality food products, who used to bring in caviar, says that it is very rare indeed to find beluga. In the days when one could lash out on caviar, osietra was my choice, recognisable by its slightly greenish-gold glints. A more affordable product now available is flying-fish roe, sometimes flavoured with wasabi.

This is the fun part. Spread out your 6 plates. Arrange the petals of fish as a flower, alternating colours, and – if you like – folding over one or two petals as if they have been stirred by the wind. With the slices of pickled ginger, add shading and emphasis to your pink petals. Spoon on the centre of each flower – that is, the salmon roe – and scatter on the black 'stamens' of caviar. The whole chives are the slender stems – admittedly a little slight for the weight of the flower, but it is, after all, a rather surreal fantasy. The daikon and carrot can become ruffles of leaves at the base of the stems.

Wrap each plate in plastic film until serving time. Refrigerate, but remove from the refrigerator at least 30 minutes before serving. As suggested earlier, it is probably more dramatic to serve the plates as they have been arranged and leave the dressings on the table. I would serve grilled country-style bread, virgin olive oil and, nearby, a small bowl of halved limes. Another version could include a bowl of one-third light soy sauce and two-thirds mirin or rice wine, with a fine mince of fresh ginger submerged in it. In the latter case, I would set each plate with an unsnapped pair of Japanese wooden chopsticks, still intact in their paper wrapper.

Pickled ginger

This Japanese condiment is frequently served with sushi, the Japanese dish of sweetened, vinegared rice often wrapped with seaweed and containing various fillings and toppings. Pickled ginger is readily available in Japanese stores, either shredded or, as is required for the petals of fish, sliced paper-thin. The rather attractive pink colour is apparently a result of the ginger being dyed. In the traditional Japanese recipe, beefsteak plant (*perilla*) was used as the dye. If you make this condiment yourself, it will have a pinkish cast but be nowhere near as dramatic as the commercially available product. Reluctantly I have to admit that for dramatic effect I buy the commercial benishoga, as it is called, but hasten to add that I have a small preserving jar full of our own make in the coolroom ready for any day when we feel that the sharp sweet-and-hot note is required.

250 g ginger, peeled and cut into fairly even-sized pieces
2 teaspoons salt
1 cup white rice vinegar
100 ml water
3 tablespoons sugar

Sprinkle the ginger with the salt and leave for 24 hours. Mix the vinegar, water and sugar in a bowl and leave until the sugar has dissolved. Lift the ginger from the salt and place in the marinade. Refrigerate for at least 1 week before using. Kept in a sealed container, such as a small, French-type preserving jar sealed with a metal clip, it will keep for months. It will become pinkish but, as mentioned above, never bright pink.

Rare-roasted saddle of hare, Sauce poivrade

2 young hares
ground black pepper
several bruised juniper berries
2 bay leaves
2 sprigs of thyme
1 large glass cognac
fruity olive oil
40 g cold unsalted butter
sea salt, pepper
watercress to garnish

SAUCE POIVRADE

1 litre sound red wine
1 kg hare trimmings
1 carrot, chopped
2 onions, roughly chopped
1 leek, washed well and sliced
1 stalk celery, chopped
200 g mushrooms
1 whole head garlic
60 g plain flour
100 ml cognac
2 glasses red-wine vinegar
1 large sprig of thyme
1 bay leaf
a few parsley stalks
20 g cracked or coarsely ground
    peppercorns
20 g bruised juniper berries
250 ml well-reduced veal stock

TO PREPARE THE HARE Using a boning knife and a cleaver, separate the forequarter and hind legs from the hares. Remove the kidneys and liver and any fat attached to the belly. With a flexible sharp knife, remove the silver-greyish membrane from the saddle of the hare. The belly section may contain quite a lot of blood, which you may wish to collect in a small bowl. Many recipes will suggest that you add this blood to the sauce to enrich it. If you wish to do this, add a small spoonful of vinegar to the blood to prevent it clotting. I never use it, as I find that it turns the sauce grey.

Cut off the lower rib section with heavy kitchen scissors and place the saddles in a glass or stainless steel bowl. Grind over a little coarse pepper, scatter over the juniper berries, tuck the bay leaves and thyme under the hare, and then pour the lightly mixed brandy and olive oil over the top. Leave to stand overnight. The forequarter and hind legs are now used for the sauce (unless you have decided to utilise the hind legs in a terrine or a braise with new season's chestnuts).

TO MAKE THE SAUCE   Place the red wine in a wide pan, bring to the boil, set alight and flame and reduce by a quarter. Set aside.

Roast the hare trimmings in a lightly oiled baking dish at 220°C for half an hour. Add the vegetables and garlic to the roasting pan and return to the oven until well browned. Place the pan over a high heat and shake the flour over. Stir and scrape until the flour also is well coloured. Pour in the cognac and vinegar, shake, stir and scrape to loosen any little brown bits with tendency to stick and then add the red-wine reduction and the thyme, bay leaf, parsley, peppercorns and juniper. Transfer to a stockpot. Bring the sauce to the boil, skim well, add the well-reduced veal stock and simmer all together for 2 hours.

Strain the sauce through a chinois, or sieve, pressing really hard on the solids so that no drop of flavour is wasted. Taste and add seasoning if it is really needed, but remember that you may still reduce the sauce a little, so be very cautious with salt. Leave the sauce to cool overnight if made the day before, or if you have made it on the same day refrigerate it until 1 hour before dinner.

TO COOK THE HARE   Preheat the oven to 250°C. Have ready a warm, deep, lidded dish in a spot where it will stay warm but not cook. Drain the hares and pat them dry with kitchen paper. Heat a little butter and oil in a heavy iron pan big enough to take the 2 saddles, or else use 2 pans. Seal the saddles well on all sides. Tip off any fat in the pan and immediately transfer the pan to the preheated oven. After 8 minutes check the meat. It should be brown on the outside, but feel springy in the centre when pressed lightly with your finger.

Using a very sharp knife, carve off the fillets from each side of the saddles and keep them warm in the deep dish. Cover. Use a ladleful of your sauce to deglaze the cooking pan and let it bubble. Strain this back into the sauce, which should now be simmering nearby.

TO SERVE   Bring the sauce to a rolling boil and boil it really hard while you carve the fillets into long, thin diagonal slices. Cut the cold unsalted butter into pieces and whisk into the sauce, have a final taste for salt and pepper, and then ladle the sauce onto your very hot plates before placing the ruby-red, rare slices of hare on the sauce. Grind some pepper over and add a flake or two of salt. I would drop on a little handful of crisp, washed watercress sprigs and serve the vegetable accompaniment on separate heated plates.

NOTE 1:   Do not panic when slicing the meat from the saddles. The uncut fillets will stay quite warm for up to 15 minutes in their resting dish before carving, and as long as the plates are hot the meat will be hot when the diners are served.
NOTE 2:   Do not waste the backbones after you have carved the saddles. When they are cold, they should be bagged, together with any drops of juice etc., labelled and put into the freezer to emerge the next time you wish to make a game sauce.

Semolina and potato gnocchi

This is a recipe from the works of Elizabeth David. It is an Italian dish and first appeared in her 1954 book *Italian Food*. It was later repeated in *French Provincial Cooking* (1960), one of the most definitive, appreciative and uncompromising guides to the regional food of France.[+]

> *500 g waxy potatoes*[✦]
> *salt, pepper*
> *a scrap of nutmeg*
> *400 ml hot milk*
> *100 g fine semolina*
> *2 large eggs, beaten well*
> *butter*

Cook the potatoes, then peel and mash them while they are still warm. Season them and gradually add the scalding-hot milk. When the purée is smooth and well blended, return the pan to the heat and pour in the semolina. Stir vigorously with a wooden spoon until the mixture is very stiff and is coming away from the sides

---

[+] I still use this recipe for gnocchi made with semolina, and have had great success serving it surrounded by a rich ragoût of oxtail. I cut it into shapes, shave generous amounts of parmesan over the top and return it to the oven resting on a piece of baking paper on a pizza tray.

[✦] One of the great advances of the last ten years has been the increased availability of new varieties of potato. I have been particularly excited by the French and Dutch-style yellow-fleshed waxy potatoes, which are absolutely delicious in salads, or crushed with olive oil, or sliced and roasted with rosemary and garlic.

of the pan. Remove the pan from the heat and beat in the eggs. Tip this stiff purée onto a buttered tray and smooth out to a thickness of about 2 cm. Leave to cool, then cover with plastic film and chill.

When ready to cook, form the mixture into little balls, roll in plain flour and fry until golden brown.

Elizabeth David notes that the potato balls can also be drizzled with melted butter and grated cheese, returned to the oven to melt the cheese, then served like this.

Roasted red pepper salad

1 clove garlic, smashed
black pepper
extra-virgin olive oil
1 hot chilli (optional)
3 large red peppers
few drops best-quality wine vinegar

Have ready a shallow salad plate containing the smashed clove of garlic, a grinding of fresh pepper, a 1 cm layer of best olive oil and the split chilli, if desired.

Over a gas flame rotate the red peppers until all sides are quite black. Wrap the hot, charred peppers in a clean towel or put them in a brown paper bag and press to seal. After 15 minutes, unwrap and rub off the black skin. Rinse the peppers under the cold tap very briefly, so as not to waste any flavour.[+] Hold each pepper over a strainer resting on a small bowl to catch the juices. Slice the top off, then scrape all the seeds from inside into the strainer. Press hard on the contents of the strainer. All juices gleaned should be poured into the salad plate. Cut the peppers into strips and stir them into the dressing. Adjust the seasoning with a few drops of vinegar.

The smell of roasting peppers is fantastic, and for me evokes Italy, the Mediterranean and Mother's barbecues when I was a child.

NOTE: Roasted peppers can be preserved in good olive oil and will keep for at least 2 weeks in the refrigerator. Pour some oil into a glass storage jar, next place a layer of peppers, cover with more oil and then more peppers. Cover the final layer with

[+] If the peppers have steamed in a bag for long enough, the skins should lift away easily. I do try not to rinse them as flavour is lost that way.

Rare-roasted saddle of hare with sauce poivrade (page 33), semolina and potato gnocchi (page 35), and roasted red pepper salad (page 36)

Puff-pastry pear tart with muscat sabayon (page 37)

more oil. Sprigs of thyme, basil or oregano could be layered with the peppers, or slivers of very fresh garlic or little pieces of hot chilli. Before using the peppers as a salad or as part of your antipasto or whatever, bring them to room temperature.✣

Hot pear tart with sabayon sauce✦

250 g puff pastry (see page 38)
3 pears
egg wash (1 whole egg, pinch of salt, whisked together)

POACHING SYRUP

2 cups sugar
2 cups water
1 cup late-picked white wine, sauternes or sherry
zest of 1 orange

GLAZE

2 tablespoons smooth apricot jam
2 tablespoons water or wine as for syrup

SABAYON SAUCE

4 egg yolks
4 tablespoons castor sugar
2 teaspoons redcurrant jelly
1 cup red wine or muscat, tokay, port etc.

Make the puff pastry (page 38) and refrigerate to rest well before cutting.

Combine all the ingredients for the poaching syrup, bring to the boil to dissolve the sugar and return to simmering point for 5 minutes. Peel the pears carefully, drop them in the poaching syrup and gently poach until just tender. Remove them

---

✣ When storing peppers, it is not so important to layer the peppers and olive oil but it is *very* important that there be no air pockets, which will result in fermented peppers. Press down very well on the peppers and, with a fine skewer, release them from the side of the jar to allow any bubbles of air to escape. Ensure that the peppers are covered with at least 1 cm of olive oil. Fermented peppers smell nasty and there will be a scum on the surface and maybe even some bubbling going on. Do not use them.

✦ Later variations on this theme were peach and pineapple tarts.

when ready and drain and cool. Slice in half lengthwise, remove the stalks and seeds and refrigerate on a tray lined with kitchen paper.

TO MAKE THE TEMPLATE FOR THE PASTRY Make a template from cardboard by tracing out a pear half, including the stem. The actual cardboard shape will be cut 1 cm larger than the tracing to allow for the shrinkage of the pastry and to ensure that there is a sufficient border to hold and frame the pear.

Roll out the pastry about 5 mm in thickness into a rectangle where the short edge corresponds to the overall length of the template. Cut out 6 pear shapes, turning the template in alternate directions to maximise efficiency in cutting. Place the shapes well apart on a baking tray and refrigerate for 30 minutes or until required.

Twenty minutes before serving time, take the pastry shapes out of the refrigerator, brush the entire surface of each one with egg wash (do not drip it over the edges or the shapes won't rise properly), carefully centre a pear half on each shape and place in a preheated oven at 220°C for 15–20 minutes until puffed and golden.

TO MAKE THE SABAYON SAUCE Whisk all the ingredients in a basin over hot water, or over a direct flame if you have been practising (see page 30). Whisk hard and do not stop when the sauce seems mousselike: remove from the heat and continue to whisk until it is warm only. Unless the sauce is well cooked at this stage it will collapse, and the whole process will have to be started again.

Do refer to the remarks about this sabayon in the introduction to this section (page 30).

Puff pastry as made at Stephanie's

Making puff pastry is a very individual skill, and if you are happy with your own method, don't bother to read this.✝

500 g plain flour
pinch salt
300 ml water
juice of 1 lemon
500 g butter

Mix flour, salt, water and lemon juice quickly into a dough. Knead quickly until it feels elastic. Place on a plate, cover with plastic film and refrigerate for 30 minutes.

Unwrap butter and pound it into a pliable square with a rolling pin. Remove dough from the refrigerator. Roll into a long rectangle so that the centre third is twice the thickness of the ends. Place the butter on this thicker section and envelop it with the two ends. The rectangle of dough should be the same width as the block of butter. Rotate the dough so that the open ends are facing you. Flatten the middle of the dough with the rolling pin, at the same time rolling a little towards each end. Using your fingers, force butter into the corners of the dough. Then close the ends over, completely covering the butter. Gently flatten the ends with your hand.

Begin the first roll. Lightly flour the top and bottom of the dough to prevent it from sticking. Roll rapidly, extending the dough as you roll. The rolling movement is a firm, even push away from you. Do not roll back and forth relentlessly. If you have any breaks in the dough, sprinkle them with flour. Fold the top and bottom ends to meet in a centre point. Then fold one end on another, like closing a book. This is the first roll completed.

Wrap in foil and refrigerate for 30 minutes. There are 4 rolls altogether, and you must rest the dough for 30 minutes between each roll. This is done in order to firm the butter and also to relax the gluten. The pastry must be refrigerated in between rolls, otherwise the butter will become too soft and the layers will break down and merge. The gluten needs to be relaxed because the pastry may otherwise retract severely when it is rolled and baked.

After the last roll, refrigerate the pastry for at least 1 hour before rolling and cutting. The cut shapes should also be rested for 30 minutes before baking.

Palmiers

There are many little biscuits that can be made from puff pastry. Palmiers are very popular because of their crunchy caramel. There are several ways of making them, but this is how we do it.

Roll out a rectangle of puff pastry after spreading castor sugar all over the workbench. Cut the rectangle into strips each about 8 cm wide. Take each strip and fold the long sides into the centre. Fold each folded section once more into the centre and then press the two folded pieces together. Chill these rolls in the refrigerator for 30 minutes.

Return the rolls to the bench and with a sharp knife slice off biscuits, then press

✢ While being able to make puff pastry is a useful skill to have, I have to be realistic. Not everyone wants to make it, and anyway, you may want to make this pear tart at a moment's notice! Sometimes good-quality pastry shops will sell you uncooked puff pastry. Ready-rolled frozen puff pastry made with butter is widely available in supermarkets.

and flatten them in a pile of castor sugar on the bench, using a flexible spatula. Space each little flattened biscuit apart on a buttered baking sheet and either freeze them to be cooked off as necessary, or rest them for 30 minutes and then bake for 4–5 minutes on each side at 220°C. The biscuits must be turned quickly as they burn easily. When cooked, they should have a glossy caramel glaze. If not, increase the cooking time by 1 minute each side. Flick the biscuits off the tray onto an oiled surface and leave to cool.

Nut twists

Roll any leftover puff pastry into a rectangle. Brush with egg wash. Mix equal quantities of sugar and any sort of chopped nuts and scatter over the pastry. Run a rolling pin very lightly over the mixture. Cut into strips. Hold a strip at each end and twist. Put onto a greased tray, pressing the ends lightly to stop them untwisting in the heat. When you have twisted each strip, chill for 20 minutes before baking. Bake in a preheated 200°C oven for 10 minutes. Cool on a rack.

Beef on a string

MENU

HAM AND PISTACHIO MOUSSE
SPICED CHERRIES

FILET À LA FICELLE . . . WITH ITS CONDIMENTS

CRÈME CARAMEL WITH VARIATIONS:
ORANGE, CARAMEL, COFFEE

TOASTED ORANGE SPONGE BISCUITS

The least appealing part of the Christmas ham is that it never ends – that is, unless you have a very large family. I usually avoid the problems by buying a piece of kassler, which is a cured and smoked pork loin. This is most delicious, and any left over can be briefly grilled as a superior ham steak. If you do have some cooked leg ham left over, this ham and pistachio mousse is very good. It should be set with a well-flavoured jelly, of which part at least will be clarified to coat the little moulds.

Not only does the robust clear taste of the meat juices lift the mousse right out of the ordinary, but it will have a delightful texture. Left out of the refrigerator too long it will collapse, but at the right temperature it is feather-light and smooth. It is important also to whip the cream until firm, but not grainy.

I use *oeufs en gelée* plastic moulds, which I bought in Paris. They are most versatile and very cheap (at least they were in Paris).

With something soft and melting like a cold mousse, I enjoy some sharp little salad with a homemade pickle of some sort. A salad of torn sorrel, watercress and corn salad or rocket would be delightful. The pistachios can go inside the mousse or perhaps in the salad for a change. I have several jars of spiced crab-apples and also of Margaret cherries that contrast well with the soft mousse. More crunch will come from the wafers of Melba toast, baked until pale gold.

Following this entrée is perhaps my favourite meal. It pays homage to the traditions of the pot-au-feu, which I also love, but *filet à la ficelle* has something extra. It is currently quite popular in restaurants searching for a new dimension for the eternally popular beef, but in my opinion they often go off the track.[+] It is meant to be a dish about broth, so you must serve the broth and a big soup spoon and a large napkin and sea salt and capers and fresh horseradish and so on. It is a ritual, and should not have its ceremony diminished. It is no doubt quite clear that I prefer my own version of this dish. I don't prefer it – I love it![✦]

No short cuts are permitted with the broth. Unlike the pot-au-feu, where the long cooking will ensure a savoury liquid, the fillet is immersed in the broth for such a short time that the bouillon must be perfection before you start to cook. Ah, the smell of the roasting onions before they go into the stockpot.

The dish also needs two marrow bones. Ask your butcher to saw the marrow bones into short pieces. This is quite difficult and dangerous to do, so don't expect slices 3 cm long. They will be more like 6 cm. They must be soaked in generous amounts of cold water overnight to draw out the blood and will be poached separately from the meat. This is a different technique from the one for steak bordelaise, where thick slices of the barely cooked marrow are set into the final rich red-wine sauce. In the latter case, your marrow bones should still be soaked as above, and then the marrow is pushed from the bone and sliced into serving pieces. Just before serving, immerse the slices into hot but not boiling water until they lose their pink look. Do rescue them before the pieces melt away into nothingness.

The big discovery we made when we were serving our *filet à la ficelle* for the first time was a fantastic method of grating fresh horseradish. Normally one scrapes

[+] A touch of bombast here, maybe defiantly sticking out my chin and daring the world to take a jab. They sometimes did, too!

[✦] Poached beef added a new dimension to the repertoire of many restaurants all through the 1980s and '90s. It has remained a popular alternative to steak and roast beef. It is also fat-free, which is not insignificant in these fat-conscious days.

the root and laboriously grates it with tears streaming down one's cheeks. We tried rigging up a board with the grater directly under our very powerful exhaust fan, but still the tears fell. (I should add that we were grating *lots* of horseradish, so a grater will do quite well for a small piece.) One clever member of staff wondered what would happen if we fed the peeled pieces into our electric juicer. Miraculous. We collect a minute amount of juice, open the machine, and there is our pulverised horseradish. Stir the juice back in, add a little salt and fold in a quantity of lightly whipped cream. Then the problem was to protect this sauce from marauding cooks.

After a great bowlful of *filet à la ficelle*, with its vegetables and garnishes, a gentle, soothing dessert is proposed. Crème caramel is perennially popular, and deservedly so. This sweet provides a lovely contrast of three flavours that marry particularly well. There are other variations possible: the classic vanilla, or sweet candied ginger steeped in the milk in place of the coffee powder. Any one flavour could be made, and will stand alone as a delicious dessert.

At Stephanie's, each diner receives three tiny custards, baked in larger-than-usual porcelain snail pots, so that each person has an orange custard, a coffee custard and a caramel custard. They look very pretty with a slivered piece of orange zest on the orange cream, a coffee bean on the next and a blow-away wisp of spun sugar on the last.

To find enough small, even-sized moulds for this dish may be a real exercise in ingenuity. If you have lots of china eggcups, they would do very well. Otherwise, try a speciality kitchen shop for aluminium moulds of a suitable size. Remember that the moulds don't have to be minute, as it is quite fiddly coating them with caramel.

Another useful tip if you are making vanilla and ginger custards is to separate the orange, vanilla and ginger from each other before they are put in the oven, as there is practically no difference in colour, and guests may end up with two of the same flavour if they are not separated at this stage.

This dessert is best baked a day in advance, as more of the caramel coating will dissolve and flow around the unmoulded custards, adding to the caramel flavour in the sauce.

The toasted orange biscuits are a great recipe. The mix is cooked as a complete sheet and then cut and returned to the oven to be crisped. All sorts of shapes could be cut, and it can be used as the base for a trifle or for lining a mould for a marquise or a charlotte.

Ham and pistachio mousse

500 g leftover ham (all fat removed before weighing)
300 ml firmly set pork jelly (see note below)
150 ml cream
2 egg whites
½ cup pistachio nuts, shelled and unsalted, rubbed to remove skins
salt, pepper
Tabasco

Place the ham in a food processor and chop it finely with the pulse action. Tip in the melted, but cold, pork jelly, and purée. Transfer the mixture to a bowl. Whip the cream until fairly firm but still foldable. Whip the egg whites to a firm snow. Fold in the nuts, cream and egg whites to the ham mixture. Taste for seasoning. Use drops of Tabasco or ground white pepper. Spoon the ham mousse into individual small moulds, or into a large jelly mould if it is to be part of a cold buffet.

If you want a very *soigné* dish, clarify the rest of the jelly (see page 68). Check that it will set firm, or adjust with gelatine. Pour a layer of the golden jelly into each mould before adding the mousse. You can embed something decorative in the jelly, such as a slice of pickled cucumber, a little cumquat zest, a few leaves of tarragon if you have infused the jelly with tarragon flavour, and so on. You must let this layer set completely before filling the moulds with mousse.

NOTE: The ideal pork jelly is a well-flavoured jelly such as results from cooking trotters, as described on page 234. The jelly must be really firm. If not, you will need to dissolve several leaves of gelatine in the stock, the amount depending on the volume of liquid (see page 14 for gelatine requirements).

Spiced cherries

2 kg firm, best-quality cherries, stems and stones intact
1 litre white-wine vinegar
500 ml water
1 kg white sugar
2 pieces cinnamon bark
3 teaspoons whole cloves
2 teaspoons whole allspice
4 bay leaves
1 teaspoon salt

Pack the fruit into 2 clean glass preserving jars.

Put all the remaining ingredients into a large pan and bring to the boil. When the sugar has dissolved, boil for a further 5 minutes. Pour the spiced vinegar over the cherries and leave for 3 days. Strain the vinegar from the cherries, and reboil it. Once again pour the vinegar over the cherries. Seal the jars and wait at least a month before opening.

Exactly the same method can be used for crab-apples, but you will need to boil the vinegar a third time, as they are much firmer than cherries. The spiced crab-apples can be used exactly as the cherries – a bowlful on a cold buffet looks wonderful near a ham or a leg of pork, and they make an interesting garnish for composed salads or to accompany pâtés and terrines. The best crab-apples are those that turn a brilliant red in late autumn – the variety is appropriately known as 'Gorgeous'.✝

✝ There are other suitable crab-apples for pickling. Perhaps the very best is 'John Downie', obtainable from specialist nurseries. In 1992 I visited the gardens of Hatfield House in Hertfordshire and marvelled at the avenues of this tree. The fruit was lozenge-shaped and brilliant in scarlet and gold. I ate one and found it just mildly tart. I have described in *Stephanie's Seasons* eating a tarte Tatin made from this fruit at Woolley Grange, a delightful country restaurant near Bath.

Filet à la ficelle . . . with its condiments

6 small carrots, peeled but with green topknot left on

6 slender leeks, root end trimmed and cut with only a very little green left,
    and very well washed

6 small turnips, peeled, but with a few green leaves attached

6 small potatoes

1.5 kg best-quality aged ox fillet, trimmed of all membrane and fat and
    cut into 6 chunks of equal weight

6 sections of marrow bone, soaked overnight in cold water to blanch

1 tablespoon chopped parsley

BOUILLON

4 onions, washed but unpeeled

2 carrots, sliced

2 leeks, sliced and well washed

2 tomatoes, chopped

200 g mushrooms, chopped

1 stalk celery, sliced

1 tablespoon olive oil

1 kg gravy beef or brisket

2 kg beef and veal bones

water

parsley stalks

1 bay leaf

1 sprig of thyme

CONDIMENTS

capers, cornichons, Dijon-style mustard, sea salt, pepper, horseradish

TO MAKE THE BOUILLON   Make the bouillon first, and start it the day before you intend to serve the *filet à la ficelle*.

Cut the onions in half and roast until dark brown by placing the cut sides directly on a hotplate.[†] Brown all the other vegetables well in the oil. Place the meat and bones in a large pot and cover with cold water. Bring slowly to a simmer,

[†] If you do not have a hotplate in your kitchen, brown the cut onions in a heavy iron pan that will not buckle.

skimming well. Add the browned onions, the other vegetables and the herbs and simmer for 6–8 hours. At the end of this time, strain the stock, let it stand, then skim off as much fat as possible. Reduce by rapid boiling until you have about 2.5 litres of well-flavoured stock.

TO COOK THE OTHER VEGETABLES   Cook each vegetable separately in small amounts of water-diluted bouillon until just tender. Drain the vegetables and return the bouillon to the original pot. After all the vegetables are cooked, bring the bouillon back to the boil. It will have reduced in quantity a little, but will have gathered extra flavour from the vegetables. Do not add salt, as the bouillon will reduce further in the actual cooking process.

When you wish to serve the dish, you must decide whether to reheat the vegetables by dropping them back in the bouillon for 1 minute, or reheat them in a perforated steamer over hot water. The first method is preferable, particularly in a home situation, where the quantities of bouillon are not large and you don't risk losing the vegetables.

TO COOK THE FILLET AND MARROW BONE   Have ready a spacious warm dish, with a cover, in which to 'rest' the pieces of meat.

Tie a double piece of string around each chunk of fillet, with the ends of the string hanging free. Tie the ends to the lid of the bouillon pot, measuring the string so that the meat will be suspended in the stock, not resting on the bottom of the pot. Bring the bouillon to a rolling boil. Cook the meat for 6–8 minutes. Remove the chunks, snip the string and place each chunk in the warm resting-dish for a further 6–8 minutes. The fillet will look an unappetising grey colour at this stage, but do not be alarmed. It will be delicious.

The blanched marrow bone should now be simmered in a little hot, but not boiling, water until the marrow has lost its pinkness.

TO SERVE   Serve the marrow bone in the dish with the beef or, to be more genteel, scoop the soft marrow out and spread it on an oven-baked crouton, which you then float in the broth.

Drop the vegetables back in the broth to reheat. Slice the fillet chunks once through the centre, exposing their rosy-red interior. This simmered meat is quite horrible if well cooked, so if your guests prefer their meat overcooked, choose another dish. Serve the meat and its vegetables in a deep dish and ladle over some of the broth. Sprinkle with chopped parsley.

THE CONDIMENTS   An essential part of this dish is the condiments. Prepare a tray of little bowls, each holding one condiment, and pass this tray to each diner. In my restaurant and in my home the condiments include capers, crunchy cornichons, Dijon-style mustard, flakes of sea salt, a pepper mill and our own prepared horse-radish. A flake of sea salt on each mouthful of meat and vegetables is fantastic.[+]

Crème caramel with variations: orange, caramel, coffee[*]

CARAMEL TO COAT THE MOULDS

2 cups castor sugar
1 cup water
1 teaspoon liquid glucose

ORANGE CARAMEL SAUCE

1 cup freshly squeezed and strained orange juice
excess coating caramel

CARAMEL CARAMEL CUSTARD

⅓ cup sugar
2 tablespoons water
300 ml hot milk
30 g castor sugar
2 eggs
2 egg yolks
garnish: spun sugar (1 cup castor sugar, ½ cup water, a drip of glucose)

[+] It is not possible to season meat that is to be poached, because any seasoning will float away. Therefore the flake of sea salt and the grinding of pepper is essential. Nowadays it is not difficult to obtain Maldon sea salt or other varieties of good-quality unrefined salt, including several Australian products. It was much more difficult in 1984. Salt has had a lot of bad press, even though it is essential to good health. As someone who does not eat highly processed food, which is frequently oversalted, I do enjoy well-seasoned food, and was delighted to read in *Good Weekend* on 27 January 2001 the opinion of a British doctor, Peter Mansfield, that 'most health-conscious people now have too little salt in their diets, and this poses a risk of dehydration. The body is more than capable of flushing out excess salt through the kidneys.' He recommends a teaspoon of salt each day.

slivered zest of 1 bright orange

350 ml milk

30 g castor sugar

2 eggs

2 egg yolks

garnish: orange zest (thinly sliced zest from ½ orange, cut in julienne shreds)

1 tablespoon instant powdered coffee

1 tablespoon hot water

350 ml hot milk

30 g castor sugar

2 eggs

2 egg yolks

garnish: coffee beans

TO CARAMELISE THE MOULDS AND MAKE THE ORANGE CARAMEL SAUCE Have all your moulds set out ready, not too close together. Have the orange juice at the ready also.

To make the caramel to coat the moulds, dissolve the sugar in the water with the glucose. Stir until the sugar has dissolved, brushing the sides of the pan with a pastry brush dipped in cold water to prevent crystals of sugar syrup sticking to the sides. Once the sugar has dissolved, increase the heat and boil steadily until you have a golden-brown caramel. Tip the caramel into the moulds a few at a time (it is a good idea to have a helper to speed up the process). Swirl the caramel around the sides of each pot and tip the excess into the next pot. Continue until all are coated.

✦ This recipe illustrates perfectly the difference between restaurant cooking and home cooking, and between 'then' as opposed to 'now'. A restaurant can serve an 'old favourite' but often feels that it must be given a twist or an extra bit of fancy technique to be seen to justify the relatively high price. And yet these home-style dishes are always very, very popular with diners, suggesting that they are not made very often at home any more. Fruit crumbles, pancakes, steamed puddings, baked tarts, custards and so on are always bestsellers. In the 1980s many home cooks wanted to cook like restaurant chefs. The dinner party as entertainment was popular and the food was very fancy. No wonder it dwindled and died! Few of us want to spend all day preparing for four or five friends to come and share our table; happily, we have stopped trying so hard to impress.

Crème caramel is an exquisite dish. The quantities given for any single flavour yield 6 x 100 ml custards. If you double the quantity for any flavour you will have sufficient for 8 serves of 150 ml each. In either case, half the quantity of caramel will be adequate for 6 or 8 individual custards.

To make the sauce, pour the orange juice into the pan with the excess coating caramel and return the pan to a gentle heat to melt the solidified caramel on the bottom. Stir until smooth and then place the pan in the refrigerator, which will help any last bits of adhering toffee to dissolve. After 2–3 hours, pour the sauce into a jug for serving.

TO PREPARE THE CUSTARDS

Caramel caramel custard: Dissolve the sugar in the small amount of water, following the method for the coating caramel. When it is a strong golden colour, add the hot milk and return to a gentle heat to melt the caramel. Stir and, when smooth, strain and measure. Add more milk if necessary to make the quantity up to 350 ml. Whisk together the castor sugar, eggs and egg yolks, pour on the flavoured milk and strain into the caramel-lined moulds.

Orange caramel custard: Drop the slivered orange zest into the milk and very slowly bring to scalding point. Leave to infuse, covered, for 2 hours. Beat together the castor sugar, eggs and egg yolks as for the caramel caramel custard, and pour on the strained flavoured milk. Strain into the caramel-lined moulds.

Coffee caramel custard: Dissolve the powdered coffee in the hot water. Stir this into the hot milk. Whisk the castor sugar, eggs and egg yolks as before, and combine with the coffee-flavoured milk. Strain into the caramel-lined moulds.

TO BAKE AND SERVE

Place a wet cloth on the bottom of a baking dish that will hold all the moulds comfortably. Carefully place in the custards and pour around some very hot water to come halfway up the sides of the moulds. Cover with foil and cook at 160°C in a non-fanforced oven for approximately 25 minutes until just set.[†] Put aside until the next day.

GARNISHES

Spun sugar: Have ready an old fork, a tray lined with silicone paper and a pan of golden-brown caramel made with the castor sugar, water and glucose (half the quantity needed to caramelise the moulds). Dip the tines of the fork into the sticky caramel and flick in fine threads over the tray. The threads are then gathered up and dropped onto the little custards. This can be quite messy until you have the knack, as the spun sugar tends to go everywhere. It must be done on the day you are to serve the custards.

Orange zest: Finely peel off the coloured part of the zest of ½ an orange and cut into julienne strips. Drop into boiling water for 5 minutes to remove any bitterness, then serve on the orange caramel custard.

[†] A family-sized crème caramel in a 1.25 litre dish will take 50–55 minutes to bake at 160°C.

Coffee beans: Either use real coffee beans if you like the crunch, or perhaps it is better to buy some chocolate-coated coffee beans. Place one coffee bean on each coffee caramel custard.

TO SERVE Unmould one custard of each flavour onto a cold plate and spoon a little of the orange caramel syrup around the custards. Add the garnishes.

The same recipe for caramel can be used if you want to dip fruits in toffee as a dramatic after-dinner treat. Strawberries work particularly well. Impale each berry on the end of a skewer, twirl in the caramel and, using a fork, push each berry off onto a lightly oiled tray to cool. Do not prepare these more than 2 hours before eating, and do not refrigerate them.

Or yet another idea. Sandwich choice walnut halves with marzipan and dip into the toffee, using tongs. Be careful of drips on your fingers.

Toasted orange sponge biscuits

———

butter

4 eggs

1 egg yolk

¾ cup sugar

1 teaspoon orange flower water

1 cup plain flour

pinch salt

1 teaspoon baking powder

1 tablespoon grated orange zest

1 tablespoon grated lemon zest

Butter a jelly-roll pan of about 25 cm × 38 cm. Line it with non-stick baking paper and brush with more butter. Preheat the oven to 180°C.

In the food processor or with an electric beater, beat the eggs, egg yolk, sugar and orange flower water until pale, thick and fluffy. Sift over the flour, salt and baking powder. Add the zests and blend gently but thoroughly with the egg mix. Pour the batter into the pan and bake for approximately 15 minutes until lightly golden and springy to the touch. Cool the cake in the pan for 5 minutes, then turn out and cool on a cake rack.

Trim the edges and cut into the desired size (e.g. finger lengths to accompany a dish or long strips to line a marquise mould). Lower the oven temperature to 150°C. Return the pieces to the oven and bake until dry but not browned. Cool and store in an airtight tin.

Pigeons I have fancied

Menu

MILLEFEUILLE OF CRAB WITH
NASTURTIUMS

ROASTED SQUAB PIGEON WITH
SWEET GARLIC AND A SALAD OF
MIGNONETTE HEARTS

FRESH 'FRUITS' . . . A PLATTER OF ICES

There are occasions when as a good cook you wish to create a grand culinary occasion and are prepared to spend quite a lot of time doing it. This menu is for such an evening. I hope that your guests will appreciate the labour of love represented by the rose-petal ice and the buttery quality of your own puff pastry, not to mention the patience needed to wrest every fragment of crab from its shell.

There are several varieties of crab available in Victoria, and for at least part of the year we have a ready supply of airfreighted live mud crabs from Queensland. Very occasionally one sees a king crab, notable for its immense size, armour-plated large claws and exquisite, sweet flesh. Probably because of the work required, not many

*Roasted squab pigeon with little potatoes, sweet garlic
and just-picked green beans on salad leaves (page 58)*

Fruit sorbets – pear, passionfruit, kiwi, rose-petal (page 61)

restaurants accept the challenge of serving crab. When they do, the response is overwhelming – everyone wants to order it.✢

I love squab pigeons. On a memorable visit to France in 1982 I tasted many. In fact, a title for this chapter kept singing in my head: 'Pigeons I have fancied'. Alain Dutournier at Au Trou Gascon served the legs in a braise and the breast roasted. At Le Pressoir, Henri Seguin delighted me with extremely rare pigeon, sliced and served on a bed of cabbage braised in the rich pigeon juices. At Taillevent my pigeon was boned and stuffed. At Pharamond, a wonderful old bistro, there were no more pigeons, so instead I was served a luscious partridge on its crouton with a dish of souffléed potatoes.

Once, in Hong Kong, Maurice took me to Sha'tin, a restaurant he had remembered from ten years previously, which specialised in pigeons. They were superb. Everywhere, tables of locals were being served large platters of crisp-skinned roast pigeon, with head, beak and, I was assured, brains intact. I tried to ask, but as I don't speak a word of Cantonese and the chef spoke only a little English, I don't think I received more than a vague idea of the method. I believe that the birds were marinated with a little star anise, steamed until tender, brushed with soy and other good things, and then roasted at a high temperature to result in the deep-mahogany crispy skins. As usual, the fingerbowls were large bowls of lukewarm tea, and most effective they were.✦

After the rich pigeon meat, you will stun your guests with this selection of ices. Any fruit can be used to make a fruit ice. They are remarkable creations, not only because they are so simple, but because they interpose nothing between the genuine taste of the fruit and the consumer. Thus if you make a peach ice from the three truly perfect peaches of the summer, your ice will be sublime. If, however, you use slightly underripe kiwi fruit, the ice will taste of slightly underripe kiwi fruit, no matter how you fiddle the sugar content.

Fruits that naturally have a high water content will always taste a little more elusive than other flavours. They are not the worse for this. It gives them a very special character. The two outstanding flavours in this category are grape and

✢ Some suppliers now sell picked crabmeat, usually from either spanner crabs or blue swimmer crabs. When it is fresh it is a wonderful resource. The problem is that crabmeat is highly perishable and often has to travel considerable distances before arriving at its destination. It is often frozen to overcome this disadvantage, with a corresponding loss of texture. There is still no substitute for cooking and hand-picking the meat yourself. It is not surprising that it is still a rare treat.

✦ Two years after writing *Menus for Food Lovers* I was a judge at the Hong Kong Food Festival – Flavour of '86. A visit to Sha'tin had been arranged. This time I visited the kitchen and watched in amazement as dozens of pigeons bobbed in huge cauldrons of stock from which dangled the threads of many spice bags. After the simmering came the deep-frying in woks heated by diesel, the flames roaring like a furnace.

watermelon. Fruits that have a sticky, 'meaty' texture will result in a firmer, more ice-cream-like ice. This is very noticeable with kiwi fruit and mango ices. And so on. The fruit you choose will be exposed 'warts and all', so don't fall for the idea that fermented, damaged fruit will make wonderful ices, because it will only make fermented ices or those that reflect back at you the damaged character of the raw material.

The character of the ice can be completely changed if you decide to cook the fruit first. Stewed plums are lovely turned into an ice. So are pears simmered in red wine, and so on and so on. Do not lose sight of the fact, however, that the appeal of these fragile creations is their iciness, their refreshing quality and their fruity purity.

The basic method consists of blending a roughly equal amount of strained, puréed fruit with sugar syrup, and adjusting this mixture with sieved sugar if it is not sweet enough, or extra water if it is too sweet. The sweetness, or 'sugar density', is best measured by using a saccharometer, otherwise you are relying on guesswork. A saccharometer is a measuring device that looks like a large thermometer and floats in the cooled syrup and records the density of the sugar. It is a necessary adjunct to good ice-making, as the sugar density not only affects the sweetness, but is very important in controlling the texture. A saccharometer should be obtainable where you buy an ice-cream churn, or at a pastrycook supplier or a medical supplier.

The basic Escoffier recipe calls for a fairly universal 18-degree sugar density (Baumé scale). Many cooks feel that these ices are too sweet for the modern palate. This is certainly the case where cooks are serving their fruit ice as a sorbet between courses, a practice that has been revived recently.[†] However, thoughtless reduction of the sugar content brings in the next problem, of iciness and granular texture. I have spent many hours experimenting and thinking about these problems and for what it is worth pass on my experience.

It is certainly easier to control some of these problems of graininess and sweetness if one has a very efficient ice-cream churn. One can reduce the sugar density to 14 or 15 degrees providing one intends to serve the ice fairly soon after it is churned. The ice will be unusable after a night in the freezer, as it will be rock hard. One must then be prepared to melt it and rechurn it before serving it again.

If, however, one incorporates some alcohol into the ice, one is dealing with a new property. Alcohol will not freeze, therefore an ice that is quite high in alcohol can afford to be quite low in sugar – hence the popularity and possibility of champagne sorbets. Even a little high-alcohol liqueur in a fruit ice will inhibit its freezing, so that the sugar content can be dropped by 1 or 2 degrees. Remember,

───────────────

[†] Fortunately the practice of serving a sorbet as a so-called 'palate cleanser' has largely disappeared. A 'palate killer' would be a better description.

however, that you started out to make, say, a pear ice, not a Poire William ice. The pear taste and texture must predominate. It is all a matter of compromise, balance and judgement.[†]

Millefeuille of crab with nasturtiums

1 cup crabmeat, tightly packed, from 1 mud crab or other variety of crab
2 cucumbers
500 g puff pastry (see page 38)
nasturtium leaves and flowers or borage flowers

MAYONNAISE SAUCE

2 egg yolks
2 tablespoons (approximately) of roe and juice from the crab
1 teaspoon wine vinegar
salt, white pepper
1 cup best-quality olive oil
few drops lemon juice (optional)
200 ml cream
1 tablespoon chopped chervil or tarragon

TO PREPARE THE CRABMEAT   If the crab is alive, drop it into boiling, salted water and simmer until the shell turns bright red, 10 minutes per kg. Lift out carefully using some sort of flat skimmer, and drain upside down until quite cool. If the crab is bought cooked, proceed with the recipe.

Twist off all the claws and set aside. Twist and lever off the soft undershell. Do this over a bowl that has a strainer placed on it. Let all the juices run into the strainer. Remove the greyish feathery gills found around the body and discard. Discard also the roundish bony sac at the top of the body. With a teaspoon, scrape the inside of the top shell and save all the creamy parts of the crab that line it. Add these to the bowl with the crab juices. Wash out this shell and save it for decoration.

[†] This whole speech regarding the technical aspects of sorbet-making has to be of historic interest only. In the early to mid-1980s most cooks churned their sorbets in hand-cranked churns with a central metal cylinder that had to be packed with alternating layers of ice and salt. It was very hard work indeed. Today, once the mix is made it is tipped into a stainless steel chamber and a switch is flicked. Fifteen minutes later the completed ice-cream or sorbet is ready.

With a heavy knife, quarter the body and patiently and carefully prise out all the flakes of delicious sweet meat stored in all the compartments. Crack the claws and remove this meat. Either add it to the bowl of body meat or keep it separately to use as a garnish.

With the back of a spoon or the pestle from a pestle and mortar, press all the solids in the strainer into the bowl, and ensure that you have removed any fragments of shell.

You should now have a well-washed body shell; a bowl of choice crabmeat; another bowl with a reddish or yellowish liquid mixed with a pasty substance (this sounds disgusting but it will add all the panache to your finished sauce); and possibly some claw meat separately.

Wash all chopping surfaces, knives etc. very thoroughly and wrap all crab debris. Refrigerate the shell and meat and juices, all covered with plastic film.

TO PREPARE THE CUCUMBERS Halve the cucumbers lengthwise, scrape out all the seeds with a teaspoon and cut the flesh into as small dice as you are able. Place the diced cucumber in a sieve, sprinkle with a very little salt and leave the sieve placed over a bowl for 1–2 hours. After this time, turn it into a clean kitchen cloth, squeeze gently and refrigerate.

TO PREPARE THE MAYONNAISE SAUCE Mayonnaise can be made most success-fully in a food processor, particularly when, as in this case, you are going to incorporate some extra ingredient with the egg yolks. It is, however, a superior sauce when hand-whisked, as there is a definite and noticeable change in the texture between a hand-mounted sauce and one made in a food processor. Hand-mounted mayonnaise has a softness on the tongue, it shines and melts and slips in the mouth, whereas mechanically mounted mayonnaise is a more solid mass, much paler, and somewhere along the way the flavour of the oil is diminished.

However, having said all this, in this particular case I suggest a compromise. Place the egg yolks, crab juices and vinegar in the food processor bowl together with a little salt and pepper, and process until very well blended. Trickle in about one-quarter of the oil with the motor running. Scrape the sauce into a bowl and then proceed to whisk in the balance of the oil. When all the oil has been blended, taste for sharpness and seasoning. Add lemon juice or extra seasonings, if desired.

Whip the cream until firm but still foldable. Fold in the chopped herbs and then fold the cream into your mayonnaise, continually tasting until you have a delicate, well-balanced sauce. The amount of cream you add is up to you. Adjust the seasoning.

TO COOK THE PUFF PASTRY SHEETS[+] Roll out the pastry to 2 rectangles approximately 30 cm × 12 cm and about 5 mm thick. Prick each rectangle very thoroughly. Select 3 clean baking sheets of the same size. Place the rectangles side by side on one baking sheet, and place the second baking sheet on top of the pastry. What you are doing is compressing all the buttery layers so that you end up with a super-crisp sheet of pastry that has been baked on both sides.

Slip the baking sheets into a 220°C oven for approximately 8 minutes. At the end of this time, remove the trays from the oven. Working quickly, invert the two trays, quickly lift off the top tray, slip the pastry layers onto the third tray, either by a quick flip or deft use of a wide, spatula-type lifter, and replace another tray on top. Press down lightly on the pastry to discourage it from rising and put the two trays in the oven for a further 8 minutes.

Check the pastry a minute or two before the end of the cooking time. The sheets should be evenly golden. Remove from the oven, remove the top tray and slide the sheets of pastry onto a cake rack to become completely cold. When quite cold, place on a board and trim the edges with a very sharp knife.

The pastry sheets could be cooked the day before, but the nutty, just-cooked quality of the puff pastry will be gone. For perfection, cook the sheets the day they are to be used, but by all means make the pastry and roll it out the day before.

TO ASSEMBLE YOUR CRAB SANDWICH
1. Set aside 2 tablespoons of mayonnaise sauce.
2. Fold enough sauce into the reserved crabmeat to make a firm filling.
3. Place a rectangle of pastry on a long, flat serving plate.
4. Spoon on the crabmeat filling, smoothing it evenly.
5. Lightly spread another pastry sheet with the reserved sauce.
6. Decorate this sheet of pastry with a border of tiny, well-washed nasturtium leaves and a ribbon of diced cucumber.
7. Place the decorated pastry sheet on top of the crab filling.
8. Put the balance of fresh cucumber and the reserved claw meat in the reserved body shell. Nasturtium flowers or borage flowers – which are, of course, edible – can be scattered around the serving platter.
9. Cut the crab sandwich into serving slices with a sharp, serrated knife. An electric knife is very effective for cutting pastry. Do not try to cut it too thinly, and be prepared to scoop some of the filling onto the plates, as it is still rather soft.

Do not assemble the millefeuille more than 1 hour before serving, as the pastry will soften if you do it too early.

✢ This is an outstanding method for making crisp puff pastry layers. Use it also to sandwich berries and pastry cream for the classic millefeuille dessert.

Roasted squab pigeon with sweet garlic and a salad of mignonette hearts

It is important to ensure that the squab pigeons you purchase are in fact *squab* pigeons. There are no doubt interesting ways of cooking older birds, but this recipe is intended to glorify the rich and tender flesh of these young fledglings.

You will need 1 squab per diner, and each should weigh between 400 and 450 g. Such birds are not always easy to find. Smaller birds are equally delicious and make wonderful salad entrées. It is also a good idea to be sure that your guests are people who enjoy picking at bones, as there is not sufficient meat on the breast alone of even a large squab to satisfy a hearty meat-eater.

In the restaurant we always have a supply of roasted backbones carved from the pigeons of the day before to make a rich game stock. Starting from scratch, one must be a little more creative.

Most squab are sold with head and feet attached; these are most valuable for the stock.

6 × 400–450 g squab pigeons (including hearts and livers)
salt, pepper
6 tiny sprigs of thyme
3 bay leaves
butter
a little olive oil
30 large, unpeeled cloves garlic
12 small potatoes
500 g best green beans, topped and tailed
2 shallots (or ½ small onion), very finely chopped
1 tablespoon chopped parsley

STOCK

1 well-roasted chicken carcass
necks, wingtips of all the squab
heads, feet of all the squab
any game scraps you can buy, e.g. more heads, feet or sometimes a squab with torn skin
1 glass dry white wine
1 bay leaf
1 sprig of thyme

1 carrot, 1 onion, 1 stalk of celery, parsley stalks, all chopped small
6 mushrooms, sliced
6 unpeeled cloves of garlic
olive oil

SALAD OF MIGNONETTE HEARTS

6–12 hearts mignonette lettuce (1–2 per person)
3 cloves garlic, finely chopped
60 g butter
3 tablespoons pigeon stock

TO MAKE THE STOCK Roast all the poultry bits and pieces in a hot oven, stirring once or twice to ensure even colouring. Lift out all the scraps into a stockpot and pour out all the fat. Deglaze the pan with the white wine, scraping and stirring to lift all browned particles. Pour the deglazing juices into the stockpot.

Cover with cold water (or, for a superior result, with any light poultry stock you might have in the freezer). Add the bay leaf and thyme, bring to a simmer and skim off any scum. Fry the remaining ingredients in a little oil until well coloured. Place into the stockpot. Adjust the heat to a gentle simmer and leave for 3 hours. Strain the stock at this time, allow to settle, skim off any fat that has risen to the top, and reduce by fast boiling to one-third. Set aside.

TO PREPARE THE BIRDS Check that the hearts and livers have been removed and are set aside. Wipe out the inside of the birds. Season well with salt and pepper, then slip 1 sprig of thyme and ½ a bay leaf inside each bird together with 1 teaspoon of soft butter. Rub the skin with a little more butter and truss with string. This is done to keep the bird a neat shape and to prevent the legs rearing up in the pan. It is also easier to move 6 birds around in a dish if they are nice and compact.

There are many methods of trussing a pigeon or any other small bird. The aim is a compact shape that will cook evenly. Measure a piece of string long enough to go around the bird loosely 3 times and thread the string through a trussing or craft needle. With the breast uppermost and the wing-tips folded underneath, push the needle firmly through the upper part of the wings and then push from the opposite direction through the thighs. Turn the bird over and tie the ends of the string together firmly at the back and cut off the excess.

Select a baking dish of a size that will hold the birds comfortably but is not too large. Pour in a film of oil. Throw in the garlic cloves and fry them for 5 minutes on top of the stove. (As the pigeons will be roasted until just rosy-pink and the garlic should be soft and sweet, a little precooking is necessary.)

Preparation to this stage can be done several hours in advance.

POTATO PREPARATION (POMMES NOISETTES)   If you grow your own potatoes, you may be lucky enough to have a supply of tiny walnut-sized potatoes, which are perfect for this dish. If not, select the smallest, newest-looking new potatoes available and proceed as follows.

Wash the potatoes, but do not peel them. Parboil for 5 minutes. Drain. Drop them into the baking dish alongside the lightly fried garlic cloves. They will later absorb all the aromas and qualities of the garlic, oil and butter, and be further enriched by the pigeon 'droppings'.

GREEN BEANS   In early summer it is possible to buy the first of the new season's stringless beans, which are round, bright green and tiny. Search diligently and change your greengrocer if he tells you that such beans don't exist. At other times of the year, buy the best beans you can find. Having topped and tailed them, have ready a large pan of boiling, salted water and a warmed dish.

Melt the shallots in a scrap of butter, stir in the chopped parsley and leave this somewhere warm until the last moment, when you will throw in the freshly boiled green beans and shake all together.

TO COOK THE BIRDS   Preheat the oven to 240°C. Heat the baking dish with the garlic and potatoes in it. Place the birds in and seal first one side, then the other, quickly over high heat (approximately 2–3 minutes). Place the birds breast-side up in the dish, and put the dish in the oven for 10 minutes.

At the end of this time, remove the dish, pick up one pigeon with tongs, let the juices run and check the colour. If they run clear to lightest pink, the birds are ready. If still red, return the pan to the oven for a further 5 minutes.

When the pigeons are done, snip the strings and remove the birds to a hot dish to rest for at least 5 minutes and up to 15. Never omit this step. They will hold their heat for some time, and there is a world of difference in rosy meat allowed to relax and rosy meat tight with its juices ready to spurt at the first stab of a fork!

Check that the potatoes are tender. If not, return the pan to the oven for 5 minutes after removing the birds. With the birds and potatoes resting on a warm plate, seal the livers and hearts in the baking dish on top of the stove with the roasted garlic. Set aside 3 tablespoons of stock for the salad dressing, and pour the rest into the baking dish. Let it bubble happily while you either joint your pigeons and drop in the green beans, or simply cook the beans and serve the birds whole.

SALAD OF MIGNONETTE HEARTS   Wash and drain the lettuce hearts very well but leave them intact. Simmer together the chopped garlic, butter and pigeon stock until the butter is golden brown. Pour this sauce over the lettuce.

TO JOINT THE PIGEONS   Have a heavy cook's knife ready. Simply sever each leg with a quick thump of your hand on the knife. Split the bird along the breastbone and cut out the backbone. (Keep the backbones and any juices for your next game stock. Bag them, label and into the freezer.)

TO SERVE   On each plate serve 1 pigeon, 2 tiny potatoes, 1 heart and 1 liver and 5 roasted whole garlic cloves. Strain over a portion of the juices. Toss your barely cooked, drained green beans into the warm dish containing the shallot/parsley mixture. Shake all together and serve either as a separate dish or on the same plate, in the juice. Serve the lettuce on a separate plate alongside.

An alternative would be to surround the lovely little mignonette salads with the green beans and offer a combined salad and bean course alongside the birds.

Fresh 'fruits' . . . a platter of ices

sugar syrup (2 litres water simmered with 2 kg sugar for 5 minutes)
saccharometer, ice-cream churn, juice extractor, blender, fine strainer

ROSE-PETAL AND CHAMPAGNE ICE

2 cups tightly packed red rose-petals with a heavy perfume
2 cups sugar syrup (see above)
1 bottle rose champagne
juice of 1 orange
2–3 drops rosewater (optional)

PEAR ICE

6 ripe pears
lemon juice
1½ cups sugar syrup (see above)
lemon zest
60 ml Poire William liqueur

KIWI FRUIT ICE

6 kiwi fruit
sugar syrup (see above)
lemon juice

PASSIONFRUIT ICE

6 passionfruit
orange juice
sugar syrup (see above)

ROSE-PETAL AND CHAMPAGNE ICE   Start 2 days before the dinner. The best roses to use for this are deep-red roses with a heady perfume. Snip off the white base of each rose petal with scissors. Discard the white base, as it is bitter. Infuse the coloured petals in a basin with 2 cups of boiling sugar syrup. Leave for 2 days, refrigerated and lightly covered.

Pass the contents of the basin through a food processor or blender and then strain the mixture through fine muslin, pressing firmly to extract every tiny drop of flavour. Combine the rose syrup with ½ bottle champagne. (You will have the rest of the champagne to drink with the dessert.) Add the orange juice, and the rose-water if the perfume is not strong enough. Taste. Measure the density. This ice will probably have a low density because of the champagne. Because of the facts mentioned earlier – i.e. that alcohol does not freeze and low sugar content means a hard ice (see page 54) – you can afford to leave the density on the low side rather than add a lot of extra sugar, which may disguise the delicate rose flavour. It should be around 13 or 14 degrees Baumé.

This ice will not last long out of the freezer.

PEAR ICE Choose ripe fruit with undamaged skins. Halve 3 of the pears lengthwise. Discard the cores and seeds. Scoop out all the fruit carefully with a teaspoon. Nick a small 'v' where the seed was, to remove the brown woody part. Brush the shells with lemon juice, stack inside one another, wrap in plastic and freeze immediately.

Peel the other 3 pears and discard the cores and seeds. Chop all the fruit roughly and poach in the sugar syrup with a sliver of lemon zest. When the fruit is just tender, blend well with the poaching syrup and pass through a strainer. Add the Poire William liqueur and sharpen with a little lemon juice. Cool.

Pour a little of the cooled mixture into the glass flask that accompanies your saccharometer and measure the density. You are aiming at around 15–16 degrees. As this ice is very thick, give the saccharometer a few minutes to find the true level. If it measures higher than 15–16 degrees, add a little water, stir well and measure again. If it measures less than 15–16 degrees (most unlikely), sieve in a little icing sugar. If the pear ice is so thick that the saccharometer will not settle at all, add an extra cup of sugar syrup and test again. When the ice registers 16 degrees, churn it according to the instructions for your churn.

When the ice is ready, quickly fill your frozen pear shells, place them on a tray, cover with plastic wrap and pack any excess pear ice into a container to be eaten on another day. Return all to the freezer.

KIWI FRUIT ICE Choose ripe fruit with undamaged skins. Halve the fruit length-wise and scoop out the pulp. Freeze the 6 most perfect shells (or freeze them all, thereby preparing a quick dessert for a further occasion). They will take at least 2 hours to freeze, but are best if placed in the freezer much earlier.

Blend the pulp or, better still, pass it through a juice extractor, which will extract all the seeds. If blended, the pulp must still be pushed through a strainer to get rid of the seeds. Measure the volume of the pulp and combine with an equal quantity of sugar syrup. Add the strained juice of 1–2 lemons and measure the density. Aim for 16 degrees. As for the pear ice, adjust with water and lemon juice if it is too sweet or add a little extra sugar syrup if the density is too low. As with the pear ice, this mix is also thick, so allow the saccharometer a few minutes to settle. Churn as for the pear ice. Pack the shells as for the pear ice and freeze any extra ice for another day.

PASSIONFRUIT ICE   This ice has a most intense flavour. Also, passionfruit has a fairly low yield of juice per piece of fruit. For these reasons I add some strained orange juice to the passionfruit juice.

Halve the fruit, scoop out the pulp and seeds and freeze the shells as before. Put the pulp and seeds through a juice extractor or simply press firmly through a strainer. Do not blend, as you wish to extract the seeds, not pulverise them. Measure the volume of juice. Add orange juice to increase the bulk to 300 ml.

Combine with an equal quantity of sugar syrup. Measure the density, adjust and churn as before. Pack the shells as for the pear and kiwi fruit ices.

TO SERVE   Have your dessert plates chilled. On each plate place a rose. Place 1 piece of each 'fruit' on the plate – that is, 1 pear, 1 kiwi fruit, 1 passionfruit, and finally a scoop of rose ice to resemble a bud.

We recently held a special spring dinner where I allowed my love of flowers to run riot. I most successfully served a posy of sorbets infused from some of the loveliest and most fragrant of spring flowers: Lorraine Lee pink roses, violets, jasmine and buddleia. The flavours were exquisite and the clear pastel colours were a delicate and astonishing delight to behold.✧

✧ I doubt that any home cook would ever consider such a labour-intensive dessert. Because it was so popular at the restaurant there was a 'razor's edge' aspect to the dish. Would we get enough of each sorbet churned in time for it to become firm enough to scoop before the first order came in? Each one had to be churned fresh every day. And we had a freezer crisis during the summer of 1984. We had to hire a portable freezer, and a member of staff spent far too much time scooping and forming these desserts wearing a padded waterproof jacket over his chef's coat.

I very nearly came undone with this dish. It was to be the finale of the second Great Chefs dinner for 100 diners at the Rothbury Estate in the Hunter Valley in 1979. There was a terrible storm in the afternoon and a power blackout. The sorbet-filled fruit shells all melted and the sorbets had to be rechurned and scooped à la minute, thanks to the many willing helpers.

The dish was supposed to trompe l'oeil and evoke a still-life arrangement of flowers and fruit. Hence the full-blown rose suggested for each plate, its scent echoed in a sorbet made from dark red petals. I must say, freezer dramas aside, the plates looked beautiful!

A few of my favourite things

I return over and over to certain dishes, certain flavours and certain influences, and often I am unaware of doing so. I suggest a dish to my colleagues thinking it fresh and new, to be greeted with knowing smiles. 'Just like we did the summer before last,' they will say. I have to acknowledge that this is how a personal style evolves. The emphasis shifts, one item has greater or lesser prominence this time, a new element creeps in, but it is still unmistakably my work, not someone else's. This is a good thing. The miniature galantine of quail is such a dish. It sums up lots of special things to me. It is intricate, and it represents lots of tender, loving care. To create a shining row of bursting little birds dotted with black truffle 'buttons' gives me astonishing satisfaction. In the mouth they

64

create an explosion of flavour, from the brilliant natural jelly to the smoothly sensual filling. The true 'amateur' of such a dish has really to get into it. Each minute bone is to be sucked and lingered over. It is impossible to be remote from this experience. The quail nestle modestly in a shrubbery of green leaves, which glisten with a touch of hazelnut oil, while the handful of violets scattered over the dish is the final poetic gesture.

For the hostess or the cook who loves a challenge, the dish has the advantage that it is complete before your guests arrive. All the drama of the clarification of the jelly is behind you, and you can present your masterpieces with proper pride.

After the quail, I am proposing a roasted loin of pork served with sauerkraut braised in champagne. The meat is rubbed with spiced cumquats, which also add a delicious flavour to the sauce. The method of roasting is a compromise between the English method, which results in the much-loved golden crackling, and the French method, where the meat is usually trussed minus the skin and roasted at a lower temperature and served in thin, elegant slices. Several years ago I was asked to design a dinner to celebrate the 1981 Vin de Champagne Award. Each course of the dinner would be partnered by a great champagne, and the organisers of the dinner had asked that at least some of the dishes include champagne as an ingredient. It was the first time I had ever cooked sauerkraut in champagne, but it was very good and very well received on the night. In fact, the triumph of the dish was that most people reading their menu and seeing roasted loin of pork with sauerkraut were rather anxious, fearing that the combination would be impossibly heavy and rich. This was not the case, for the dish was light and festive in feeling.

As with all the meat that I serve roasted, the sauce is light in body and uses every drop of flavour created by the actual cooking process. I find it most worthwhile to spend a little time thinking creatively about what will sit in the baking dish with the joint of lamb, pork, beef or whatever, as the most subtle juices can result. I frequently choose the sweetness of whole garlic or small pickling onions in their skins.† Think also of pieces of dried orange or mandarin zest, or lots of a single herb, so that it becomes lamb with thyme, not just lamb with a sprig of thyme. Cumquats are magical. Also roughly chopped fennel allowed to caramelise in the baking dish, or celery prepared in the same manner. Or lots of carrots – sprinkle over a spoonful of sugar to ensure the caramelising. You will have to cook other vegetables to accompany the meat, as the flavouring carrots, fennel or whatever will have given up their goodness and be pretty lifeless by the time the pan is deglazed and bubbled

---

† Cooked garlic was very frightening to many in the early 1980s. Restaurants had to introduce it gently, with encouraging words such as 'sweet' or 'tender'. Many cooks would now automatically add a clove or three of garlic to almost any roasting bird or piece of meat, and enjoy its mellow flavour and soft, melting centre.

with some wine. A classic roasted duck is one of the best-known examples of how a change in a flavouring can completely change the character of the dish.

Think also of green olives or stoned cherries or slivered, shredded Seville orange zest, or glazed turnips or ripe purple figs, or even peeled muscat grapes. In each case one might well add something else to the pan juices, perhaps some *concassée* of fresh tomato with the olives, a few drops of kirsch with the cherries, a spoonful of fine Rose's tangerine marmalade in the juice with the Seville oranges, a few drops of the pickling vinegar if using spiced cumquats, plums or crab-apples, and so on and so on.

In this menu I have given the recipe for the spiced cumquats that will accompany this pork.[+] It is becoming rare to stock a pantry cupboard with one's own jams, jellies and preserves. However, I find it soothing, satisfying work, cutting up the fruit and weighing the sugar. To me it is the essence of housewifery – or should it be husbandry? – to use resources when they are bountiful and then to set them by for bleaker days.[✦] It reminds me of the grasshopper and the ant. Agricultural shows provide myriad ways of demonstrating to city-dwellers the riches and richness of country life. The country women's cooking section has spectacular displays of jams and jellies. The rows and rows of products are backlit, and the glorious warm pinks and cornelian glow of the quince and currant jellies are superb. One year, in the marmalade section, I was transfixed by the artistry of a cook whose contribution was a jar of clear golden-orange marmalade in which long shreds of orange zest were tied in butterfly bows and were held suspended in the gold like an insect in amber. How did she do it?

I have included in this section a recipe for jelly that I make once a year from my friend Helen's loquat tree, a fruit so often ignored and so common in older suburban gardens.

[+] I do claim responsibility for reviving interest in cumquats. My mother loved them and not only made marmalade and liqueur, but used to crush the fresh fruit all over the skin of a chicken before roasting it. She then pushed the spent skin either under its breast or into the cavity. That marvellous perfumed bittersweet flavour will always have a special meaning for me. I have been writing about cumquats since 1976 and now read of many cooks using them in puddings and sauces. They are usually spelt 'kumquats' but my mother wrote 'cumquats', so I'm sticking to that.

[✦] Having a restaurant in the late 1970s and throughout the 1980s and with no formal training, just a love of sharing good food, I naturally drew on the resources I had available to me. This included my own garden, my mother's garden, the herb garden of at least one friend, and what I could buy in times of abundance to bottle, pickle or otherwise preserve. This was a traditional and practical way of maintaining a household, only 'new' in that the skills had been largely forgotten, and in any case had been found in private homes, not in public eating-houses. I believe I changed this situation and opened the minds of many to what they had either never known or had forgotten.

All this musing on pantry shelves and larders leads me to contemplate other old-fashioned treats. I have decided to complete this menu with the very famous English summer pudding. It is very well known, but each time we have it on the menu at the restaurant I am surprised at how many people ask for the recipe. It can have a variety of red fruit in it, but it *must* have redcurrants. In the early 1980s one was lucky to see half a dozen punnets of redcurrants for the whole summer. Each year I have asked my greengrocer for them and I think many others must have asked also. We now have a plentiful supply of redcurrants in the summer months. They are always expensive, possibly because they are very fiddly to pick. I have a token three or four canes in the garden, which I grow mainly so that I can use their delicately scented leaves in creams and custards, or to layer amongst the spiced blood plums to increase the flavour in the juice. And when in fruit the little clusters of jewels look amazing – the birds certainly enjoy them!

Truffled galantine of quail

6 quail
salt, ground pepper
60 ml cognac
1 split pig's trotter
a little light oil
30 g butter
1 small carrot, chopped
1 onion, chopped
1 stalk celery, chopped
1 leek, well washed and sliced
4 mushrooms, chopped
1.5 litres chicken stock
1 tomato, skinned and seeded
3 egg whites
1 eggshell
2 extra slices carrot
1 stalk parsley
juice from 50 g tin of truffles (optional)
port or Madeira
1 truffle

DUCK MOUSSE

100 g duck livers
60 g hard pork fat, diced
1 sprig thyme
1 bay leaf
¼ cup port or Madeira
salt, pepper
60 g butter
100 g canned foie gras
1 tablespoon cream

needle and strong linen or
    other thread

TO PREPARE THE QUAIL   Cut out the backbone of each bird with poultry scissors and carefully remove the ribcage with a sharp knife and your fingers, leaving the wings and legs intact. Keep the knife blade always angled into the carcass to avoid cutting your fingers. Reserve the bones. Sprinkle the opened-out birds with salt, pepper and cognac.

Cover and refrigerate for a few hours.

TO MAKE THE STOCK AND THE JELLY   Sprinkle the quail bones and the trotter with a few drops of oil and roast in a hot oven until well browned. Heat the butter in a large, heavy stockpot and brown all the vegetables except the tomato. Stir often to ensure even colouring and to prevent sticking. When this *mirepoix* is well coloured, add the quail bones and the trotter. Deglaze the roasting pan with a little of the chicken stock and add the juices to the stockpot. Add the balance of the stock, and the tomato. Bring to the boil, skim, adjust the heat and simmer for 2½ hours.

Strain the stock into a smaller, clean pan and discard the bones and vegetables. (As the trotter will be tender, bone it, cut it into small pieces, mix with a few pickled cucumber slices, some parsley and some oil and vinegar and eat this little salad for lunch as you work.) Reduce the stock by one-third over high heat. Cool, and when cold lift off any fat particles with a piece of kitchen paper and proceed to the clarification.

To clarify the stock: Combine in a food processor the egg whites, eggshell, extra carrot slices and parsley stalk. Whiz until a light froth. Tip into the cold stock and stir continuously over moderate heat until the mixture comes to simmering point. Draw to one side and let simmer gently for 20 minutes. Turn the heat off and leave for 5 minutes.

Line a colander or chinois sieve with a damp, clean cloth and suspend it over a bowl. With a wire skimmer, gently lift part of the 'raft' of coagulated egg and vegetable and discard it, then ladle the limpid clear broth through the damp cloth. Flavour with the truffle juice (if using), port, salt and pepper. Place the stock in the refrigerator until quite cold and test the set. It should be set, but will still wobble a little if you tilt the bowl. If you had no trotter to use in the stock, you may now have to add several leaves of gelatine, the amount depending on the volume of liquid. (See page 14 for gelatine requirements.)

TO MAKE THE MOUSSE   Place the duck livers and pork fat in a bowl with the thyme and bay leaf and pour the port over. Season with salt and pepper. Cover and leave for 2 hours. Remove the livers to a sieve and drain well over a bowl. Pat dry with a paper towel. Cook the livers rapidly in the butter until browned on the outside but still quite pink in the middle, no more than 2 minutes. Remove the livers and set aside.

Strain the port marinade into the pan, scrape and boil until reduced by half (1 minute). In a food processor, process the pork fat until paste-like, then add the duck livers and cooking juices. Rub through a fine sieve to remove any sinews, then return to the cleaned food processor and incorporate the *foie gras* and cream and check for seasoning. Chill the mousse.

TO PREPARE THE GALANTINE Stuff each quail with 1 heaped tablespoon of duck mousse and sew up, leaving a long thread for easy removal. If you have not been very skilful with the initial boning, you may need to make a few extra seams in the quail with your needle and thread. It won't matter, as the jelly will cover up the evidence. Do, however, remember to remove the extra thread. Tuck the legs in neatly and roast in a preheated oven at 220°C for 12 minutes until lightly golden. (Do not cook longer as the flesh must remain pink. There is nothing more horrible than trying to eat a hard, cold piece of poultry.) Cool and refrigerate.

When cold, gently pull out all threads, snip off any extra skin around the neck, and wipe off any excess butter with a clean, damp cloth.

TO GLAZE Chop the truffle into very fine dice and set aside on a small plate. Place the quail on a cake rack over a tray. Melt the jelly over gentle heat and tip into a bowl that is set over another bowl half-full of crushed ice. Swirl the jelly until it thickens. Quickly spoon generous amounts over each quail and scatter each with a little chopped truffle. (A less extravagant version would be to scatter ½ a teaspoon of cracked peppercorns per quail instead of the diced truffle.) Quickly transfer the rack to the refrigerator to set the first layer. While the layer is setting, scrape all the jelly from the tray back into the pan, melt again, strain back into the bowl over ice, swirl to thicken again and repeat the spooning-over process.

Repeat this process of melting and thickening the aspic until the quails have a sufficient coating, or until all the aspic is used up.

Serve the quails on a nest of carefully selected greenery with violets peeping out. Fingerbowls will be needed so that the legs and wings can be enjoyed.[✢]

[✢] I obviously do enjoy being fanciful. Here, the quail are arranged in a nest of greenery to suggest under-brush. In 1980 I was invited to participate in a reception for the International Wine & Food Society, held in the Great Hall of the National Gallery of Victoria. Various chefs had to provide one signature dish. I chose these quail and laboured over 100 of them. I then arranged a field of leaves and edible blossoms, where they rested until seized upon, with here and there a hard-boiled quail egg still in its speckled shell.

Roasted loin of pork with cumquats and sauerkraut braised in champagne

1 loin of pork, approximate weight 2 kg, rind finely scored by the butcher
salt, pepper
a light little oil
2 cloves garlic, smashed but unpeeled
12 spiced cumquats (see page 72)
1 onion, roughly chopped
1 carrot, roughly chopped
1 bulb of fennel, roughly chopped
1 teaspoon whole coriander seeds
1 bay leaf
60 ml spiced vinegar from the cumquat jar
1 glass dry white wine or champagne
1 litre light veal or chicken stock

RENDERED PORK FAT

500 g minced port fat
2 cloves garlic, unpeeled
1 bay leaf
1 sprig thyme

SAUERKRAUT

100 g rendered pork fat (see above)
3 onions, sliced
1 sprig thyme
1 bay leaf
1 teaspoon peppercorns
20 juniper berries, lightly crushed
1 bottle dry champagne
2 kg sauerkraut (buy the fresh variety, not tinned, and wash well
*   under cold water and then squeeze dry)*
2 large potatoes, grated
1 liqueur glass of kirsch

TO RENDER THE PORK FAT Place the minced pork fat in a pan with the garlic cloves, bay leaf, thyme and a spoonful of water and set to melt gently over a low heat. Stir once or twice to stop the particles sticking. Strain the fat through a conical or other strainer, pressing on the solids. Discard the solids.

This flavoured fat will keep well for months in the refrigerator, and can be used for cooking pieces of poultry or pork in the tradition of south-western France.

TO PREPARE THE PORK Rub the scored rind of the pork with salt, pepper and a little oil. Season the bony side of the joint with salt and pepper and massage in the smashed cloves of garlic and the cumquats. In a little oil in a baking dish, lightly colour the onion, carrot and fennel. Drop in the spent garlic cloves, the coriander seeds, the crushed cumquats and the bay leaf.

Place the joint of pork directly on a rack of the oven halfway up, with the baking dish placed underneath it. Pour 1 cm of water into the dish to prevent the fat burning. Roast the meat at 220°C for 30 minutes to crisp the skin, then reduce the heat to 180°C. Every 30 minutes, pour off the fat into a clear container so that it can easily be identified later on. The meat is cooked when the juices run clear, after 1½–2 hours depending on the thickness of the piece of meat.

When the meat is cooked, remove it to a board. It can rest happily for 30 minutes before serving. Using a sharp knife, lift off the sheet of crackling and leave it in a warm place. Slice off any excess layer of fat and discard it. Still with the sharp knife and probably protecting your hand with a cloth, remove the bones and set aside. Wrap the joint of meat in aluminium foil and leave in a very warm spot, or reduce the oven temperature to 140°C and leave the foil parcel in the oven on a tray, while you make the sauce.[+]

TO MAKE THE SAUCE Pour off any remaining fat in the baking dish. Place the pork bones back in the baking dish and transfer to a fast flame on top of the stove. Stir all the vegetables around over high heat for 1 minute until they 'grip' well. Tip in the cumquat vinegar and the wine. Keep the heat high. Add the heated stock. Boil all together for 5 minutes, then strain into a pan, pressing hard on the solids and then discarding them. Skim any fat and then boil hard to reduce the sauce for a further 5–10 minutes. Taste for seasoning and strength of flavour. With this *jus*-type sauce it is never necessary to have more than enough to thoroughly moisten the meat, and it does not need to be reduced so much that it starts to develop a sticky, tarry quality.

[+] I really haven't progressed in how I like to cook a joint of pork. Rind on or off seems to be the only variable, otherwise I still use the same method.

TO COOK THE SAUERKRAUT   Heat the rendered pork fat in a large enamelled cast-iron casserole dish that has a tight-fitting lid. Sauté the onions until transparent, then add the thyme, bay leaf, peppercorns, juniper berries and champagne and simmer for 5 minutes. Add the sauerkraut, stirring and lifting well so that it mixes with the other ingredients. Place the dish on a simmer mat and simmer for 1½ hours. Stir every 20 minutes or so to ensure that it is not sticking. Taste for seasoning, stir in the grated potato and simmer again for 20 minutes. Add the kirsch immediately before serving.

TO SERVE   When the sauerkraut is ready, cut thinnish slices of pork, break off a generous piece of crackling, pour over a little sauce and serve the rest separately. If you wish, an extra pickled cumquat can be served as a garnish – however, the flavour is very intense. A separate dish of baby carrots or whatever can be cooked as a further accompaniment.

NOTE 1:   The fat you collected in the glass container will taste absolutely wonderful, far superior to the fat you have already rendered for your sauerkraut. Ladle it off the sediment at the bottom of the container into a clean jar (if left there the sediment could send the fat rancid) and store this beautifully flavoured treasure to cook some more sauerkraut or to fry some onions and potatoes for a simple meal some other time.

NOTE 2:   The sauerkraut takes quite a long time to cook, so it should be started after the meat has had its initial 30 minutes at the higher heat. Both dishes will then be properly synchronised for service.

Spiced cumquats

1 teaspoon salt
600 ml water
500 g cumquats
150 g castor sugar
½ cinnamon stick
1 teaspoon whole cloves
600 ml white-wine vinegar

Dissolve the salt in the water and bring to a boil. Pour the water over the cumquats in a bowl or basin and allow to stand for 12 hours. Drain. Simmer the sugar and spices in the vinegar for 5 minutes. Pour the hot vinegar over the cumquats, bottle and store in a cool place.

As with all pickled and spiced products, the flavour will mellow with keeping.

Helen's loquat jelly

Pick the available amount of fruit – ripe, but not overripe, and absolutely dry. Put the fruit in a saucepan and barely cover with water. Boil until soft, approximately 15–20 minutes, and then strain through a fine strainer, pressing very hard on the fruit pulp to extract the maximum juice. Discard the solids.

Measure out 1 cup of sugar for each cup of juice and combine in an enamelled cast-iron or stainless steel pan. Boil together, skimming until it jells, using the usual test of a teaspoonful dropped into a saucer. Cool, then push your finger or a spoon through the jelly. It should wrinkle and leave a clear path where the spoon or finger has been.

The same method can be used with gooseberries, and one year I had great creamy panicles of flowers on my elder tree so that I was able to add elderflowers to my gooseberry jelly. It gave a rather grapelike flavour, as promised in *Summer Cooking* by Elizabeth David, whose idea it was.

Loquat jelly makes a lovely glaze for fruit tarts made with pale-coloured fruit, such as grape or pear.

Another friend of mine who shares my enthusiasm for turning one's produce into edible treats gave me a Christmas present of a jar of her apple jelly in which she had imprisoned a tiny Cecile Brunner rosebud. It added fragrance to the jelly and a sense of romance to the pantry shelves. What about crab-apple jelly with a crinkly leaf of nutmeg geranium?✠

✠ My interest in edible flowers and leaves was soundly based on the best English traditions of the still-room and larder, but again it was considered very avant-garde by my customers. 'Nutmeg geranium indeed!' they exclaimed. Some, of course, found it pretentious.

Summer pudding

It is possible to make this sweet with *some* frozen fruit. However, it is not possible to use *only* frozen fruit, as the quality of the juice is dramatically diminished. All sorts of combinations are possible. I have used combinations of the following: blackberries, youngberries, boysenberries, loganberries, raspberries, blueberries, redcurrants and blackcurrants. Strawberries are not good and too many blackberries or blueberries will result in purple juice rather than the ideal rich crimson. If using some frozen fruit, add it to the sugar syrup and allow it to thaw before adding the other fruits.

The recipe I have given here is my idea of the perfect combination of berries and makes a sufficient quantity for a 1 litre pudding basin.

1 loaf day-old white bread, thinly sliced
125 ml water
125 g sugar
125 g redcurrants, weighed after stripping the fruit from the stalks
125 g loganberries
375 g raspberries

TO PREPARE THE PUDDING   Trim the crusts from the bread. Cut sufficient triangles of bread to line the base of your basin carefully. The bread lining should be a good fit to prevent premature or excessive loss of juice. Cut more slices to line the sides. Reserve 2 or 3 slices to form a lid.

Place the water and sugar in a pan. Simmer, stirring, until the sugar has melted. Add any frozen fruit now, cover and allow to thaw. Tip in all the fruit. Give a good stir and cover again until the fruit returns to the boil. As soon as this happens, remove the pan from the heat. Have ready a large stainless steel strainer or colander that fits over a large bowl. Tip all the fruit and liquid into the strainer and let the excess juice strain into the bowl. Don't press the fruit. Place the fruit in a basin and leave to get cold.

Place the bread-lined basin on a tray with a rim all around it, or on a large rimmed plate. Spoon in the fruit right to the top of the basin. Level the top and pour over a little of the reserved juice so that the filling looks wet but is not swimming in liquid. Put the slices of bread in place for the lid. Place a doubled sheet of foil over the pudding and then press in a saucer which just fits inside the rim of the basin. Weight this saucer with jam tins or whatever and return the whole edifice to the refrigerator overnight.

TO SERVE   Next day, remove the weights, saucer and foil. Place a deep serving plate over the basin and invert carefully. Your pudding will be a deep crimson and some juice will ooze and seep onto the serving plate. Add to this by pouring over and around some more of the strained reserved juice and you now have a ruby-red castle in a crimson moat. Enjoy it with the best-quality cream you can find.✝

FINAL NOTE: In the restaurant we make individual puddings. It is very time-consuming lining the moulds. We use stackable coffee cups and weight each pudding by stacking another coffee cup on top.

✝ Nowadays we have the choice of rich farm cream of 45 per cent butterfat, clotted cream and good-quality crème fraîche. When I originally wrote this, you could only buy thickened or unthickened cream, and the only rich farm cream available was if you lived on a dairy farm, or knew someone who knew someone who did.

Summer nights

MENU

∽

TOMATO JELLY WITH CRISPY BACON
AND OTHER GOOD THINGS

LA FRITURE WITH SALSA VERDE,
SKORDALIA OR MEDITERRANEAN
TOMATO SAUCE

PEACHES IN CHAMPAGNE
LADYFINGER BISCUITS

∽

On a perfect summer's day I was driving along
Beaconsfield Parade, St Kilda, watching the brilliant butterfly wings of the windsurfers and planning my
'hot summer's night' menu. Memories of other nights, other
places, slipped through my thoughts. A hot summer's
night years ago when a friend had enchanted me with a
simple but beautiful gazpacho served splendidly at a formally set table in her garden, the only light being from
swinging Chinese lanterns. More recently, a week spent
at a *pensione* on Lake Maggiore, where the whole village
seemed to take the air in the evenings – such balmy air
it was, too. Couples rocked in swinging chairs at the
sidewalk cafés and small children squealed and slipped
amongst the shadows.

Also long ago there was a student holiday in Greece, where my most vivid and pleasurable experiences gastronomically were warm evenings spent eating crisply fried little fish within sound of the water. The wooden tables and chairs were all at the water's edge – the cafés were across the road. All evening, the agile waiters darted across the traffic bearing platters of golden nameless little fish and squid and generous quarters of wonderful lemons. Eating near water is a magical experience, and rare in Melbourne unless you have a swimming pool.✝ It is one of the pleasures of Asian villages, too, be it the relative isolation of the east coast of Malaya or the bustle of the floating restaurants in Hong Kong. The flare of the braziers adds to the excitement in Asia, but for me the best part is the soft, warm air, the bare legs, the immediacy of the food and the lapping and shimmering of reflected light and dark, rippling water.

Where deep-frying is a part of any meal, there must be no compromise permitted with the quality of the oil, the cleanliness of the pan and the readiness of the diners. Although such delicacies as deep-fried sardines or prawns are often the choice for casual meals, do not confuse the casual with the inadequate. Deep-fried food must be drained on copious clean paper towels and then quickly transferred to a folded napkin on a large plate. I prefer to use olive oil or a blended, good-tasting vegetable or grapeseed oil. I do not like peanut oil at all, and as for solid frying fats, the less said the better.✦

So, if my meal is to feature a *friture* as the centrepiece, I would prefer to start with something sharp and acid on the palate. Either a gazpacho or, as in this case, I would settle for my favourite wobbly little tomato jelly surrounded by a few piquant tastes. Tonight I can muster a few crisply fried rashers of smoked bacon, some Japanese-style salted and vinegared carrot and cucumber, some sweet water-melon rind, and some curls of Melba toast.

With the *friture*, the choice of ingredients is tantalising. Very occasionally we see small red mullet, a fish much admired in Mediterranean countries.❖ There, it is frequently grilled, scaled but never gutted. The liver of the mullet is considered a great delicacy. The fish is a very pretty pinky-red, and I have even seen it sold here

✝ Happily, Melbourne has discovered its watery boundaries since I wrote this. Several councils now lease spaces right on the sand to enterprising restaurateurs, and added to this are a growing number of establishments that overlook the Yarra River, not to mention our new Docklands waterfront.

✦ Deep-frying may be thought of as evil by some, but demand would suggest these people are in the minority. One has only to think of the popularity of fried potatoes! Or, at the other end of the price scale, tempura in Japanese restaurants. I enjoy beautifully fried food and feel that my remarks of two decades ago are just as valid today.

❖ Red mullet is seen more often these days. Much appreciated by the Greek population, it is often sold in the markets as 'barbounia'.

by its French name, *rouget*. More often you will find sand whiting, another small, sweet fish, and both are suited to frying. Be aware that both fish are bony, and many people have no training in eating small fish so are very frightened of bones. Sardines and garfish are ideal for the *friture*, and here the simple rolling-pin trick (see below) will help to remove the bones.[+]

Gut the fish, rub off the scales of the sardine, rinse and, with a small knife, completely slit the belly so that the fish is opened completely. Take a rolling pin and roll firmly down the backbone. Gently ease out the spinal column and with it will come at least 80 per cent of the bones. For those who really can't handle bones, it is easy to buy a large fillet of snapper, blue eye, groper or rock ling and cut chunky strips known as *goujons*. Variety is introduced with prawns and squid, and the tentacles are especially wonderful. All of these fish and shellfish are to be seasoned, dipped into a batter and fried quickly in clean oil. I have given recipes for two batters. Both are quite well known. The beer-and-riceflour batter has a little more substance than the other. I prefer the lighter batter if my *friture* is to be made up of vegetables, such as miniature flowerets of cauliflower and broccoli or slices of aubergine, fennel and zucchini, as somehow the colours of the vegetables always peep through the egg-white-only batter. It makes for easy identification when selecting morsels for your plate.

The two sauces I have given recipes for could both be served. A third choice would be a classic sauce tartare. The salsa verde is an Italian sauce, and the skordalia is of Greek origin. The three together pay homage to the three southern European regions where I have enjoyed a *friture*.[♦]

A special friend was showing me her infant espaliered white peaches – she is hoping for great things. We had espaliered white peaches against an ugly brick wall in the first house I remember living in. Sliced peaches, warm from the tree, sprinkled with some castor sugar, topped with another layer of the same and then another – all left to macerate and bruise for an hour – were then enjoyed as a very special breakfast. I have taken liberties with my mother's treat and will serve my grown-up version to finish this meal. My version is no more delicious than the original – just a little more heady from the addition of champagne. Ladyfinger biscuits are an elegant way of indulging in the usually forbidden childish habit of dunking biscuits in your tea. Funnily enough, no one will object to your dunking of this sugary treat in your peachy champagne.

[+] I have failed to mention one of the best of all local fish for deep-frying: flathead.

[♦] These sauces were relatively unknown when this book first appeared. Most of us have now become familiar with salsa verde and skordalia. The recipe given on page 85 is a rather luxurious version of skordalia. In *The Cook's Companion* I have a simpler recipe that was given to me by a Greek friend. It has no eggs or almonds, but does feature potato and milk.

Tomato jelly with crispy bacon and other good things

This refreshing entrée permits the cook to design an original *salade composée* of infinite variation to stimulate the palate rather than overload it. It is ideal served before a heavy or rich or fried main course.[†]

1.5 kg ripe tomatoes, unpeeled and roughly chopped
1 piece of celery stalk, 7.5 cm long, roughly chopped
few leaves basil or *other herb*
12 leaves Dr Oetker gelatine or *20 g powdered gelatine*
juice of 1 lemon or *to taste*
Tabasco to taste
Worcestershire sauce to taste
bacon

TO PREPARE THE JELLY   Place the tomato, celery and basil in a food processor. Process until a thick mush. Pass this thick purée through the fine disc of the Mouli or press it through a sieve. Put one-quarter of the mixture in a basin and stand the basin over a pan of simmering water on a gentle heat.[✦] Sprinkle the gelatine on top, reduce the heat and let the gelatine dissolve completely. Mix with the balance of the mixture and add the seasonings to taste. If using leaf gelatine, soak the leaves in cold water for 5 minutes. Heat one-quarter of the tomato mixture until simmering, drop in the soaked leaves, swish to dissolve completely, then mix with the balance of the mixture and season. Pour into your selected moulds and leave to set in the refrigerator. The flavour is better if the jelly is brought out of the refrigerator half an hour before serving.

CRISPY BACON   Slice bacon very finely and cook in a non-stick pan. When crisp, drain on kitchen paper.

[†] *Salades composées* were one of the most attractive discoveries of nouvelle cuisine. See my remarks on pages 228–31 for guidelines for creating your own.
[✦] If this tomato mixture is allowed to come to the boil, simmered for a few minutes and then strained, the resultant liquid will be almost clear and yet still have the intense flavour of tomato. Then add the gelatine as directed. During the late 1980s I used this exquisite jelly to set poached bantam or quail eggs, and accompanied them with a salad of white and green asparagus.

Tomato jelly as the centrepiece of a salade composée: Choose foods that underline flavour relationships, or make contrasts, or both, such as sharp v. smooth, salt v. vinegar, egg and bacon, soft v. crunch. For example: crispy bacon or pancetta (salt, hot crisp), smoked beef (soft, slightly sweet and smoky), vinegared vegetables (see below), snippets of herbs to echo the taste in the jelly, hard-boiled quail eggs with their shells shone with a drop of oil.

Tomato jelly with crudités: For example, tiny dice of sweet red and green peppers; slices of avocado or peeled cocktail avocados, brushed with a lemony vinaigrette; julienne of celeriac tossed with mayonnaise; home-pickled mushrooms (page 82); marinated olives (page 81). Serve with thin curls of Melba toast or toasted triangles of wholemeal unleavened bread. Make your own bread and flavour it with more basil for unusual flavoured Melba toast.

Tomato jelly combined with seafood: Serve cooked shelled prawns, bugs, yabby tails or sliced crayfish alongside with a mayonnaise, or embed the prawns or shrimps in the jelly before it sets.

Tomato jelly as a filling: Trim some large artichoke bottoms and cook in a blanc made by whisking a scant handful of flour into salted water to which you have added the juice of a lemon. Simmer until just cooked. Drain and sauté the bottoms in a little butter or oil. When cold, fill the hollows with a scoop of tomato jelly and perhaps serve with sliced smoked salmon or smoked trout.

Blanched, hollowed-out cucumbers can be filled with the jelly. Stand the hollow cucumbers on end in a narrow saucepan, fill the extra space with crumpled foil to hold them steady, pour in the jelly and leave to set. Slice when set and serve as appetisers on freshly fried croutons made from a crunchy wholegrain bread.

Japanese-style vinegared vegetables

1 × 10 cm piece daikon (Japanese radish), cut into slim batons
2 medium carrots, peeled and cut into slim batons
1 teaspoon salt
¾ cup white rice vinegar
2½ tablespoons mirin (rice wine)
¼ cup water

Put the vegetables in a stainless steel or glass bowl and sprinkle with salt. Leave for 15 minutes, then turn the vegetables in the salt, squeezing them hard. The radish will give up a lot of liquid.

Transfer the squeezed vegetables to a clean bowl. Pour over ¼ cup of vinegar, mix well and drain well.

Heat the remaining vinegar with the mirin and water, cool and pour over the vegetables. Stir, cover and refrigerate. Leave until the next day to serve.

Home-style green olives

Choose firm green olives sold in brine. Make a slit in the side of each one and layer them with pieces of garlic, little sprigs of thyme or oregano and a few slivers of very hot red chilli. Place in jars and fill the jars with olive oil. Leave at least 2 weeks. The olives can be stored for months.

Watermelon-rind pickle[+]

1 kg watermelon rind
¼ cup salt
1 litre water

PICKLING SYRUP
1 kg sugar
600 ml white-wine vinegar
600 ml water
1 lemon, thinly sliced
1 cinnamon stick
1 teaspoon whole cloves
1 teaspoon whole allspice

Cut the watermelon rind so that just a blush of pink is left on and trim it into even-shaped pieces, approximately 6 cm × 1 cm. Soak the rind overnight in the salt and water.

Next day, drain the rind, put it in a pan, cover with fresh cold water and simmer for about 30 minutes until the head of a pin will easily pierce the skin.

Make up the pickling syrup by combining all the ingredients and simmering for 10 minutes. Add the drained rind and boil rapidly until the rind is translucent. Fill hot, clean jars with the rind and syrup and leave for about a week. It is even better if you can bear to leave it for a month.

VARIATIONS: Add 1 or 2 slices of ginger to the syrup, or add ½ a cup of grenadine syrup if you prefer a pink pickle.

[+] In 1994 I was delighted to find 'Stephanie's pickled watermelon rind' served with prosciutto at one of my favourite London restaurants, Clarke's in Kensington Church Street.

Pickled mushrooms

1 kg firm, white button mushrooms
600 ml white-wine vinegar
300 ml water
2 bay leaves
12 peppercorns
12 coriander seeds

Trim the stalks of the mushrooms and wipe the tops to remove any dirt. Bring the vinegar, water and spices to the boil. Simmer for 5 minutes. Drop in the mushrooms and simmer for 10 minutes. Pack the mushrooms into hot, sterilised preserving jars and pour over the pickling liquid. If there is too much liquid, it can be used to make a second batch of pickled mushrooms.

La friture – salsa verde, skordalia, Mediterranean tomato sauce

olive oil, grapeseed oil or *sunflower oil for frying*
plain flour
1 egg, beaten
fine fresh breadcrumbs

SEAFOOD

small fish, served entire
strips of large fish fillets
small fillets, curled or *left flat*
prawns
squid
scallops
oysters
mussels

MEATS

brains, poached and drained
sweetbreads, soaked, blanched and braised in stock
tripe, simmered in stock until tender

celeriac, blanched (optional)
zucchini
cauliflower, blanched
fennel, blanched
eggplants
broccoli, blanched (optional)
parsley, celery leaves and/or *sorrel leaves*
whole garlic cloves, blanched
artichoke hearts (see pages 158–9)

ETCETERAS

sliced cheese, hard Greek kasseri, chilled mozzarella, goat's milk cheese
leftover risotto or *rice pilaf, formed into balls*
sticky purées, e.g. sweet potato or *salted codfish*

Set the oven at 120°C and warm a large platter in it to receive the fried food. Line another large platter with several layers of kitchen paper and have it ready for draining the food. Choose a mixture of ingredients, or decide that your *friture* will be all vegetables, all fish etc. Any single ingredient can become a first course on its own with one of the sauces mentioned, or it can be a robust vegetable course to follow something quite light.

Some vegetables will cook sufficiently in the brief frying time. Others, such as fennel, will need prior blanching. They must then be refreshed quickly to stop the cooking and drained very well so as not to become soggy or to cause the hot oil to hiss and boil up.

Usually one will need to trim and prepare artichoke hearts, as described on page 158. Very occasionally, early in the season, or if you grow your own, you can find tiny artichokes, sufficiently tender to be eaten whole. This is, in fact, a speciality in some Roman restaurants. The artichoke leaves are trimmed, opened out like a flower, deep-fried in oil, then finally splashed with a few drops of water. They become golden brown and quite crisp.

If cooking any of the 'Etceteras', before frying dust them in flour, then dip into egg and then breadcrumbs.

REMEMBER: Do not crowd the food. The oil must be clean and hot. Most foods are best fried at 180°C. Use a thermometer to check the temperature of the oil. If it drops below 180°C, wait for it to reheat before adding any more food.

Frying batter 1

250 g plain flour
pinch of salt, pepper
6 tablespoons olive oil
400 ml warm water
2 egg whites

Place the flour, salt and pepper in a food processor. With the motor running, dribble in the oil, stopping at least once to scrape the bowl and ensure that there is not a layer of sticky flour trapped on the base. Again with the motor running, pour in the warm water until the mixture is like thick cream.

Pour into a bowl and, just before using, fold in the firmly whisked egg whites. You can incorporate finely chopped herbs into the batter with the flour and salt, if you wish.

Frying batter 2

175 g self-raising flour
30 g rice flour
salt, pepper
2 tablespoons olive oil
300 ml beer
2 egg whites

Place the flours, salt and pepper in a food processor. Combine with the oil while the motor is running. Slowly add the beer, stirring at least once to ensure a smooth mix. Leave for at least 1 hour. Just before using, fold in the firmly whisked egg whites.

Wobbly tomato jelly (page 79) with yabbies,
avocado and hand-mounted mayonnaise (page 56)

Crudités with anchovy vinaigrette (pages 90, 92)

Roasted rock lobster with scorched fennel stalks and watercress,
drizzled with beurre blanc (page 93)

*Filet à la ficelle – poached beef with young vegetables in a savoury broth
and bone marrow, scattered with sea salt (page 46)*

Sauces for La friture

Salsa verde

1 large handful parsley, washed and finely chopped
1 tablespoon capers
2 cloves of garlic
2 anchovy fillets
1 thick slice stale bread, soaked in 2 tablespoons olive oil
1 tablespoon lemon juice or red-wine vinegar
pepper
6 tablespoons (approximately) olive oil

Combine all ingredients except the olive oil in a food processor. Taste for seasoning. Dribble in the olive oil while the motor is running. The sauce should be sharp, highly seasoned and thickish.[†]

Skordalia

2 egg yolks
6 cloves of garlic
pinch of salt, pepper
125 ml olive oil
60 g ground almonds
60 g fresh white breadcrumbs
lemon juice
freshly chopped parsley

Combine the egg yolks, garlic, salt and pepper in a food processor. Dribble in the oil while the motor is running, as for a mayonnaise. Add the ground almonds, the breadcrumbs, lemon juice to taste and a little chopped parsley.

[†] There are many versions of salsa verde. Since originally writing this book, I have been served a very loose salsa verde in northern Italy to accompany a boiled chicken. I don't think it had any bread in it at all. I enjoyed it just as much as the thicker version.

Mediterranean tomato sauce

Another simple but delicious sauce. Roast a panful of ripe tomatoes with some unpeeled cloves of garlic in a moderate oven for 30 minutes. Process the tomatoes with lots of basil, some salt and pepper, and the flesh of the garlic. When it is a rich, red purée, drizzle in a few spoonfuls of olive oil until thick. Serve the same day if possible, as it will probably separate. It still tastes good the next day and can be rewhirled for a dinner *en famille*, perhaps with fried eggs or grilled sausages.

Peaches in champagne

There really is no need for a recipe. You must choose perfect peaches. There is nothing more infuriating than asking a greengrocer for ripe peaches and getting them home to find that one is nearly ripe and the rest may possibly be ripe next week. Be assertive and pick them yourself.[+]

Choose 1½ good-sized peaches per guest. Over a bowl, slip the skins off. (The ultimate test of a ripe peach is that the skins really do slip off.) Slice the peaches into the bowl, scattering each layer with castor sugar. When all the peaches are sliced, pour over 1 glass of champagne and press a piece of plastic film down over the surface. Leave the peaches to blend and mingle with the juices. Unless it is a very hot day, don't refrigerate the bowl. Just before serving, spoon the peaches into a flute and top with good champagne.

[+] In the last couple of years I have noticed a giant leap in the quality of the white peaches (and white nectarines) I have been buying. Horticulturalists acknowledge that the best growers now recognise the extra marketing benefits that result from picking their fruit riper and more often, so it is ready to eat and enthuse over rather than disappoint, as so often used to be the case.

Ladyfinger biscuits

100 g castor sugar
100 g plain flour
3 eggs
icing sugar
2 baking trays lined with silicone paper
1 piping bag with plain 1.5 cm nozzle
fine strainer

Have the oven ready at 190°C, the baking trays prepared and the piping bag at hand before you start.

Have all the ingredients measured, the flour sifted and the eggs separated. Whisk the egg yolks with 70 g of the sugar until pale and thick. Beat the egg whites until firm, add the remaining sugar and beat until stiff and glossy. Gently tip this meringue into the bowl containing the whisked yolks. Fold in the meringue gently but quickly. Add the sifted flour and blend well but lightly. Spoon the mixture into the piping bag. Pipe fingers about 5 cm long onto the trays, well apart. Sift over some icing sugar.

Bake for 8–12 minutes until pale gold. You may have to change the position of the trays halfway through the baking time. The biscuits should look a deeper gold around the edges than in the centre. Allow to cool for a few minutes, then lift off the paper and cool completely on a rack.

Toast to Eze

MENU

❦

LES CRUDITÉS WITH SEVERAL SAUCES
BLACK OLIVES IN TWO WAYS

CRAYFISH 1: ROASTED, WITH MELTED BUTTER
or
CRAYFISH 2: STEAMED, WITH BUTTER SAUCE
AND BASIL LEAVES

ROSE-SCENTED GERANIUM JUNKET
WITH RASPBERRIES
TUILES

❦

One Sunday my husband Maurice and I lunched at a little café at Eze, near our rented villa at Beaulieu on the Côte d'Azur. It was 1975. The line of cars parked outside suggested that something good was in store. It was another of those French experiences that confirm me as a Francophile, and which I relate when attempting to convert others.

Sunday lunch is *the* meal for eating in restaurants in France – for French families, that is, rather than tourists. This restaurant was busy! They were doing what food lovers dream of – serving simple, direct food that was not only well conceived and prepared, but had that little extra, which titillated other senses and induced an instant frisson of anticipation. The maître d'hôtel had an air of theatre with his large handlebar moustache, his exaggerated gestures, his charm and concern towards the ladies and his bonhomie for the men.

The *spécialité de la maison* was fresh rock crayfish grilled with *herbes de Provence*. As many an experienced waiter knows, he is often required to 'sell' the house speciality, and so often for the wrong reasons – the meat is perhaps old and won't last another day, the wine is over the hill and needs to be drunk. But the best reason is always that the product is in prime condition, is often hard to get, and you must have it because it is so good. So it was with the snapping, dripping crayfish paraded before our eyes. We had to have it.

At every second table one heard either the crack of claws or the splutter of exploding dried twigs as the langoustes were liberally doused in Armagnac in the final libations.

'Perhaps a few crudités to start, M'sieur, Madame?'

'Yes, yes,' we cried, saliva dripping.

Oh, what a delight. A better-than-still-life basket came to the table, Jim Dine rather than Cézanne. Wet, perfect little radishes, young fennel with pale fronds waving, shiny sweet peppers both yellow and red, broad beans still in their pods, bumpy tomatoes, *champignons de Paris* and little rounded carrots washed but unpeeled – and that is all I can remember. The whole was presented in a cane basket complete with a wickedly sharp cook's knife, a big plate each and a bowl of vinaigrette. Alongside was a stoneware crock with an olive-wood dipper. A scoopful of those intensely flavoured, shiny boot-bottom niçoise olives were offered as a condiment with the crudités.

Yet another happy French memory was being served a simple junket, in this case drained of its whey and tied into a long parcel. The wrapping was green hay, which added an aroma of the haystack and looked a little like the stick insects that cling to buildings. It was sufficient, however, to send me home to make junket, and this is our version.

Either version I have provided of the crayfish dinner remains a rich and rather aggressive main course. I think a soothing finale is in order and have suggested a rose-scented geranium junket to be served with fresh raspberries. Have your prettiest bowls ready, as the junket sets almost instantly. Of course, each guest must have his/her own bowl as the perfection of junket exists only as long as its surface is unbroken.

The tuiles that are served with the junket are also a useful and versatile biscuit to accompany ice-creams or sherbets, and all cooks should feel comfortable about making them. Keep the mixture thin, don't cook too many at once, and don't remove them *before* they are cooked in your anxiety not to burn them, or they will bend and not be crisp at all.

Les crudités with several sauces

This is stating the obvious: there is not point serving a raw vegetable that is not beautiful. Quality must precede quantity or variety. Perfect radishes are a gourmet's delight on their own, and if that's all there is – serve radishes. Otherwise, imagining the perfect garden or supplier, choose a selection of:

> *young broad beans presented in their pods*
> *small zucchini, picked that day with blossom still attached*
> *zucchini, a little older but still lovely, slivered and spread to a fan shape*
> *sections of young fennel (try to leave at least a little tuft of pale leaves attached)*
> *home-grown florets of cauliflower, which are delicious if young*
> *fresh tomatoes, especially the little red cherry and pear-shaped yellow ones*
> *aforementioned radishes, trimmed, but with a topknot of leaves left intact*
> *the hidden inner stalks of celery*
> *garden-fresh green peas left in their waxy pods and/or sugar peas*
> *finely curled spring onions*
> *crunchy cucumber*
> *avocados*
> *olives (see page 91)*

My own feeling is that once one starts selecting larger vegetables and cutting batons or strips, the point of crudités is lost. I have a similar reaction to a plate of food-processed shreds. However, a cross-cultural addition that I like is a few very fresh bean shoots.

On holiday in South Australia a year or two after our experience at Eze, I was excited to see olive trees laden with black shiny olives growing at the sides of the road. They were everywhere, so we picked them on the slopes of Mount Lofty and later amongst the vineyards in the Coonawarra region. I am including my two tested recipes for olives – one given to me by my friend Cath, whose mother is French and swears by this recipe, and a second given to me by my very dear Greek friend Melita.[+]

[+] As the local olive industry goes from strength to strength we have all become much more aware of olives on trees, and each year cases of olives appear in the markets in the autumn ready for pickling. I have collected several more recipes for pickling olives and refer interested readers to one of my favourites, the recipe for Cracked Green Olives in *The Cook's Companion*.

Black olives in two ways

Cath's black olives

Slit each olive with a sharp knife and put into a bucket of water. Change the water every couple of days for 14 days.

Pack the olives into jars and cover with pickling brine. Seal and leave for at least a month. When ready to use, take from the jar what is needed, rinse well in cold water and toss in olive oil. Serve flavoured if you like with a little chopped spring onion, grated orange zest and coarsely ground cumin.

Pickling brine is made up of half good red-wine or white-wine vinegar and half brine.

Brine solution: Fill a bowl with water. Continue to add salt to the water until an egg will float.

Melita's olives

Select your olives scrupulously; the fruit must be firm and spotlessly clean. Discard any damaged fruit – they will ruin the whole batch. Put the olives into a bucket of water (no need to slit them). Leave for 40 days, changing the water every 2 days.

After 40 days, drain the olives and cover with coarse salt. Leave for 2 days. Wash the olives well.

Pack into clean jars with pieces of lemon, slivers of garlic and little sprigs of thyme or rosemary. Cover with either olive oil or red-wine vinegar, or half and half.

Seal and leave for 2 weeks before eating.

Sauces for Les crudités

Soft-boiled-egg vinaigrette

This is a lovely cold sauce that I find most versatile. It is delicious with a salad of cray-fish, or as a sauce for freshly boiled warm prawns. It is my favourite for crudités as it is less rich than mayonnaise, but has more body than a vinaigrette or a *sauce ravigote*.

It can be varied to feature one special herb or to include a distinctive extra taste, such as the mustard and juices from the head of a crayfish or from the body of a mud crab.

1 shallot or *¼ mild onion, finely chopped*
1 tablespoon finely chopped parsley
1 tablespoon other herb (one only, such as basil, or *a mixture)*
1 three-minute soft-boiled large egg, yolk scooped out, white finely chopped
    (it is best if the sauce is made while the egg is warm)
50 ml best olive oil
salt, pepper
lemon juice

In a food processor or blender, combine the shallot, parsley, herbs and egg yolk. Add the oil while the motor is running. Season with salt, pepper and lemon juice and fold in the finely chopped egg white.

Anchovy dipping sauce

This extremely versatile sauce can be used for crudités, fried or steamed fish, grilled steak, and a thousand other things.

6 fillets of anchovy (either tinned in oil or, *if salted, soak the fish overnight in milk,*
    strip the fillets from the bones, pat dry and proceed)
3 teaspoons capers
1 tablespoon white-wine or *red-wine vinegar*
½ small onion, finely chopped
1 clove garlic, finely chopped
½ cup chopped parsley
¼ cup lemon juice
1 cup olive oil
Tabasco, to taste

Place all the ingredients in a food processor or blender and combine. The sauce can be coarse or smooth. You could add chives or finely chopped crunchy pickled cucumber. If you want a thicker sauce, add a little crumbled homemade bread. You may substitute tinned tuna for the anchovies.

A simple vinaigrette

I use 4 parts olive oil to 1 scant part vinegar, and I choose my vinegar with great care. Some of the superior red-wine or sherry vinegars, if they are old and well matured, are needed only in very small quantities, and then I frequently use nearly 5 parts of oil to 1 of vinegar. Season lightly with sea salt and freshly ground black pepper. I like a little *fresh* garlic in my vinaigrette. I abhor garlic cloves left in bottles of made-up sauce in refrigerators. They are almost always rank and rancid.

With crudités and simple vinaigrette I might stir in some finely chopped *fines herbes*, particularly chervil, tarragon and parsley, and a scrap of chives.

Blue cheese sauce

In a food processor, blend together equal quantities of full-fat cream cheese, or low-fat cheese if you prefer, and pieces of blue cheese. Add a few drops of cognac and a few drops of Tabasco, then moisten with enough cream, sour cream or yoghurt to make a dipping consistency. Taste for salt. I would add none, as I enjoy the texture and taste of a fine grain of sea salt and would prefer to place a tiny soy-sauce cup on each plate and scatter a few flakes of Maldon salt in each.

Crayfish 1: Roasted, with melted butter

The two recipes that follow are both superb, and each is better suited to a certain-sized crayfish.[✝]

You must buy live crayfish. A twice-cooked crayfish is hard and horrible. Be aware that crayfish dishes in restaurants are frequently based on cooked crayfish, perhaps purchased 1 or 2 days previously, topped with a tomato sauce, cheese sauce or other sauce and reheated in the oven or under an overhead grill. It is a strange fact that a diner is often so out of touch with the realities of food preparation that he never wonders how his crayfish can appear any day of the week at a few minutes' notice.

The home cook has an advantage over the restaurateur when roasting crayfish. To organise and serve 6 people is a possibility, but to provide for a possible demand of up to 50 portions is a lot more difficult.[✦]

[✝] What is commonly known as 'crayfish' is more correctly named 'rock lobster' (*Jasus edwardsii*). The term crayfish is more correctly applied to the various varieties of freshwater crayfish, such as redclaw, yabby and marron. It is important to name species correctly, and I try to do so on menus, but nothing will stop fish-shop proprietors in seaside towns chalking 'Fresh crays' on blackboards when they mean 'rock lobsters'. Customers know what to expect, too.

[✦] I will never forget the magical evening when Robert Castellani, now chef at the Melbourne seaside restaurant Donovans, roasted 100 rock lobsters in a beach pit under a layer of seaweed as part of the 1997 Melbourne Food & Wine Festival – without question my best-ever rock lobster experience.

3 × 1.5 kg live crayfish (rock lobster) (i.e. ½ crayfish per person)
melted butter
2 tablespoons chopped herbs of your choice
salt, pepper
lemon quarters

Most home cooks will prefer to drown their crayfish in cold water before splitting them. We kill them quickly with a smart blow to the back of the head and then split the crayfish in two. An obliging fishmonger will almost certainly drown and split the crayfish for you, but arrange things so that he does it the day of the dinner, not the day before.

Remove and discard the head sac and the intestinal thread. Scoop out any roe and the greenish liquid found in the head. Reserve the roe and either pass it through a fine sieve and incorporate it in your melted butter, or whiz it in the food processor with some soft butter, Tabasco and a few drops of cognac, press it through a sieve, roll it and freeze. This is a simplified crayfish butter, which can be whisked into some future sauce.

Paint the flesh liberally with some melted butter into which you have stirred the chopped herbs, then season lightly. Place the crayfish in the top of a preheated very hot oven (250°C) for 8–10 minutes until the shells are bright red and the flesh has lost its translucency. Paint again with butter and pass quickly under a preheated grill to brown and bubble the surface. Let the crayfish rest and relax for 1–2 minutes. It is best to slip a very sharp knife around the edges of the tail meat before serving, as it attaches very firmly to the shell and can splatter all over your guest's silk dress instead of lifting cleanly away. Serve quickly now with a wedge of lemon and perhaps an extra little jug (heated) of melted butter. Fingerbowls are needed, as are crackers for the claws, and very big napkins. Any other garnish is simply a nuisance. I make an exception for a bowl of crisp young watercress in the centre of the table, served quite plain. It is fantastic to fork a little watercress into the empty tail shell and enjoy it all perfumed with the herbs, the crayfish and the butter, and yet the finish is clean and tangy.

If on the day of the party your fishmonger has only very large live crayfish, do not despair. Here is an alternative dish, which is the one we serve more often.

Crayfish 2: Steamed, with butter sauce and basil leaves

1 × 3–3.5 kg crayfish (rock lobster), drowned or *stabbed but not split*
basil leaves for garnish

CRAYFISH FUMET

crayfish head and shell
1 small onion, chopped
½ carrot, diced
½ stalk celery, chopped
1 small glass brandy
1 bay leaf
parsley stalks
sprig of thyme
500 ml dry white wine
1 litre water or *light fish stock*
1 tablespoon tomato paste
pepper

BUTTER SAUCE

4 shallots or *1 mild onion, very finely chopped*
250 ml crayfish fumet (see above)
1 teaspoon tomato paste
1 tablespoon cream
250 g unsalted butter, cut into chunks

TO PREPARE THE CRAYFISH Twist the tail section and detach it from the head. With a heavy knife or poultry scissors, release the tail meat from the shell by cutting along each edge of the soft undershell. Peel back the shell, lift out the tail meat and carefully pull out the intestinal thread. Cut the meat into 6 sections with kitchen scissors. Check that there are no pieces of intestine left in the sections, cover with plastic wrap and refrigerate. Reserve the best claws and legs to steam with the meat. Discard the gravelly sac in the head.

TO MAKE THE FUMET Smash up the head and shell with a cleaver. Sauté the vegetables in a little butter until softened and starting to colour. Add the smashed head and shell, increase the heat and stir until the shell takes on a good colour. Flame with the brandy, warmed before lighting. Add the herbs, wine, water, tomato paste and pepper. Simmer for 1 hour over moderate heat. Strain, pressing well on the debris. Set aside 250 ml for the butter sauce. (Bag, label and freeze the rest for another day. If you reduce this right down to a near-glaze and then whisk it with a little butter, either plain unsalted butter or a slice of the crayfish variety as described in the earlier recipe, you will have a well-flavoured sauce for a fish mousse, steamed fillet of fish etc.)

Both the finishing of the butter sauce and the actual cooking of the crayfish are very fast, so ensure that you have everything prepared. The plates must be hot and the guests assembled and eager. The steamer should be steaming well. Sections of tail meat should now be placed in lightly buttered containers that fit easily in a single layer in the steamer.

TO MAKE THE SAUCE   Simmer the shallot in the reserved crayfish fumet until well reduced and moist. Add the tomato paste and cream and bring to the boil. Carefully whisk in each chunk of butter, removing the pan from the heat entirely if the butter is melting too fast. It should emerge as a creamy emulsion, not an oily sauce. When all the butter has been incorporated, return to the heat for 1 minute, whisking vigorously. Pull off and leave in a barely warm place. Taste for seasoning.

TO COOK THE CRAYFISH   Place the buttered containers of tail meat in the steamer and add the reserved claws and legs. Check after 4 minutes – the tail meat should be steamed until just no longer transparent.

The actual flesh could be wrapped in buttered spinach, sorrel or basil leaves, but this makes it a bit hard to see when the tail meat is cooked.

TO SERVE   Spoon some butter sauce onto hot plates. Place the cooked tail meat on the sauce. Arrange the legs and claws to garnish. Sprinkle over some fresh basil leaves and serve at once.

Crayfish meat is very rich, and this is enough for 6 people with normal appetites.

Serve no vegetable course until the dish is cleared from the table. Whether to serve your salad at the same time or after is optional. As mentioned on page 94, some diners really love to use their undressed salad to mop up the last bits of sauce, and then again, others dislike it. Decisions, decisions . . .

Rose-scented geranium junket with raspberries

~

300 ml milk
12 rose-geranium leaves, washed+
1½ tablespoons castor sugar
300 ml cream
3 plain junket tablets, crushed with ½ tablespoon water
raspberries

Bring ½ a cup of the milk to a boil with the leaves and sugar. Let sit about 30 minutes. Strain the sweetened milk back into the rest of the milk and the cream, pressing hard on the leaves. Warm the milk/cream to 37°C, i.e. blood heat. Remember the old rule that if it feels just warm on the inside of the wrist it is correct. Mix in the crushed junket tablets very briskly and thoroughly, and pour into bowls.

Arrange the raspberries in an opulent pile and serve castor sugar and extra cream for those who are gluttons.

VANILLA OR NUTMEG JUNKET: To enjoy a delicate junket at times of the year when raspberries are not available, follow the ingredients and method for Rose-scented Geranium Junket, substituting the geranium leaves with a split vanilla bean for a vanilla junket, or some freshly ground nutmeg for a nutmeg junket.

+ The rose-scented geranium I used in this recipe was grown from cuttings taken from my mother's garden. She died nearly twenty years ago, just before this book was originally published, but part of her garden has followed me wherever I have settled since. There are several rose geraniums. Mine, *Pelargonium capitatum*, has rounded leaves and a very delicate rose scent. It is a low-growing, scrambling plant ideal for rockeries. A more commonly found variety, *Pelargonium graveolens*, has deeply cut leaves, is much larger and is altogether more robust. I find its scent less subtle.

Tuiles

A classic biscuit to accompany custards and ices.

    125 g unsalted butter
    3 egg whites
    1 cup plain flour
    pinch of salt
    ½ cup castor sugar
    1 cup flaked almonds

    baking paper or *other non-stick cooking parchment*

Preheat the oven to 160°C. Line an oven tray with baking paper.

Whirl all the ingredients except the flaked almonds in a food processor until quite smooth. Smear 4 thin circles onto the baking paper with the back of a spoon. Sprinkle with the flaked almonds. Cook for 3–5 minutes until well browned at the edges and golden in the centre. Remove and quickly flip each biscuit with a flexible spatula over a rolling pin or a tumbler resting on its side, or into a curved breadstick pan.

Leave to cool completely before removing and storing in an airtight container. Do not make more than 4 tuiles at once, and don't try to have 2 trays on the go unless you have had lots of practice and have lots of rolling pins. It is possible to buy professional tuile tubes, which are like breadstick pans and facilitate forming the biscuits correctly. In the restaurant we paint the batter onto the baking paper with a wide pastry brush. They are, however, very delicate and fragile.

Surprise parcels

MENU

ASPARAGUS WITH A CODDLED EGG

PAPILLOTE OF FISH WITH A
JULIENNE OF VEGETABLES

PINK ICED STRAWBERRY CAKE

I love surprises, especially when they are in the form of parcels. Perhaps this is why I love parcelled and stuffed food.

One can create a beautiful parcel with buttered parchment,[+] which is altogether more aesthetic than aluminium foil. It crinkles and sputters and puffs up when ready, and can conceal anything from a fillet of fish and assorted slivered vegetables chosen to suggest eastern or western tastes, to vegetables on their own, steamed and then buttered, to a single portion of a vegetable stew such as ratatouille. Individual parcel meals can include braised sticky veal shanks wrapped with similarly braised carrots and potatoes. In this case, scatter the gremolata after you have slit the papillote with your knife. (Gremolata is normally scattered over osso buco. It is a mix of grated lemon zest, finely chopped garlic and fresh parsley, too good to keep for just one dish.) The act of presenting, slitting and saucing your parchment parcel adds suspense and ceremony to a dinner party – both rather stimulating qualities. The trapped aromas make for astonished cries of delight as they waft upwards.

As an alternative, your parcel wrap can be rice paper filled with some quick-cooking mixture, such as chopped prawns and ginger, or slivered breast of chicken marinated for half an hour in a little rice wine, ginger and garlic and topped with the finest shreds of spring onion. You can moisten your rice paper with butter or egg white, fold it over and fry the little parcels. As you only want the parcels to crisp and turn golden and the filling to cook very rapidly, keep this type of parcel small.

Filo pastry has become very popular as a wrap for almost anything edible: cheese, nuts, strudel mixes, minced meats and salted fish (as in the special Greek Easter pie). Always butter between the layers of the filo if you are making a roll or a layered cake. Little cheese triangles, or *tiropetes*, are made quickly by cutting a long strip, brushing it with butter, putting a spoonful of your cheese mixture in the corner, folding over a triangle of filo and continuing to fold the little triangle over and over to seal and complete the package.

Among my favourite wrappings are vine leaves – fresh ones for preference, but the preserved ones are fine as long as they are well rinsed of their brine.

Hearts of mignonette and butter lettuces are also excellent wrappings, either for a savoury meat mixture or for a richly flavoured mix of field mushrooms simmered with onions, parsley, fresh white breadcrumbs and some quality grated Gruyère.✦ Dip the washed and drained lettuce hearts in melted butter, season them, spread the leaves gently and re-form the hearts into little balls. If the stuffing is already cooked, you have only to reheat by gently sautéing (no need for extra butter if you are using a Teflon pan), or, if you have used a raw meat filling, you should add a few spoonfuls of good meat juice or stock and braise gently.

Everyone knows cabbage rolls. A whole cabbage briefly blanched and its leaves spread is an excellent way of showing off a creative filling and feeding lots of people. It is re-formed, bound with tape and braised for at least two hours and should be presented entire at the table before being cut into wedges like the Magic

Asparagus with a coddled egg and toasted breadcrumbs (page 103)

Pink iced strawberry cake with crushed strawberry cream (page 108)

Pudding. Both red and crinkly savoy varieties are excellent. Ingredients that combine well with a basic pork–veal mince are: crumbled, cooked chestnuts; cooked, boned and chopped trotters; puréed or finely chopped poultry livers; and fresh herbs, a little allspice and some cognac or Madeira. Remember to bind it with cream rather than eggs for a less dense stuffing. Good stock is essential, preferably with a good piece of pork rind tucked under the cabbage or, failing this, a slab of lightly smoked bacon.✢

Caul fat is another wonderful wrap. The same *farce* that goes into your whole cabbage will become a crépinette if it is formed into a flattish hamburger topped with a sprig of sage or thyme and a fresh bay leaf and then wrapped in an adequate but sparing layer of caul fat. You should buy at least 1 kg of caul fat at a time, as it is often not easy for your butcher to obtain, and he is more likely to succeed with a request for a reasonable amount.✦ Soak the caul overnight in clean cold water. Drain, separate into four bags and label and freeze them until you need them. Crépinettes, or faggots as they are known in the north of England, are gently fried and served with a purée of lentils, apples, potatoes or anything else you fancy. The stickier they are, the better. The caul fat itself fries to a most appetising brown. Apart from these luxury hamburgers, remember caul fat when you are stuffing a roast of veal. It not only firmly holds the stuffing but gently bastes the meat, keeping it moist. Its other most useful purpose is to line a dish before making a simple country terrine. Once again the caul will brown during the final stage of cooking when you have removed the lid from the terrine, marking the top with its distinctive lacy pattern.

Most parcelled and wrapped food is prepared in advance and is either cooked slowly for a long time or requires the cook to do nothing until 15 minutes before serving. Don't, however, become so converted as to serve filo-wrapped cheese triangles, followed by papillotes, followed by apple strudel. Surprises are really best one at a time!

My menu for this dinner has a fish papillote as the main dish, and fresh asparagus served with a nursery-style coddled egg as the starter. A pink iced cake for dessert has its own surprise (it is filled with strawberries).

Like many others, I have fond memories of eating a soft-boiled egg spooned onto soft breadcrumbs mixed into a delicious-tasting mess with salt, pepper and a

✢ I am intrigued that I went into such detail about a whole stuffed cabbage here. In my 2002 book on south-west France, such a dish gets star treatment – a good example of how most of the dishes I relate to have a history and tradition.

✦ I wonder how many butchers in 1984 would have been able to supply caul fat as I so blithely assumed? It would be much easier today, although my remarks about ordering a substantial quantity are just as valid now.

little parsley. I have refined this combination and serve it with the choicest new-season's asparagus. Essential equipment is, per person, an egg-coddler or a boilproof small buttered cup. The asparagus is dipped into the runny egg and rolled into the dish of chopped fresh herbs and buttery toasted crumbs and eaten with the fingers. The buttered asparagus is served on a large plate lying on a folded napkin, and a fingerbowl will be required.✠

Having already evoked the nursery with the entrée and encouraged your guests to feel like children by eating with their fingers, and probably licking them, the paper parcel is even more fun.

It seems right to finish with a dessert that, to me, is like a grown-up version of the iced cakes served at children's birthday parties. The butter sponge is hollowed out and filled with firmly whipped cream mixed with crushed strawberries. Slices of strawberry are allowed to peep out, the lid is replaced (rather like the top of an egg) and the whole is iced with a thin, pink glacé icing. Only by carefully exercising restraint have I prevented myself from scattering over the hundreds and thousands.✦

Your special friends should go home feeling relaxed, ten years younger, and ready for all sorts of childish games.

✠ This fantasy of using asparagus as 'dippy toast' for a boiled egg has been much copied in the years since this book was first published. I still serve it, although it is not so easy to find egg coddlers. A small ceramic ovenproof dish holding one buttered baked egg is an alternative. Cook in a bain-marie covered with foil or the egg white on the bottom of the dish will set solid before the top is lightly set.

✦ Can't get away from that whimsy!

Asparagus with a coddled egg

———

1 tablespoon melted butter
6 large eggs, preferably new-laid free-range eggs[+]
salt, pepper
2 tablespoons chopped parsley
1 tablespoon chopped chervil
1 tablespoon chopped chives
1 tablespoon chopped tarragon
24 good stalks of asparagus of even size
60 g butter
1 cup fine, white breadcrumbs from day-old bread
3 tablespoons cream

6 porcelain egg-coddlers with metal lids or *6 porcelain* or *china egg-cups*
6 large folded napkins
6 large oval plates for serving or *other plates long enough to hold the*
stalks of asparagus

TO PREPARE THE EGGS AND THE ASPARAGUS Use the melted butter to brush the inside of each egg-coddler. Break an egg into each coddler and lightly season with salt and pepper.

Mix all the herbs together and divide between 6 little saucers. (I use the small saucers sold very cheaply in Asian shops and intended for soy sauce.)

Prepare the asparagus. Snap off the stalk at the point where it becomes woody. With a potato peeler, peel the bottom 3–4 cm to ensure that every scrap of asparagus is tender.

Melt the 60 g of butter in a small frying pan and tip in the breadcrumbs. Spoon over and over until all the crumbs have become a lovely toasted-biscuit colour. Tip onto kitchen paper for a few minutes, then divide the crumbs between 6 other saucers.

TO COOK Have ready a tall pan of lightly salted water in which you have placed a can opened at both top and bottom. The ideal-shaped can or cans, as you might

[+] There has been rapid growth in the consumer demand for free-range eggs, and this is the perfect dish to show off superior-flavoured, very fresh ones. I have found that people who have never registered much difference between eggs are surprised by the colour and the rich, deep flavour of such eggs.

need two, is the tall tomato-juice type. Tie your asparagus lightly with string into bundles of 4 and stand upright in the pan so that the tips steam, rather than boil, and the stalks all cook evenly. Obviously this is a poor man's version of an asparagus cooker. If you eat lots of asparagus, you may feel that an asparagus cooker is a sensible buy. They are certainly very efficient and have an added bonus: the perforated basket that can be raised or lowered inside the cooker also makes an excellent steamer for a few vegetables or prawns, and a million other things.

Have ready a further pan of simmering water that will hold your 6 egg-coddlers. Screw on the lids – not too tightly, as they are red-hot at the end of the coddling time – and carefully place them in the barely simmering water, which should come two-thirds of the way up the sides of the coddlers. Time them for 4 minutes.

The asparagus will take 6–10 minutes depending on the thickness, so time its cooking with the coddled eggs so that they are ready simultaneously.

When the asparagus is ready, hook out the bundles with tongs or a fork and gently lie them in a warm dish. Snip the strings and brush with a little butter remaining from the buttering of the coddlers.

Carefully remove the egg-coddlers from the pan. Unscrew the lids, protecting your hands with a cloth, and pour in a little cream.

Transfer the buttered asparagus spears to your hot cloth-lined plates and to each plate add a saucer of herbs, a saucer of buttered crumbs and a coddler, with its metal lid on the side.

Papillote of fish with a julienne of vegetables

100 g melted butter
60 g butter
6 tablespoons carrot julienne
    (i.e. carrot cut into thin matchstick strips[+])
6 tablespoons turnip julienne
6 tablespoons celery julienne
6 handfuls small, choice spinach leaves, well washed
6 × 180 g skinned, bone-free fillets of white fish (rockling, John Dory,
    coral trout and blue eye are varieties I have used frequently)

[+] It was wise in 1984 to be specific rather than leave readers wondering. The term 'julienne' was not widely understood – the era of the cooking class was just beginning.

salt, pepper
tarragon leaves
small amount of egg white

6 large pieces cooking parchment (think of the total area
    covered by 2 large dinner plates)

On the cooking parchment, trace the outline of 2 dinner plates slightly overlapping, as if they were Siamese twins. Cut out this design 6 times. Generously butter the inner side of the shapes using a pastry brush and the melted butter.

Melt the 60 g butter and stir the julienned vegetables over heat for 1 minute. Barely cover with water, bring to the boil and simmer for 1 minute. Strain and reserve.

Place a handful of the spinach leaves on one half of each paper wrapping, then a fillet of fish, then the julienne, scattered attractively. Season with salt and pepper and add some tarragon leaves.

To seal, generously brush the edges of each paper shape with egg white. Fold the package in half, press and fold the edges firmly to seal.

Cook in the oven at 180°C for 10 minutes. The parcels will be puffed, and if you listen carefully they will 'sing' to you. I promise you!

Each person opens their package at the table with a sharp knife, and spoons on a little sauce, which is best served separately and individually. Some will prefer to pour on their sauce. I prefer to dip a forkful of fish in the sauce rather than create the sorry effect of diluted sauce mixing with the fish juices exuded in the cooking.

A classic *beurre blanc* is hard to better as an accompaniment. I have given a recipe for *beurre blanc* on page 214 in the recipe for grilled scallops. If you wish, you could make a little concentrated fish fumet with the bones and skin of the fish and replace part or all of the dry white wine in the initial reduction with this fish essence for a stronger-tasting sauce. A lovely addition would be 1 tablespoon of chopped tarragon stirred into the *beurre blanc* before dividing it into your individual sauce dishes.

Tiropetes with a simple cheese filling

250 g ricotta cheese
100 g Gruyère cheese
1 egg
2 tablespoons chopped parsley or dill or mint
salt, pepper
6 sheets filo pastry
melted butter

Combine the cheeses, egg, herbs, salt and pepper in a food processor. Lay out 1 sheet of pastry and brush it all over with melted butter. Cut it into strips of whatever size you please, say, 6 cm wide. Place 1 heaped teaspoon of filling in one corner of a strip and fold it over to make a triangle. Continue folding until you fold over the last triangle at the end of the strip. Repeat with the other filo sheets and the remaining filling. Place the *tiropetes* on an ungreased baking tray and cook for 8–10 minutes in a 200°C oven until puffed and golden brown.

Variations
- Instead of 250 g of ricotta, use 125 g of fetta and 125 g of ricotta for a stronger flavour.
- Add 100 g of fresh walnut halves to the basic ingredients.
- For a petit-four filling, mix ricotta with vanilla sugar to taste, and add a spoonful of brandy-soaked sultanas.

Stuffed vine leaves (dolmades)†

24 vine leaves, fresh or canned
½ onion, finely chopped
100 ml fruity olive oil
½ cup long-grain rice
1¼ cups water
¼ cup currants
¼ cup toasted pine nuts
¼ cup chopped parsley
1 tablespoon chopped dill
salt, pepper
1¼ cups tomato juice

If the vine leaves are fresh, rinse them briefly and cut off the stems. If using canned vine leaves, rinse them well to remove the brine. Pat dry and spread on a clean surface.

Sauté the onion in the oil, add the rice and stir well for 2 minutes. Add the water and all other ingredients except the tomato juice. Simmer very gently, stirring from time to time, until the rice is cooked, approximately 10 minutes. Taste for salt and pepper. Allow the stuffing to cool.

Divide the filling between the vine leaves and roll up each leaf tightly, tucking the ends in well. Pack the rolls tightly into a saucepan that holds them exactly in 1 layer. Pour over the tomato juice. Put a plate on top of the rolls and weight it lightly to hold them firm while they cook. Bring to a boil and then simmer very gently for approximately 45 minutes until the leaves are quite tender. When cool, remove to a non-metal dish and store, covered, in the refrigerator. Serve at room temperature.

† Here and there readers may notice a Greek influence. From 1977 until 1982 Janni Kyritsis worked as my right-hand man at Stephanie's Restaurant – I don't think we went in for the traditional title of 'sous-chef' in those days – and we taught each other many things. Janni's dolmades were fought over by the kitchen staff. After five years he moved to Sydney and spent twelve years in the kitchen at Berowra Waters Inn. He was a partner in the acclaimed restaurant MG Garage until late 2002.

Pink iced strawberry cake

6 standard brioche tins of 10 cm diameter
melted butter for preparing tins

BUTTER SPONGE CAKE MIX

5 × 60 g eggs
150 g castor sugar
150 g plain flour, sifted
60 g cooled, melted butter

FILLING

1 punnet strawberries
few drops fraises des bois liqueur or strawberry vermouth or Cointreau
300 ml cream

ICING

2 cups pure icing sugar, sifted
juice of ½ lemon
few drops pink food colouring
warm water to mix

TO MAKE THE CAKES Preheat the oven to 180°C. Butter the brioche tins well and dust with flour. Shake out the excess.

Place the eggs and castor sugar in a bowl over hot water and whisk until the mixture feels quite warm. Transfer it to a heated electric mixing bowl and continue to whisk until the mixture is thick and mousselike. This will take about 10 minutes. Quickly sift the flour over the egg/sugar mix and speedily fold in the flour with deft, purposeful strokes using a large metal spoon. When the flour is well incorporated, drizzle the cooled melted butter around the sides and fold in well but quickly. Immediately spoon the mix into the 6 prepared tins and place them on a tray in the preheated oven. Bake for about 10 minutes. The little cakes should feel firm but light, and a skewer test will be clean. Remove them from the oven, allow to cool in the tins for 2–3 minutes and then turn out and cool for a few minutes on a wire cake rack. Do not leave them too long on the cake rack, as the wires can cut into the delicate surface of the cake. When no longer hot to the touch, invert them onto a plate or a sheet of aluminium foil.

TO MAKE THE FILLING   When the cakes are quite cold, take a very sharp, small knife and turn them upside down, i.e. with the broadest diameter as the base of the cake. Cut off a thin slice as a 'hat' from the narrow end of each 'brioche', and then proceed to hollow out the cake, leaving the sides intact. Run the cake pieces (not the 'hats') in the food processor and then transfer these cake crumbs to a small bowl and dampen them with the chosen liqueur.

Reserve 6 beautiful strawberries for a garnish, and crush the rest. They can be crushed in the food processor, but be careful as you don't want a sloppy purée. Rather, you are aiming at mashed strawberries. Mix the mashed strawberries with the wet crumbs, cover and refrigerate. These cakes are best made the same day they are to be eaten, and the filling should definitely not be made more than 1–2 hours before serving.

TO ICE THE CAKES   Combine the icing sugar with the lemon juice. Add the pink food colouring in drops, and add 1 tablespoon of warm water. Add more water in drops if necessary. Adjust the colouring if too discreet. (The best way to add a very small amount of colouring is to dip the point of a metal skewer into the bottle and hold that over the bowl, rather than attempting to pour single drops from the bottle.)[+]

When you have a pourable but not runny icing, place the 'hats' back on the hollow cakes. Place them on a rack over a tray and generously spoon over the icing. If too much runs off, scrape it back from the tray, warm briefly, strain and pour again. Allow to firm and then delicately separate the 'hats' from the cakes.

TO SERVE   Whip the cream until very firm, fold in the cake-crumb/strawberry mixture and fill the hollows. Slice each garnishing strawberry into 4 and arrange these quarters to peep out from under the 'hats', which you now place on the top.

For total perfection in presentation, wreath each plate in strawberry leaves and perhaps place a Cécile Brunner rosebud on the plate.

NOTE: This method of making a delicately tinted glacé icing can be used on another occasion to coat small shapes of the same butter sponge to serve as petits fours. Always be generous with the icing – pour it on and allow to run off. Never dab at the cakes. Professional cooks would use fondant diluted with a little water and warmed over hot water. You can buy fondant in small quantities in speciality cake-decorating shops.

[+] Today I would moisten the icing sugar with some strawberry purée rather than use pink colouring. Put a little of the mashed strawberry in the food processor, then add the sifted icing sugar and mix. If it is too stiff, thin the mixture with a few drops of hot water.

All my own work

MENU

~⌀~

MUSSEL SOUP WITH ITS ROUILLE

STUFFED TRIPE WITH VARIOUS SAUCES

BREAD-AND-BUTTER PUDDING
CANDIED CITRUS PEEL

~⌀~

This recipe for mussel soup is one of my favourites. It has a full, restorative flavour, and is gutsy but light in body. Each time I holiday in the south of France I have to eat a *soupe de poissons* the very first day – rather like kissing the ground on arrival. There are lots of versions of fish soup. Because I am addicted to them, I try them all and have become something of a connoisseur. There are the grainy-type soups, where minute fragments of fish and fish cartilage are forced through a sieve so that there is a sort of fine purée held in suspension. There are the soups bound with a little garlic mayonnaise, which finish as creamy, pungent and delicious. This type of soup becomes the *bourride* of the south by adding an assortment of fish. There are the broths of the Atlantic coast made without saffron. There are American chowders, which seem to be completely different in feeling. There are Italian fish soups encountered along the Adriatic coast, which are sweet and thick with clams. And there is of course *bouillabaisse*, a complete meal of fish and crustaceans in a saffron-tinted fish soup, and so on and so on.

The simple *soupe de poissons* as served in the old town of Nice or in countless family cafés along the coast is served in a glazed earthenware bowl with three smaller bowls accompanying it. In them is usually rather dried-out, oily Gruyère (either it has not been stored correctly or it is old), oven-dried rough croutons and a bowl of *rouille*. *Rouille* means 'rust' in French, and refers presumably to the colour of the sauce. Once again, there are many different versions of *rouille*. Some are a type of *aïoli* with hot pepper and saffron added. (*Aïoli* refers to the very powerful garlic mayonnaise used as the sole condiment in a dish of boiled vegetables, meat and fish and eaten in the south of France.) Others are sauces built up on pounded, dried and soaked bread, and the most specialised recipe I have is based on the pounded liver of the red mullet. All versions have in common saffron, hot pepper, lots of garlic and olive oil. The *rouille* is plopped into your soup and allowed to melt and spread, and results in a wonderful glow in the mouth.

My version of *soupe de poissons* has mussels added, and uses the fumet of the mussels. It has genuine Spanish saffron stamens and a touch of *pastis*, and the *rouille* is an unusual recipe that I adore. It is based on the stickiness of potatoes cooked in the broth with chilli and saffron and then pounded and mounted with virgin olive oil. Sometimes I throw into the soup a handful of basil, sometimes a *chiffonnade* of spinach, sometimes a dice of peeled, seeded tomatoes. The *rouille* floats on the top of the soup in a scrubbed mussel shell, like a bobbing fishing-boat.✢

This same recipe for *rouille*, if blended with some soft, unsalted butter, can be spread onto mussels on the half-shell, sprinkled with fresh crumbs and then passed briefly under a very hot grill to bubble and brown. Don't stop at mussels. Try it with small pipis or cockles. With the pipis, cook them open in a little wine as for mussels. Check them carefully for sand. If they are still sandy, wash them in the carefully strained cooking liquid and then proceed. Spread a layer of the hot butter on the half-shell to cover the meat and grill as above.

In 1981 I was invited to contribute a main course for the third Great Chefs of Australia dinner held in the Cask Hall at Rothbury Estate in the Hunter Valley. This seemed an appropriate place to display my proudest creation: stuffed tripe. Perhaps there is no such thing as a truly original recipe – that is, one that does not

---

✢ Without question this is still my favourite fish soup. Regular diners at both Stephanie's and Richmond Hill Cafe & Larder will know how often this rich saffron/tomato/*rouille* combination has occurred on my menus.

draw from one's own experiences, things read or eaten. But the creative buzz comes from knowing, once in a while, that you have put together something of which you are very proud. For anyone who is interested in understanding personal style, the clues are all there to see. Here is the ancestry of my stuffed tripe.

Reading Richard Olney's *French Menu Cookbook* for the hundredth time, I once again lingered on his description of stuffed pig's ears. I remembered the stuffed ears on the menu at Alain Chapel's at Mionnay on my first visit in 1979. As they were not part of the *menu dégustation*, I did not taste them. (Trap for inexperienced players, these *menus dégustations*. Good value for money, but not always what you wished to try – anyway, that is a different story.)

The Alain Chapel cookbook (*La Cuisine c'est beaucoup plus que des recettes*) has a long recipe for stuffed ears. I do serve unusual dishes from time to time and believe that I have reliable instincts about what the public is willing to try. I am proud of the acceptance given to dishes served at Stephanie's that are unusual, such as the ear, tongue and trotter salad on page 233, or the beautiful stuffed cabbage braised in sticky veal broth, or our woodland fantasy, which we call autumn salad (page 237), or our shimmering rock pool (page 128). But stuffed ears as a main course? I don't think so – yet.[+]

Years ago I served deep-fried tripe with great success in the manner frequently encountered in the bistros of Lyon under the charming name of *la tablier de sapeur* (the fireman's apron). Tripe is a superb wrapper. I also had great success with a mixed charcuterie platter of which one ingredient was pickled hocks, boned, stuffed and simmered with a mix that included pistachio nuts. The brilliance of the red meat in contrast with the pale stuffing was very pretty.

I determined to put together an interesting and highly flavoured filling for tripe. My very dear colleague Janni Kyritsis understood the concept perfectly, and together we created this fabulous dish. Modern surgery relies on dissolving sutures, but how could we make our 'sutures' dissolve? The answer, of course, was to sew up the tripe with hog casings, rather than string or thread. No need to remove them, and they are very strong. We were very excited.

The dish was voted a great success at the special dinner. I have served it on several seasonal menus since, and most people love it. We make no attempt to persuade people to order such an unusual dish, but it is most gratifying to see how well it stands up next to the usual bestsellers of duck and beef. At the dinner I served a purée of soaked French morel mushrooms with the tripe. I liked it, but most people didn't. It cost the earth, with morels selling at $250 a kilogram, so I decided to forget that sauce, to put the morels inside the stuffing instead of ordinary mushrooms,

[+] I may not have been prepared to serve stuffed ears in 1985, but others were. One of them was Janni Kyritsis, who served it at Berowra Waters Inn in 1984.

and to serve a quite different sauce.⁺ With this dish I like salsa verde, which is described on page 85 to accompany *la friture*. I have also given two other sauces as alternatives.

I love to 'embroider' with food. A stitch here, an unexpected little pleat there, a blend or contrast of colours, and lots of texture changes.

A final word on 'originality'. After working on this dish for some time, and displaying it proudly at the Great Chefs dinner and serving it in three menus spanning nine different months of the year, I bought the *Offal* title in the Time-Life series *The Good Cook* three years later. Lo and behold, on the cover, a dish of stuffed tripe! Thank goodness the stuffing was entirely different.

After such a stimulating main course, a soothing dessert. This is the grown-up version of bread-and-butter pudding, made from sultana brioche. The fruit in the pudding is soaked in brandy, and the custard is based on cream. Boarding-school version was never like this.

⁺ Fresh morel mushrooms are gathered in Victoria and Sydney in the springtime by those in the know. They are less sandy than the imported dried French ones, and although full-flavoured they lack the perfume of the French fungus. As one might expect for a hand-gathered, chance-occurring wild product, morels are expensive.

Mussel soup with its rouille

⌇

2 kg mussels
1 stalk parsley
1 bay leaf
600 ml dry white wine
salt, pepper

FISH STOCK (SOUP BASE)

2 kg fish heads and bones
butter, oil
2 onions, sliced
1 stalk celery, sliced
2 carrots, sliced
2 leeks, well washed and sliced
½ head garlic, unpeeled
1 bulb fennel, sliced
1 bay leaf
1 sprig of thyme
parsley stalks
1 small glass Pernod
300 ml dry white wine
2 envelopes powdered saffron
    (packaged in envelopes in
    Italian groceries for risotto)
4 tomatoes, peeled, seeded and
    quartered
1 tablespoon Spanish saffron stamens

TOMATO PURÉE

6 large tomatoes, peeled, seeded
    and roughly chopped
30 g butter
1 bay leaf

ROUILLE

2 red peppers
2 hot chillis
2 large potatoes
4 cloves garlic
1 envelope powdered saffron
fish broth to cover
150 ml virgin olive oil
salt

CROUTONS

1 day-old breadstick
olive oil
1 clove garlic, peeled and halved

GARNISH

all or some of: spinach leaves,
    shredded; tomatoes, peeled,
    seeded and diced; basil leaves,
    sliced or torn

TO PREPARE THE MUSSELS AND MUSSEL STOCK   Scrub the mussels well in cold water. Do not bother to de-beard them, as each mussel will be handled again. Place them in a large baking dish.✣ (Try not to have the mussels more than 2 deep, as they steam much less evenly.) Add the parsley stalk, bay leaf and wine. Cover the dish and place over high heat. Shake once or twice and stir the mussels around. They will all be open after about 3 minutes of vigorous steaming. Draw the dish from the heat and, as soon as the mussels can be handled, pull each one from its shell,

✣ Mussels also steam beautifully in a covered wok.

snip off the beard and drop the meat into a small bowl. Continue until all the mussels are shelled. Reserve 6 beautiful shells for the *rouille*. Discard the rest of the shells. Cover the shelled mussels with plastic film pressed down tightly to prevent them drying out. Pour the mussel stock through the finest strainer you own into a glass jug and leave to settle. After 2 hours, carefully ladle off the mussel stock through the same fine strainer into another jug, leaving all traces of sand and sediment behind. You should now have about 200 ml of rather salty mussel stock.

TO PREPARE THE FISH STOCK (SOUP BASE)   Wash all the fish heads and bones and chop up any large pieces. (This enables more gelatine to be extracted from the bones in the relatively short cooking time.) Place in a stockpot. In a separate baking dish heat a film of butter and oil and lightly colour the onion, celery, carrot, leek, garlic, fennel and herbs. Deglaze the pan with the Pernod and white wine. Sprinkle over the powdered saffron, scrape and stir and transfer all the contents of the baking dish to the stockpot. Add the quartered tomatoes and enough cold water to barely cover. Very slowly, bring to simmering point, skimming well. Simmer for 20 minutes and then strain through a conical or chinois sieve, pressing very well on the debris to extract the maximum flavour. You should have 1½–2 litres of stock. Combine the mussel stock gradually with the fish stock, tasting as you go to ensure that it doesn't become too salty. (It should, however, have a briny quality – after all, mussels and fish are of the sea!) Add the saffron stamens.

TO PREPARE THE TOMATO PURÉE AND THE SOUP   Cook the tomato gently in the butter with the bay leaf. Simmer until a moist purée. Stir this into the fish stock. Simmer all together and taste for seasoning. This is your basic fish soup. Leave aside until needed. (On another occasion you could use this broth to poach some fish fillets, and if there were no mussels left but you still had some soup, you could add some dried croutons and cheese. It becomes a delicious fish broth in its own right.)

TO MAKE THE ROUILLE   Roast the red peppers following the method on page 36. Peel, seed and slice. Remove the stems and seeds from the chillis. Peel and quarter the potatoes. Peel the garlic cloves. Place all of these into a small pan with the contents of the envelope of saffron, and barely cover with fish soup. Simmer gently until the potatoes are quite tender (15–20 minutes). Tip all the solids into a food processor, blender or Mouli and combine to make a thick paste, using a little of the saffron cooking liquid. In a food processor or blender, gradually add the olive oil with the motor running. (If using a food mill, the oil should be added drop by drop at first, and then in a thin stream, as for a mayonnaise.) Taste for salt. Set the *rouille* aside until needed. It will last 2–3 days in the refrigerator, but the potatoes will turn sour, so do not use after a few days without tasting it first.

Any saffron cooking liquid not needed to make the paste for the *rouille* should be tipped back into the basic fish broth.

TO MAKE THE CROUTONS Cut slanting slices from the breadstick about 1 cm thick. Paint each slice with olive oil and bake the slices in a slow oven until dry and a pale gold in colour. Rub each slice on both sides with the garlic and store the croutons in an airtight container for 1–2 days. They will start to smell and taste rancid after more than a few days, so don't bother to keep them for some vague future occasion.

TO SERVE Heat 1 generous ladleful of fish soup per serving to boiling point. Throw in 6–8 mussels, garnish with a handful of spinach and 1 teaspoon of diced fresh tomato and/or basil, and pour immediately into a shallow bowl. Float a shell of *rouille* on the top and serve with some garlic croutons.

Stuffed tripe with various sauces

This recipe has so many processes and takes such a lot of work that it doesn't seem practical to make too small a quantity. Save it for a grand dinner when you have assembled a collection of true food lovers with a sense of adventure. It probably can, however, be made in half the quantity. The quantities given will provide a main course for 8–10 people. (Any left over is delicious cold.)[+]

Practically all tripe sold in Australia is precooked. In fact, if you are looking for the beige (unbleached), uncooked variety to make a *tripes à la mode de Caen* or some other long-simmered dish, you will have great difficulty finding it. This recipe presumes bleached honeycomb tripe that has been precooked. Simmer the tripe in a light stock for around 30 minutes and then eat a little piece. It should be tender, but still *al dente*. There is nothing more certain to turn people off eating tripe than to serve a dish where the texture resembles wet rags.[✦]

[+] I am amazed that I prepared this dish over and over again. It certainly had its devotees. But the work! Consider this a curiosity left over from the days when we did not consider how long a dish took to prepare if it was sufficiently interesting. There can be very few establishments left that offer themselves or their customers this luxury.

[✦] Having had occasion recently to quiz my butcher regarding tripe, the up-to-date story has not changed very much. It is still not easy to buy unbleached tripe, certainly not from a mainstream butcher, but you can order raw tripe. Almost all tripe sold has been precooked.

Mussel soup with rouille and croutons (page 114)

Rock pool with various sea creatures, seaweed and a rippling, spicy jelly (page 128)

1 small pickled ox tongue

2 pickled hocks

100 g dried morels or 400 g fresh button mushrooms

2 large onions

butter

½ cup dry white wine

½ cup port

500 g large veal sweetbreads (export quality, if possible – warn your butcher)

1 litre veal stock

1.5 kg honeycomb tripe

400 ml cream

500 g pure chicken breast meat, weighed without skin and scraped free of tendons

salt, pepper

4 egg whites

3 tablespoons chopped parsley

pinch ground ginger

pinch ground allspice

flour for dredging

3 eggs, beaten

fine white breadcrumbs, dried in the oven

clean, blended vegetable oil for deep-frying

parsley sprigs or celery leaves

POACHING INGREDIENTS

1 onion stuck with 3 whole cloves

1 carrot, sliced

1 leek, washed and sliced

1 bay leaf

1 sprig of thyme

3 parsley stalks

200 ml port

water to barely cover

TO POACH THE TONGUE AND HOCKS   Place the tongue and the hocks in a large pan and add all the poaching ingredients. Simmer for 2–3 hours until quite tender. The tongue may be ready before the hock. Test with a skewer and cook until there is no resistance. When the tongue is cooked, run it under cold water, peel off the skin and trim off any gristly bits from the root end. When the hock is tender, peel off the skin and any excess layer of fat, reserving the skin to enrich a cassoulet or a dish of lentils or dried beans. Cut both meats into 5 mm cubes, place in a basin and cover with enough of the poaching liquid to prevent the meat drying out while the rest of the preparation takes place.

As mentioned in the section on composed salads (pages 228–31), this highly flavoured stock can now be clarified (see page 68) and will set to a beautiful jelly. It is ideal for the simple ham mousse on page 44. Unclarified, it will make the base for a delicious soup. (Simmer some slate-brown lentils in it until just tender and garnish with fried slices of your favourite sausage.)

TO PREPARE THE MUSHROOMS AND ONIONS   Soak the morels either overnight or for several hours in warm water, changing the water at least twice. Lift the mushrooms from their soaking water and allow to drain in a colander. Trim off any hard stem ends and then cut the mushrooms into large even-sized pieces. (The strained soaking water should be added to your next stock, if you can organise to have a stock to start the same or the next day.) Finely chop the onions and cook very slowly in butter until they are limp and golden. Meanwhile, gently simmer the mushrooms in the wine and port until all the liquid has been absorbed. Set the mushrooms and onions aside.

TO PREPARE THE SWEETBREADS   Soak the sweetbreads overnight in cold salted water to draw out the blood. Put the sweetbreads into a saucepan, cover with cold water and bring slowly to simmering point. Strain and rinse. Pull off the large pieces of membrane and gristle, cover with the veal stock and simmer gently for approximately 15 minutes until the sweetbreads are tender. Once again handle each piece of sweetbread and remove all connecting tissue. Drop each piece into a bowl with some of the stock to prevent them drying out.

If you have no veal stock, simmer the sweetbreads in some of the stock from cooking the hocks.✢

TO PREPARE THE TRIPE   Simmer the tripe as mentioned in the recipe introduction, until it is *al dente*. You should use a light chicken stock, or a little diluted veal stock, or dilute some of the stock from cooking the tongue and hocks. Cut the tripe in such a way that you will have 2 pouches like fat sausages. (Any scraps can be crumbed to deep-fry the same evening for the children, or else frozen and added to a casserole of oxtail some other day.)

Using a tapestry or leathercraft needle and a length of hog casing, sew up the pouches to form a rough sausage with the honeycomb on the outside, leaving one end open for the filling. Refrigerate the tripe sausages on folded kitchen paper.

✢ If using the hock poaching liquid, expect the sweetbreads (and the tripe) to take on a slightly pinkish hue from the pickling salts used to cure the hock.

TO PREPARE THE CHICKEN MOUSSELINE   Chill the canister of your food processor for 2 hours. Also chill a large metal bowl for folding in the other ingredients. Measure and chill the cream thoroughly. Cut the chicken flesh into cubes. Process with some salt and pepper and the egg whites until the mix is really firm and shiny – at least 5 minutes. Press this purée through the fine disc of a Mouli or through a drum sieve to extract all scraps of non-puréed tissue. Chill the purée for at least 1 hour. Return the washed food-processor canister to the freezer. When everything is very cold, return the purée to the food processor and incorporate the cream. Scrape out the purée and poach a small ball of it in lightly salted water. Taste. Add extra salt and pepper if needed.

TO ASSEMBLE   In the chilled metal bowl combine the well-drained and chopped hocks and tongue, the cooked mushroom, onion and sweetbreads, and the chopped parsley. Add the ginger and allspice. Gently combine with the chicken purée, mixing lightly but well with a large metal spoon. Poach a further ball of stuffing to check the seasoning.

Fill the tripe sausages with this mix, either with a spoon or using a piping bag with a very large aperture. The tripe can be well filled, as it will expand as necessary to accommodate the swelling of the stuffing. Sew up the open ends.

Generously flour each sausage, roll in the beaten egg and then liberally coat with the breadcrumbs. Deep-fry the sausages in good, clean oil at approximately 160°C for 25 minutes. Leave each sausage to drain on a clean cloth or a thick wad of kitchen paper in a warm place for a good 5 minutes before cutting. Cut into 1 cm slices with a sharp, serrated knife. Deep-fried parsley sprigs or young celery leaves can be scattered around. Serve your preferred sauce separately.

TO DEEP-FRY THE PARSLEY SPRIGS OR CELERY LEAVES   The leaves or sprigs must be washed and very dry. The oil must have completely recovered temperature and be very hot. Remove the leaves after only a few seconds and transfer immediately to kitchen paper to drain.

NOTE ON DEEP-FRYING: If you choose the shape of your tripe carefully, you should have only 2 sausages. Even so, this will need a lot of oil. You will need a deep-fryer with a thermostat or, failing this, a heavy pan, such as the base of a pressure-cooker, with an accurate thermometer attached. After the correct temperature is reached, you will need to adjust the heat of the jet or hotplate so that a *satisfactory sizzle* is maintained throughout the frying time. If you have only one receptacle, you will need to fry the sausages one at a time. Don't forget to allow the temperature to recover, and although there will be a slight difference in the texture of sausages 1 and 2, both will taste delicious as long as sausage number 1 has been lain to rest in a warm place.

Sauce suggestions for Stuffed tripe

Salsa verde (page 85)
Skordalia (page 85)
Mediterranean tomato sauce (page 86)

Sauce ravigote

A very popular French sauce for all sorts of cold meats. It is basically a vinaigrette thickened by the addition of a generous amount of chopped herbs. The herbs are not chopped so finely that they lose their character. One can still see that parsley, tarragon, chives and chervil are present. The usual additions are a few capers, a dice of crunchy cornichons and sometimes a little anchovy.

This sauce goes particularly well with *les restes* of the tripe. That is, any left over should be sliced quite thinly and served cold as an hors d'oeuvre with the *sauce ravigote* spooned over.

Sauce béarnaise

A classic and delectable sauce, but quite rich. Serve small portions![+]

250 g unsalted butter
2 shallots or ½ small onion, very finely chopped
60 ml white wine or white-wine vinegar
1 tablespoon tarragon vinegar
salt, white pepper
2 tablespoons cold water
4 egg yolks
fresh tarragon, finely chopped
few drops lemon juice (optional)

Have assembled a pan half-full of hot water with a small basin that fits well over the water but doesn't touch it.

[+] Béarnaise sauce and hollandaise sauce fell under a cloud for a few years after the then British Minister for Health, Edwina Currie, suggested in 1987 that most eggs in the UK were likely to carry salmonella. This suggestion was not substantiated. Nonetheless, at the time many London hotel dining rooms ceased making these classic sauces.

In a small pan melt the butter, skim off the white foam and leave aside. In a separate pan combine the chopped shallots, wine or wine vinegar, tarragon vinegar, salt and pepper and reduce until the shallot is very moist but not completely dry. Add the cold water to this reduction and transfer it to the top of the double-boiler together with the egg yolks.

Using a comfortable small whisk, whisk the yolks until they are thick and foamy. Remove the basin from the hot water and continue to whisk for 1 minute to further firm the egg mousse. Slowly trickle in the melted butter, whisking well. If you have a friend nearby, have him or her pour in the butter in a continuous stream while you just keep whisking. Taste the sauce, stir in the chopped tarragon and, if necessary, a few drops of lemon juice, and return the finished sauce to its position over the hot water to keep warm. Push the pan away from the heat, however, as it will curdle if it gets too hot. Béarnaise and hollandaise sauces are always served warm.

Bread-and-butter pudding

This recipe will make 2 × 500 g loaf tins of brioche. You will need only 1 loaf for the pudding, so either freeze the other loaf so as to simplify a repeat performance of this dessert or else serve the second loaf for Sunday brunch or for a luxury breakfast treat.

butter
½ cup mixed dried fruit, e.g. currants, sultanas, chopped dried apricots etc.
castor sugar for sprinkling

SIMPLE BRIOCHE DOUGH

30 g sugar
250 ml milk
2 teaspoons dried yeast
6 egg yolks
500 g plain flour
1 teaspoon salt
150 g soft unsalted butter
100 g sultanas soaked overnight in a little brandy

75 g castor sugar
4 whole eggs
seeds from 1 split vanilla bean
375 ml milk
375 ml cream

TO MAKE THE BRIOCHE   Heat the sugar and milk in a pan until lukewarm. Sprinkle over the yeast and leave to foam. Beat the egg yolks lightly and add to the warm yeast/milk mixture. Sift the flour and salt into a separate bowl and form a well in the centre. Pour in the liquid and mix into a dough. I place this sticky mass in an electric mixer, attach the dough hook and beat the dough well for about 5 minutes. Add the softened butter in about 4 lots, beating well after each addition. Continue to beat the dough until it is shiny and smooth and comes away cleanly from the sides of the bowl.

Lightly butter a mixing bowl and put the dough in it. Cover with a damp cloth and leave to rise in a warm place for approximately 2½ hours. When well risen, knock down, scatter over the brandy-soaked sultanas and form into 2 loaves. Put into buttered tins and leave to rise again for approximately 1 hour.

Cook at 190°C for 30 minutes. Tip the loaves out of the tins onto the oven rack and continue to cook for a further 10 minutes to brown the crust. Leave to cool on a wire rack.

TO MAKE THE CUSTARD AND ASSEMBLE THE PUDDING   Mix the sugar, eggs and vanilla seeds. Stir in the milk and cream. Butter slices of the cooled brioche and toast lightly on one side under the grill. (They toast quickly!) Cut each slice into triangles or leave whole.

Put the brioche pieces into a 6 cup (1.5 litre) pie dish and sprinkle with the dried fruit. Ladle the custard over, right to the top of the dish. Sprinkle with castor sugar. Stand the pie dish in a deep baking dish. Fill the baking dish up to the halfway mark with boiling water and bake at 180°C for 40 minutes, or until the pudding is golden brown and just firm. Serve with pouring cream.

Candied citrus peel

My family used to throw away the skins of oranges and grapefruit after juicing them. They don't now. There is a plastic container in the refrigerator in which all spent skins are collected. Once a week I make or, more accurately, *they* make candied grapefruit and orange peel. In its syrup, in a tightly closed jar in the refrigerator, it keeps forever. Take out what you need with tongs, rather than your fingers, if making a fruit cake or the pudding in this menu. Or, if you wish to serve the pieces of peel as a sophisticated sweetmeat with coffee, drain the requisite number on a cake rack over a tray on the morning of the party, or even the night before, and roll them liberally in sugar just before dinner. A little of the syrup added to plain sugar and water will greatly improve the subtlety of a simple poached pear.

TO PREPARE THE PEEL   Slice the halved skins into wedge-shaped pieces. Put into a pot with a large amount of cold water. Bring slowly to the boil, then tip the contents of the pan through a colander. Return the peel to the pan, add fresh cold water and repeat the process. The peel should be blanched 3 times until it no longer tastes bitter. Drain well.

Make a heavy syrup using 1 kg of sugar dissolved in 1 litre of water. Pour the syrup over the peel. The quantity of peel must be covered by the syrup. If you have too much peel, cook it in two batches, using the same syrup again.

Simmer the peel until it is quite soft and the rind is translucent and can be pierced easily with a fine skewer, approximately 45 minutes to 1 hour. Store in clean jars, covered with syrup. The peel will keep indefinitely.

Chicken in a pot

MENU

～

ROCK POOL

POACHED CHICKEN WITH
SPRING VEGETABLES

RICH ALMOND TART

～

We first served this entrée in our first year in
Hawthorn (1981). It came about one day after I had
shared my image of a cool, clear rock pool with colleague
Janni Kyritsis. I wanted to present a shallow bowl into
which one could almost dive – clear, with little ripples
around the half-submerged rocks, with waving fronds and
hidden sea-creatures. It had to taste delicious, so as not to
be a mere exercise in cleverness. I have served it several
times since then, and one of the pleasures is that the pool
changes, perhaps not with the tide, but certainly with the
market availability of produce. Sometimes there are green
periwinkles, the 'door' ajar and the fish nearly exposed;
sometimes a delicate tentacle of baby squid hooks around
an oyster rock. A diver friend has occasionally produced

some delicate sea-lettuce, which spreads into a flower shape. Prawns are easy to accommodate, and waving sea-anemones can be suggested by a piece of turnip cut as a flower (described on page 240).

The dish, however, relies on the purity and flavour of the lightly jellied consommé. We have experimented with several recipes and find that the best flavour comes with a consommé that has some shellfish in it. The extra sweetness counteracts the dulling effect that cold food can have on the palate. Recipes often suggest adding extra salt and pepper if a dish is to be served cold. Another approach is to put into the dish some lively ingredient that has its own flavour-sharpener. The consommé could be served hot and garnished with filled pasta shapes or slivered fish or shellfish, or vegetables left crunchy or raw, or a simple handful of herbs.✝

The second dish is a poached chicken. If you have a supplier of superior hens, this is an admirable dish for six or even eight. In the French repertoire this dish is often styled *poule au pot, Henri IV*. Legend says that when Henri became king he declared his aim to improve the lot of the French people so that they could all enjoy a *poule au pot* every Sunday. *Poule* means a boiling fowl, not a chicken, but I do not recommend using a boiling fowl, as they are often so tough that they require hours of simmering. This concept of a chicken simmered in broth and then sauced with a sauce based on the broth is much appreciated in many European cuisines. I think there is a great prejudice against poached, i.e. white, chicken in this country. How much of this feeling can be attributed to the mass marketing of formula-produced, takeaway fried chicken, I wonder?

The bird can be boned or not. If it is tied in muslin it will stay whiter than if it simmers naked in the broth. If not in muslin, you will need to sew it rather than rely on poultry pins. If boned before stuffing, it is easier to slice. If poached whole, the stuffing can be inserted in the cavity and sliced separately or formed into little balls and simmered as dumplings in the broth alongside the chicken, added at the same time as the fresh vegetables to be served on the plate. If you grow little six-week turnips, it can become poached chicken with turnips. Serve the turnips still with their green attached. Similarly, if you are able to grow or buy young leeks, no thicker than your thumb, it becomes poached chicken with leeks.

✝ The rock pool became a signature dish. Over the years the consommé varied in character and the selection of seafood changed, but the jelly was always spooned into the bowl in such a manner that the surface was rippled. I served it to over 100 guests at a special dinner in New York held at the Ritz-Carlton in 1992. Many other cooks have been attracted by the same idea. Phillip Searle filled a fish tank with jellied consommé and seafood for one of his fantastic dishes at the banquet for the first Symposium of Gastronomy in Adelaide in 1984. (Guests were enticed into the dining space and later waited upon by actors dressed as white-faced clowns, among them a young and relatively unknown Geoffrey Rush.)

A selection of young vegetables – carrots, turnips, leeks, peas – can become a springtime special dish, as could a dish of poached chicken with asparagus. In all cases, drain the chicken well before carving as it is unpleasant to be faced with a poached chicken in a pool of liquid.[+]

A simple velouté sauce is probably the easiest to make, whereby you make a blond roux with 30 g of butter and 30 g of flour and whisk in 500 ml of well-reduced hot poaching stock. Toss in lots of fresh garden parsley or tarragon, and the dish will taste very good. Or enrich the sauce with three egg yolks and three tablespoons of cream whisked together with a little of the hot sauce and reheated without boiling before adding the same herb combinations and perhaps a few drops of lemon juice. Or soft-boil an egg and then whirl the yolk in the processor with a little of the reduced broth and lots of parsley to create a pale green sauce. Finally, stir in the finely chopped white of the egg and even more parsley or a *fines herbes* mix. Offer flakes of sea salt with the chicken. A poached dish looks magnificent on one of my collection of old and faded Victorian meat platters. I have one that is patterned in a soft grey–green and it has a beautiful sauce boat with a patterned china ladle. I proudly bring it out for my *poule au pot*.

Probably every cook has some skill or dish that he or she feels anxious about. I am still not very happy about making puff pastry, and for years I had what amounted to a near-phobia about flour in general. I was convinced that I could not make pastry. My mother and sister were both always fast and confident when whipping up the family's traditional North Country paste, which uses a combination of flours and lard. Mine was always tough and brittle, overworked and quite unrollable. Theirs was plastic, and they could swing it, I promise you! The recipe for Grandma's bramble cake on page 164 uses this dough, and, after tuition from my sister, I can now make it.

I owe a debt to my great friend and colleague Damien Pignolet, who, with his wife, Josephine, runs the delightful restaurant Claude's, in Sydney.[+] Apart from his skill as a cook, Damien is an excellent teacher and in half an hour he taught me

[+] All these comments regarding the problematic supply of high-quality poultry and young vegetables are interesting. Nowadays almost every supermarket offers free-range and grain-fed poultry, and small, delicately flavoured carrots, leeks and turnips are no longer a rarity. I am intrigued that nearly twenty years after writing *Menus for Food Lovers* I once again included details of the preparation and eating of a poached and stuffed chicken in my most recent book, *Cooking & Travelling in South-West France*. Some dishes are classics and fortunately defy fashion.

[+] Josephine was tragically killed in an accident in 1987. She was a true friend and a superb cook and will forever be missed. Damien sold Claude's to his long-time colleague, Tim Pak Poy, in 1995. It continues to delight customers with its exquisite food. Damien (and his present wife, Julie) are now the owners (with business partners) of Bistro Moncur in Woollahra.

all I know about *pâte brisée*. The parsley tart I once ate at Claude's remains for me the yardstick of what shortcrust should be: crisp, almost flaky, unmistakably made with butter, with no effort made to force its layers to lie flat. It crinkled and wrinkled and in the mouth shattered into crisp little pieces. Never soggy, never hard. It is made entirely by hand. It should be obvious by now that I *love* my food processor, but as with all relationships it is a big mistake to feel that any one relationship can fulfil all one's needs. All *pâte brisée* tart shells made at Stephanie's have been made by hand since The Great Breakthrough. I have included Damien's recipe with its cautionary notes exactly as he gave it to me. Use it for both sweet and savoury tarts. I personally never add sugar to it.

We have a new house by the sea. It is a house for relaxing and resting.[+] I was enchanted to see that there were two very romantic trees on the property – an almond tree and a pear tree. The almond tree is a true harbinger of spring – its delicate blossom the first to burst after the winter. I have therefore included my favourite almond tart as a lovely spring dessert, made even more delicious with Damien's crispy pastry.

After the blossom, the fruit. It was a joy to taste the chewy, sweet fresh almonds. Some of them I roasted in almond oil and dusted with a shake of cayenne pepper. Most were eaten fresh from the tree. I have included here a recipe for old-fashioned almond bread. Probably everyone knows how to make it, but it is a very popular biscuit in the restaurant when we cut it into fingers before the second baking and serve it as a petit four. Its great charm is that it is not very sweet.

[+] Maurice and I designed and had built a lovely retreat at Barwon Heads where we could escape from the all-consuming restaurant. In the mid-1980s Barwon Heads was a sleepy seaside town. This all changed in the late 1990s with the success of the ABC series *SeaChange*, when Barwon Heads became 'Pearl Bay'.

Rock pool

CONSOMMÉ

1.5 kg fish heads and bones
1 leek, well washed and sliced
1 onion, sliced
1 carrot, sliced
3 slices lemon
1 bay leaf
1 sprig of thyme
several parsley stalks, roughly chopped
6 mushrooms, sliced
½ stalk celery, sliced
1 tomato
1 teaspoon sugar
10 peppercorns
2 tablespoons white-wine vinegar
1.5 litres water
300 ml white wine
2 slices ginger
1 small green crayfish (rock lobster), approximately 700 g (ask your fishmonger to drown or stab the crayfish before you collect it)[†]

CLARIFICATION

crushed shell of the crayfish and all its mustard and coral, if any
2 egg whites
2 eggshells, crushed
2 tomatoes, peeled, seeded and chopped
½ leek, washed and finely shredded
1 tablespoon roughly chopped parsley
½ stalk celery, finely chopped
100 g skinless fillet of fish, finely chopped

GARNISH

6 periwinkles, steamed, trimmed and replaced in the shell
ringlets and tentacles of 1 small squid
12 steamed prawns
12 oysters in the shell
sea-lettuce and/or soaked and sautéed Chinese tree fungus and/or soaked wakame seaweed
meat from the crayfish head and claws
caviar (optional)
anything else that takes your fancy and reminds you of a rock pool

TO PREPARE THE CONSOMMÉ Rinse the fish heads and bones. Chop roughly. Combine all stock ingredients, except the crayfish, in a pan and heat. Just before the liquid boils, skim and adjust the heat to a simmer. Simmer gently for 30 minutes, skimming well. Strain. Reheat to simmering point. Plunge the green (i.e. uncooked) crayfish into the stock and cook for 8 minutes. Draw the pan off the heat and leave the crayfish to cool in the stock for 15 minutes.

[†] I have already commented on the correct name of this crustacean (see page 93).

Take the crayfish from the pan. Remove the tail meat and set aside for another dish.[+] Extract the meat from the claws and head and reserve for the garnish. After removing the gritty sac from the head, place the shell, head and claws in a clean rubbish bag and pound well. For the clarification, lightly process the crayfish mustard and coral, if any, in a food processor with the egg whites, eggshells, tomatoes, leek, parsley, celery and chopped fish. Process for 1 minute and then mix with the crushed carcass of the crayfish. Whisk into the cooled stock. Stirring gently but constantly, bring the stock slowly to a simmer. Cover and simmer very gently for 20 minutes, then draw to one side, turn off the heat and let stand undisturbed for 5 minutes.

Over a large bowl, suspend a sieve lined with a damp, clean cloth. With an egg lifter, gently lift off part of the coagulated 'raft' and ladle the clear consommé through the cloth. Taste for seasoning and leave to get quite cold to test the set.

The 'set' of the consommé will depend in large part on the gelatine content of the fish used. When completely cold, it should be very lightly set. If it is still liquid, use the leaf gelatine quantities given on page 14 and reduce the quantity by half. That is, if you have 1 litre of consommé, which would normally take 12 leaves to form a light jelly, use only 6 leaves. Your rock pool should *almost* be a soup, barely scoopable, and if the temperature is very warm it will quickly melt. Once you are happy with the texture of the consommé, proceed to assemble each rock pool.

THE GARNISH

Periwinkles: Place the periwinkles in a small, covered pan with a little white wine and steam for 4–5 minutes until the 'door' opens. Extract the fish gently with a pin or the point of a skewer, trim off the black tip and half-replace in the shell. I leave the 'door' on for decorative effect, but it is not edible.

Squid: To clean the squid, cut off the tentacles in one piece with scissors, just below the hard bony piece known as the 'beak'. Discard the ink sac and pull out the intestines and backbone, which is like a pliable piece of plastic, from inside the body cavity. Rinse the body cavity well in salted water and then proceed to rub and pull off all the blackish-grey skin on the body and fins. Also rub the tentacles to remove as much grey skin as possible.

Cut the tentacles into 6 cm pieces. Cut the body crosswise into rings about 5 mm thick. Place both the body rings and the pieces of tentacle in a pan with a pinch of salt. Add 1 tablespoon of water for each squid. Cover the pan and place over moderate heat. After 1 minute, remove the lid and give a good stir. Replace the lid

[+] My favourite would be simply sliced tail meat accompanied by green leaves and a fine mayonnaise, for a delicious lunch.

and simmer for about 2 more minutes. Eat a piece. It should be deliciously tender. Tip onto a shallow plate to cool.

Incidentally, this is the best method for cooking squid and will always result in rosy-pink, tender meat. If you then add a handful of fresh parsley, a little good olive oil and a squeeze of lemon juice, you will have a delicious squid salad. Stir in some olives and some warm pasta and you will have a substantial lunch dish.

Prawns: It looks most dramatic to use small Harbour prawns still in their shells, but it does make the rock pool messy to eat. It is probably best to steam the prawns first, leaving the heads on, and have 1 or 2 prawn heads with long curled feelers peeping out from under a rock.

Oysters: The oysters are the rocks. I slip an oyster from its shell and put it in the shell with another one. In this way the empty oyster shell can be presented upside-down in the bowl – it looks very rocklike.

TO ASSEMBLE Select plain, shallow soup bowls. Place the upside-down rock first. Drape over a bit of sea-lettuce, soaked and sautéed tree fungus, or soaked seaweed. Arrange your periwinkles, squid, prawns, oysters and shreds of crayfish meat. Carefully ladle over some consommé and let it settle into the assemblage. With the tines of a fork you can 'shirr' the surface, if you like, to create a feeling of rippled water. If you are using a final scatter of caviar, scatter it over the rock pools just before serving so that it doesn't bleed or lose its flavour into the consommé.

The rock pools should be refrigerated until serving time.

If you have ever spent time bending over rock pools you will know that you see fine pink strands of seaweed, small smooth, washed pebbles, darting little black fish and waving anemones. Does this give you other ideas?[†]

[†] Nowadays I would possibly include steamed pipis, or a whole baby abalone (now being successfully farmed in several Australian locations) separately braised until tender.

Poached chicken with spring vegetables

1 large chicken, approximately 2 kg
salt, pepper
2 litres good chicken stock with some gelatinous ingredient added (simmer it for
    1–2 hours with a veal shank or a pig's trotter)
a selection of choice vegetables in season (e.g. baby carrots, peeled; young leeks,
    trimmed and well washed; baby turnips, peeled)

STUFFING

3 slices white bread
⅓ cup milk
1 onion, finely chopped
1 tablespoon butter
1 slice ham 5 mm thick, finely chopped
250 g minced pork
2 chicken livers, chopped
2 tablespoons chopped parsley
1 tablespoon chopped tarragon
salt, pepper
1 tablespoon cognac
1 egg

VELOUTÉ SAUCE

30 g butter
30 g plain flour
500 ml reserved well-reduced poaching stock
3 egg yolks
3 tablespoons cream
1 tablespoon chopped tarragon
1 tablespoon chopped parsley
salt, pepper
few drops lemon juice

poultry pins
1 metre butter muslin
string

TO BONE THE CHICKEN   Cut the chicken skin down the spine to the parson's nose. Release the parson's nose from the spinal column, but do not cut it in half. Using a small sharp knife angled always to the bone, and with the tail end of the chicken towards you, gently free the skin and flesh from the bone. It is easier to do than explain, and there are innumerable books with step-by-step illustrations of the process. One of the clearest and most comprehensive is Diane Holuigue's *The French Kitchen*.✝ The bits to watch out for are: (a) freeing the knuckles from the sockets of the leg and wing joints and (b) not piercing the breast skin when you are severing the flesh and skin from the breastbone.

For this dish I would remove only the thigh bones of the chicken, leaving the wings as they are. Season the chicken with salt and pepper and leave in the refrigerator.

TO MAKE THE STUFFING   Soak the bread in the milk. Sauté the onion in the butter until soft and yellow. When the bread has absorbed all the milk, put all the stuffing ingredients except the egg in a food processor and blend briefly. Add the egg and blend. Taste a little of the stuffing for seasoning or, if you can't bear the idea of raw stuffing, poach a little ball of it in lightly salted water and taste that.

TO ASSEMBLE AND COOK   Spread the bird out on your workbench. Place the stuffing in the centre of the chicken and, using poultry pins, pin together again into the shape of a chicken. Wet the muslin and wring it out well. Wrap the chicken firmly in the muslin and tie (not too tightly) in three places around the circumference, like a sausage.

Bring the chicken stock to a gentle simmer and place in the chicken parcel and simmer for 1 hour. Then add the vegetables and simmer for a further 15 minutes. Check the vegetables at this time. If they are tender, remove them to a warm plate and keep warm. Using two lifters, remove the chicken parcel and drain it on a rack for a few minutes, then transfer it also to a warm place.

Pour the stock into a wide pan and reduce by fast boiling to half the quantity. Measure it. Keep 500 ml simmering for the sauce.

TO MAKE THE SAUCE AND SERVE   Melt the butter in a small pan and add the flour. Stir and blend, then cook over low heat for 5 minutes until the roux is well cooked and the colour of sand. Gradually whisk in the 500 ml of hot stock and simmer, stirring, until it comes to the boil. The sauce will improve in flavour if allowed to simmer for 5–10 minutes before finishing it.

✝ This book was out of print at the time of writing this footnote, but you may be able to find a second-hand copy.

Have ready in a small basin the egg yolks lightly beaten with the cream. Add a little of the hot sauce and return the mixture to the pan. Stir in the herbs and adjust the seasoning with salt, pepper and lemon juice.

Remove the muslin from the chicken. Cut the chicken into thickish slices and surround with the vegetables on your favourite platter. Ladle over a little of the herb-speckled sauce and serve the rest of the sauce in the heated sauce boat.

Damien's pâte brisée – buttery shortcrust

180 g unsalted butter
240 g plain flour
pinch of salt
60 ml cold still or *sparkling mineral water*

pastry scraper

Remove the butter from the refrigerator 30 minutes before making the pastry. Sieve the flour and salt onto a marble pastry slab or workbench. Chop the butter into smallish pieces and toss lightly in the flour. Lightly rub to only partly combine. Make a well in the centre and pour in the mineral water. Using a pastry scraper, and mindful of the technique I'm sure you have observed of mixing cement, work the paste to a very rough heap of buttery lumps of dough.

Using the heel of your hand, quickly smear the pastry away from you across the board. It will lightly combine. Gather together, press quickly into a flat cake, dust with a little flour, wrap in plastic film and refrigerate for 20 minutes. Roll out, dusting with flour as necessary, then drape the pastry over the pin and roll it over a 26 cm removable-base fluted flan tin. Prick the bottom with a fork and place in the freezer or refrigerator for at least 20 minutes before baking.

Line with a double thickness of foil only, pressed well into the corners. Cook for 10 minutes at 200°C, then remove the foil and lower the temperature to 180°C. Cook for a further 10 minutes until quite dry, golden and crisp.

If the tart shell is to be filled with a liquid (e.g. custard filling for an onion tart), have the filling hot and pour it straight into the tart while the crust is still hot. In this way you will have no seepage of liquid into the base of the tart and it will still be crisp after a further 15–20 minutes at 180°C to set the filling.

- Always roll the pastry out after a short rest only. It should never be hard.
- Chill it in the freezer for 20 minutes before baking.
- Do not fill the pastry shell with beans or rice. The pricking of the base will prevent undue rising, and will permit a little bubbling of the surface, which adds to the flaky quality
- Do not combine the butter and flour in a food processor. It will not work.
- Completed shells can live happily in the freezer for days until needed. Do not defrost them. They go straight from freezer to oven at 200°C.
- Do not delay between the cooking of the shell and its filling. In other words, time the operation so that it is continuous. If you wish to serve a tart as a dessert (as for the almond tart below), bake it before your guests arrive and serve it warm or at room temperature.
- Liquid fillings should be hot.

Rich almond tart

1 quantity Damien's pâte brisée (see page 133)
240 g unsalted butter
300 g castor sugar
200 g ground almond meal
4 eggs
100 ml cognac
200 g finely chopped, blanched almonds
2 tablespoons smooth apricot jam
2 tablespoons flaked almonds

Make and cook the *pâte brisée* as instructed on page 133. While the pastry is cooking, cream the butter and sugar in a food processor. Add the almond meal, eggs and cognac and blend well. Add the chopped almonds and blend very briefly.

Remove the cooked tart shell from the oven and spread with the apricot jam. Pour in the almond filling and return to the oven. Reduce the heat to 160°C and cook for 15 minutes. Open the oven and sprinkle over the flaked almonds. Continue to cook for a further 10–15 minutes until the tart is brown, the almonds are golden and the centre feels springy, not liquid. The tart will become much firmer as it cools. Serve with whipped cream and in smallish portions, as it is very rich.

Almond bread biscuits[+]

3 egg whites
90 g castor sugar
90 g plain flour
90 g unblanched almonds (i.e. shelled almonds, skins on)

Whip the egg whites until stiff. Beat in the sugar and then fold in the flour and almonds. Bake in a greased and parchment-lined log tin for 45–55 minutes at 180°C. When the bread is cooked, it will look golden brown and feel firm to the touch. Cool the loaf on a wire rack and, when cold, cut it carefully with a serrated knife into thin slices.

Spread the slices on a tray and place in the oven at 140°C for 15 minutes. Check after this time – the slices should look light gold. If so, turn them and repeat the process on the other side. If not, check again after a further 5 minutes.

Once it is quite cold, almond bread can be stored for weeks in an airtight tin.

[+] The recipe for almond bread is very well known. A delicious variation is to use Australian-grown pistachios. The green colour of the nuts looks lovely, and the flavour is very good, too.

The compleat housewife

MENU

Prawn Quenelles with Tiny Onions
Simmered in Red Wine

Seared Sliced Duck Breast with Turnips
and Cumquat Butter on Salad

Chocolate and Almond Cake with
Redcurrant Jelly

Cherries Preserved in Eau–de–vie

This menu is sure to be a crowd-pleaser. Soufflés, mousses and quenelles seem to be perennial favourites.[+] It is, I think, to do with the magic of all that captured air, which puffs and fluffs so splendidly. I have here chosen to make a quenelle from prawns and sauced it with a garnish of wine-simmered onions and a sauce built on a reduction of fish stock and tomatoes. Although there is some butter in the sauce, it is much less rich than a *beurre blanc* or *beurre rouge*.

The duck breast with sliced turnips was created in the kitchen in order to combine some of my favourite tastes: grilled crispy skin (I love its texture, too), sweet caramelised turnips and the pungency of cumquats. In order to rescue the tastebuds from a near-overdose of intense flavour, the dish is designed to be wreathed in watercress.

The chocolate cake is also a favourite. It is the French classic Queen of Sheba, now well known from Elizabeth David's *Summer Cooking*, and, apart from tasting delicious, is made without recourse to mixers or food processors. It is the perfect dessert for making in a tiny kitchen or, as I discovered one summer in a holiday house, with the minimum of utensils. A wooden spoon, a fork and a whisk or egg-beater and the cake is made.✦

As I said earlier, I am very attracted to the idea of the larder or pantry. I believe that a jar of one's own crunchy cornichons, spiced cumquats or spiced cherries is a wonderful resource to draw on. Redcurrants are increasingly available in the markets and greengrocers' shops. I am delighted by the brilliant jewel colour and perfection of form of these miraculous fruits and have made lots of redcurrant jelly. As I add no pectin, it has a very light 'set' but is perfect spooned around the chocolate cake. The advantage of the recipe is that one doesn't bother with any stripping of stems and stalks. Just take an equal weight of sugar and currants, boil for 8 minutes, skim, strain and bottle.

We have also put down several bottles of cherries in *eau-de-vie*, a clear spirit distilled from fruit, which is fiery but is the ultimate *digestif* after dinner. After a month we will get to taste our first batch, which will have been dipped in melted fondant and then enrobed with best couverture chocolate and settled in little cases for a further two weeks before being served to our lucky customers.❖

The husbandry continues with the preparation of the tarragon and basil butters, made so much easier by the purchase of my new stainless steel $100 drum

---

✝ It is difficult to remember the days before kitchen food processors, but they were still very new in the early 1980s. One of the most arduous tasks in any kitchen is pushing a large quantity of anything through a sieve. So for a restaurant to offer quenelles, or a mousse of chicken or fish, in pre-processor days was very labour-intensive and most impressive. With the advent of the food processor, suddenly *everyone* was making mousses and fish terrines and mousseline stuffings for everything. Combined with the other great skill of these machines – making smooth purées – kitchens across the land were in danger of being seen as offering baby food. Smooth, soft shapes and slices surrounded by pools of pale, pastel-coloured vegetable and fruit sauces known as *coulis* became ubiquitous. I was no exception!

✦ This chocolate cake is now probably being made by every cook in the land. It is still my favourite because of its intense flavour and soft texture.

❖ In the 1980s many people took up home chocolate-making and most cookware shops started to sell the best couverture chocolate in small quantities for home use. I don't see the same enthusiasm for this very highly skilled art any more. Couverture chocolate has a high level of cocoa butter as opposed to the more generally available compound chocolate, in which fats such as palm kernel oil or coconut oil are substituted for cocoa butter to cut costs and increase stability. The flavour suffers as a result.

sieve. Food processors are wonderful, and we couldn't operate without them, but it is also part of the game to recognise what they cannot do. If one aims at a perfect result, the herb butters and the fish mousse and quenelle mixtures must be painstakingly pushed through a fine sieve. A Mouli does an excellent job for a small household quantity, as does a hand-held small sieve and a wooden spoon, but when there is a 4-litre bucket of heavily concentrated tarragon butter to be dealt with, we need a heavy-duty mesh and a firm wooden 'mushroom' to push the butter through. Our youngest apprentice cheerfully copes, but admits to sore arms.

What richness we have provided with these butters! We can now mount our *beurres blancs* with a little of this concentrated flavour along with the mass of the sweet butter. Or we can melt a little sliver of concentrated flavour on a simple grilled chicken. A pat or two can be whisked into the braising juice of a neck of pork, a leg of veal, and so on. We frequently add chopped fresh herbs to our fettuccine, so perhaps I can add a little of this butter to other baked goods. The very thought of a tarragon-flavoured brioche sends me dashing to the flour bin.

Prawn quenelles with tiny onions simmered in red wine

QUENELLES

1 kg fresh (i.e. not frozen) green (i.e. uncooked) prawns
3–4 egg whites
180–240 ml cream
salt, white pepper
chives or *parsley, not too finely chopped*

RED-WINE SAUCE

1 tablespoon finely chopped shallot or *mild onion*
1 clove garlic, finely chopped
2 tablespoons unsalted butter
4 large tomatoes, peeled, seeded and finely chopped
1 tablespoon cognac
reserved prawn shells (not heads)
½ cup fish stock
¼ cup red wine

½ bay leaf
1 small sprig of thyme
ground pepper
4 tablespoons cold unsalted butter for thickening sauce

ONIONS

½ cup red wine
½ cup red-wine vinegar
1 teaspoon sugar
12 small white onions, peeled

TO PREPARE THE QUENELLES   Chill the canister of the food processor for 1 hour. Shell and de-vein the prawns. Weigh after the cleaning process. You will have about 300–400 g of pure meat. For each 100 g of prawn flesh, use 1 egg white and 60 ml of cream.

Process the prawns in the chilled food processor. Add the egg whites and process until the mix is very firm and really shines. Scrape the mixture from the sides at least once.

Transfer the purée to a bowl and return the washed canister to the freezer. Press the purée through a fine sieve to extract all fine shreds of tissue, etc. Chill the purée in the refrigerator for at least 1 hour. Return to the chilled canister and add the cream in two batches, plus salt and pepper to taste. The cream should be well incorporated. Because everything is so cold there is little danger of the cream curdling, so don't be frightened to let the processor run. Poach 1 teaspoon of the mixture in a pan of very lightly salted water to test for salt and pepper. Cover the bowl of quenelle mix with plastic film and store in the refrigerator until needed. It can be made on the morning of your dinner, but not the day before.

TO MAKE THE SAUCE BASE   Soften the onion and garlic in the butter for 1–2 minutes. Add the tomato and cook for 5 minutes until the mixture is soft and starting to look dry. Add the cognac, increase the heat and bubble for 1 minute, stirring. Add the prawn shells, stirring and lifting. Pour in the liquids and seasonings. Cover and simmer all together for 5 minutes. Press the liquid through a fine sieve, extracting every drop of juice. You should have about 1 cup. You can make the sauce to this point several hours before dinner and finish it while the quenelles are poaching.

TO COOK THE ONIONS   Bring the liquid and sugar to the boil in an enamelled or stainless steel saucepan. Simmer the onions slowly with a lid on for about 30 minutes, or until they are tender and the liquid has been absorbed. Keep warm until ready to serve.

Bring the sauce base to a simmer in a pan and quickly whisk or swirl in the extra butter. Keep warm for the few minutes it takes to poach and drain the quenelles.

Have ready a shallow pan of water at simmering point. With 2 tablespoons dipped in hot water, mould 6 small, egg-sized quenelles from the mixture and float them in the water. Turn over after 1–2 minutes, depending on their size. One quenelle per person is sufficient for an entrée.

As the quenelles are ready, lift each one out with a slotted spoon and rest it briefly on a folded, clean cloth to drain.

TO SERVE   Spoon the sauce onto hot plates. Add 2 small onions, then 1 quenelle. Sprinkle over the chopped herbs. If the onions and sauce base were completed before the meal, steam the onions hot before adding them to the hot sauce.

NOTE: If you want really tiny quenelles, as a garnish for a consommé or a poached trout, for example, put the mixture into a piping bag with a small open nozzle and squeeze tiny balls into simmering water to cook. Do not poach them directly in your consommé, as they will cloud it.

Seared sliced duck breast with turnips and cumquat butter on salad[+]

6 duck breasts, as firm, red and thick as possible
1 cup fine rock salt (ask your butcher for a little:
    do not waste your precious sea salt on this)
4 medium turnips
2 tablespoons unsalted butter
1 tablespoon sugar
1 cup veal stock
pepper, salt

MARINADE

½ cup light olive oil
½ cup red wine
1 bay leaf, crumbled
sprig of thyme

cumquat butter (see page 142)
watercress and/or *other salad leaves*

1 very heavy cast-iron frying pan
6 × 12 cm squares of foil, brushed with butter

TO PREPARE THE DUCK BREASTS   Mix the marinade ingredients and marinate the duck breasts overnight. Drain and pat dry. Up to several hours before dinner, heat the frying pan with an even layer of rock salt to very hot. (My pans for this purpose are heavy and black and were inexpensive in an Italian hardware shop. They do not rust.) Place the duck breasts skin-side down on the hot salt. Adjust the heat so that there is a steady hiss and crackle but no explosions, and leave to cook, skin down, for 5–8 minutes, depending on the thickness of the breasts. Be a little wary, as hot salt does jump about a bit. Turn the breasts to seal the fleshy side. After 2 minutes, remove the breasts and feel them critically. They should feel firm and crispy on the skin side, but give quite easily when pressed on the flesh side. Brush off any salt and leave to rest skin-side down in a dish. There is no need to keep them warm, as the last-minute searing will do all the heating necessary. The breasts should be quite rare at this stage.

TO COOK THE TURNIPS   Peel the turnips and cut in half if large. Melt the butter and sugar in an enamelled dish in which the turnips will fit comfortably in one layer. Roll the turnips in the lightly syrupy liquid. Add the stock, cover and simmer quite gently for about 15 minutes. Check, and if the turnips are nearly tender, remove the lid, turn the heat up and shake the pan so that the turnips acquire a golden caramel coating as the liquid evaporates. If the turnips are not cooked and the stock seems to be evaporating too quickly, add a little water and turn the heat down so that they cook more slowly. Put the turnips aside until they are cool enough to handle.

TO ASSEMBLE THE DISH   On a board and using a sharp knife, place the duck breasts skin-side down and cut into thin slices on the bias. Discard the slices that have only fat and a bit of skin attached. (Keep these pieces of duck skin. Sliced and sautéed, they make duck 'crackling' to scatter over a salad.) Slice the turnips into even slices, keeping them as shapely as possible.

✢ I do wonder if any reader ever attempted to prepare this duck dish. The flavours are lovely and I would happily serve it in my café today, but I think I was being unrealistic to suggest that it would be possible at home for more than two absolutely dedicated food lovers!

On each buttered square of foil arrange the duck and turnip slices like the petals of a flower, overlapping the slices a little. Lay the pattern carefully, as this is how the 'flower' will be presented on the serving plates. Season each flower with pepper and a very little salt. Brush with any oil and juices that have accumulated in the resting pan and the turnip dish.[+]

TO COOK AND SERVE   This is very fast, so the serving plates must be very hot, the washed and dried watercress or salad sprigs at the ready, the cumquat butter sliced and ready. You will need a wide spatula or fish lifter, and 2 Teflon-coated pans.

Preheat the pans to hot! Lightly film the surface with a trace of oil. Slap 1 duck flower into each pan. Let them hiss and sizzle. Place 1 slice of cumquat butter on each serving plate, peel off the foil and invert 1 flower onto the butter, steadying with a spatula if necessary. Place another slice of butter on top, scatter the watercress around and serve. Continue with this process twice more.

This sort of cooking takes much longer to describe than to do. In a professional kitchen, 4 pans will be at work, but if you are prepared and calm and you flip while your co-host butters, watercresses and serves, all 6 diners will be served their aromatic crisped 'flowers' in less than 5 minutes.

Cumquat butter

500 g unsalted butter at room temperature
2 tablespoons spiced cumquats (see page 72), seeded and finely chopped
1 tablespoon spiced cumquat liquor
4 tablespoons glace de volaille (see Glossary)
pepper
½ teaspoon finely chopped garlic
2 tablespoons finely chopped parsley

Whiz all the ingredients in a food processor. If the butter is to be whisked in a sauce, press through a sieve for a very fine texture. As long as it is well mixed, however, there is no need for the extra step for the duck and turnip recipe (page 140).

Scrape the cumquat butter into a large, doubled piece of foil and form into a roll by smoothing and twisting the ends in opposite directions.

Chocolate and almond cake

125 g chocolate
1 tablespoon brandy
1 tablespoon black coffee
100 g unsalted butter
100 g castor sugar
100 g ground almonds
3 eggs, separated
icing sugar for dusting

Preheat the oven to 160°C. Combine the chocolate, brandy and coffee over hot water or in a double boiler. Stir when melted and add the butter and sugar. Mix well. Add the almonds and stir all very well together. Stir in the lightly beaten egg yolks. Scrape into a bowl. Beat the egg whites to a snow, but not 'rocky', and lighten the chocolate mix with 1 spoonful. Fold in the rest of the whites and turn into a buttered, paper-lined round cake tin of 18 cm diameter × 4 cm deep, or a heart-shaped tin.

Bake for 45 minutes. The cake will develop a crust on the top and be very fragile. Turn out when it is cool and invert again onto a serving plate. Dust with icing sugar and serve with a sauce of redcurrant jelly (see below) and a bowl of whipped cream.

Simple redcurrant jelly

500 g redcurrants (no need to strip the fruit from the stems)
500 g sugar

Combine the redcurrants and sugar in a pot, bring to the boil and stir once. Boil for 8 minutes. Skim and strain into scalded, hot jars. Seal.

‡ This dish is a perfect example of the way in which home cooking has changed. A dish designed specifically for a restaurant situation (imagine a stack of duck and turnip 'flowers' in a refrigerator) is being suggested as suitable for a home cook. I can't think of many home cooks today that would be prepared to go to this amount of effort.

Chocolate tart

This recipe is called a tart although it has no separate crust. As it bakes, the outside forms a hard crust and the centre stays chewy and very chocolatey. It is a useful recipe in that it can be made 2 or 3 days ahead of a special party and will keep after cutting. It always fractures and cracks on the top as it is cut, but if you sift the top generously with icing sugar you can disguise the crater and eruptions. Cut the tart with a sharp knife dipped in hot water.

> *100 g best-quality dark chocolate*[+]
> *100 g unsalted butter*
> *50 g plain flour*
> *150 g castor sugar*
> *3 eggs*
>
> *1 × 22 cm springform pan*

Preheat the oven to 180°C. To prepare the tin, brush the inside all over with melted butter. Cut a circle of silicone paper to line the tin, but cut it 5 cm larger than the base. Nick the outside circumference of the paper and line the tin, folding the slit sections over each other so that you have a smooth, lined surface for the chocolate mixture.

Melt the chocolate with the butter in a double boiler or in a basin over simmering water. Beat together the flour, sugar and eggs in an electric mixer until thick and pale. When the chocolate and butter have melted and are quite smooth, pour the chocolate mixture onto the egg mixture and combine thoroughly.

Pour into the prepared tin and bake for 35–40 minutes. The tart rises a lot in the baking and then settles down in the tin as it cools (hence the cracks). It will appear to be still sticky in the centre, but do not cook it any longer. When it is cool, release the sides of the springform tin and transfer the tart to a flat plate. After cutting, protect the cut edge with plastic wrap. Do not refrigerate.

[+] It is always worth spending the extra on good couverture chocolate when making any dessert where the chocolate flavour is the whole point of the dish, such as this 'tart'.

Cherries preserved in eau-de-vie[+]

2.5 kg cherries
250 g sugar
2.5 litres eau-de-vie or vodka
2.5 kg extra cherries, bought 2 weeks after the first lot

Stone the first lot of cherries and wrap the stones in a cloth. Crush the stones with a mallet or hammer and put the crushed pits, pitted cherries, sugar and *eau-de-vie* into a glass container. Leave for 2 weeks to macerate.

Strain the marinade. Snip the ends of each cherry stem in the second lot of cherries and put them, unstoned, into the marinade. Leave for at least 1 month. The cherries will keep for up to a year or even longer, if there are any left.

Serve as they are with a little of their liquor, or buy a small amount of fondant from a cake-decorating shop, melt it over hot water with a spoonful of syrup, tint it a delicate rose, and dip each cherry. Allow them to dry and serve in paper cases as a powerful petit four.

[+] This is a very extravagant way of making an extremely potent after-dinner sweet. The recipe was given to me by a French chef who worked with me at Stephanie's in the early 1980s. Since then I have studied how fruits are macerated in alcohol in the south-west of France, and in every example I was shown the fruit was put to marinate in *eau-de-vie* and sugar without any additional crushed fruit being added to reinforce the flavour.

To freeze or not to freeze

To freeze or not to freeze is often the question among gourmets. People are surprised to discover that I have four freezers in my restaurant. But surely, they exclaim, all your food is fresh! French restaurants raise their hands in horror at the mention of *surgelé*, and yet several of their most renowned chefs now present ranges of frozen food.

No, I am not suggesting that when we are short of this or that portion, we pull one out of the freezer, but simply that by intelligently treating the freezer as a resource, we can gain immense benefits. We save money, we reduce waste, and we can often cope well with emergency situations. Most of what we have discovered is relevant in the home situation. Perhaps the most important point is the sensible and profitable recycling of products often thrown away when no imme-diate use can be envisaged. What to do with one extra fish fillet? Freeze it, then use it finely minced to clarify a fish stock. What to do with two chicken necks and a few wingtips? Freeze them and add to your next stock, which might have to be made with a small roasted carcass. It will greatly benefit by the addition of the raw material.

If you are one of the many who have misgivings about the place of the freezer in the kitchen of a 'serious' cook, I would like you to consider my inventory of freezer contents. I also propose a three-course meal that can be presented speedily using food from the freezer, with no sacrifice of gastronomic quality.[†]

First, we have stocks and glazes. They freeze perfectly. Save yoghurt, sour cream and ricotta containers with their lids. Wash them well and store unlidded in a dust-free container. Use them for small quantities, allowing room for expansion as the contents freeze. Always label and date each container.

If you have lots and lots of chicken stock on hand, reduce it right down by fast boiling and label the result *glace de volaille* or, indeed, chicken glaze. Gouge out a tablespoon any time you want to add intensity to, say, a pilaf of rice that was cooked in very little stock or maybe even water, or to boost the flavour of a delicate velouté sauce to nap a poached chicken. Or melt it and mix it through the *farce* of a poultry-and-pork terrine or a compound butter. Think of all the infamous suggestions made by the producers of chicken stock cubes (which I HATE) and use your genuine flavour-enricher instead. I feel prepared for anything with my tubs of chicken stock, chicken glaze, duck stock, duck glaze, fish stock, demi-glace, game stock etc.

Next is the huge field of compound butters. We have rolls of them and squares of them. If you have half a cup of some delicious, thick, syrupy gravy left from a roast of beef, scrape it up, heat it, strain it and whirl in the food processor with 250 g of soft butter (unsalted for preference), a squeeze of lemon juice and some chopped parsley and you have created an exquisite compound butter that will transform a cooked-in-a-hurry piece of steak into something a little more special. The same principle applies to creating a *marchand de vin* butter. If I have a few 'ends' of sound red wine left after a party, I refrigerate them before I fall into bed and the next day reduce the wine by half with half a small onion or a shallot, finely chopped, a sprig of thyme and a scrap of bay leaf, and then whiz the strained and pressed reduction with some soft butter, some parsley and a little finely chopped

[†] Much of the advice in this chapter is still sound, although the suggestions come so thick and fast that I imagine many readers will feel exhausted. My advice is to consider one suggestion at a time. I do not suggest that you make a full-scale assault on the freezer and make stocks, compound butters, bread-crumbs and so on all at once! Rather, it is the idea that a little of what seems to be extra can become something rather special.

garlic. Apart from being a great sauce for the chops at a barbecue, this red-wine butter is excellent if used to deglaze the pan after a few duck livers have been sautéed, or if allowed to melt over a pan-fried slice of calf's liver.

Perhaps you had a freshly boiled crayfish for dinner? After the meal, don't stuff all the shell debris in the rubbish bin. Instead, take a clean heavy-duty rubbish bag, tip in the shell and pound it with a rolling pin. Place this debris into a wide pan, warm it gently, add a bouquet garni, flame with a glass of brandy and then add at least 250 g of unsalted butter (depending on the amount of shell). Melt the butter and allow it to foam for 5 minutes, stirring well. Do not allow the butter to do more than foam, and then strain it through a conical sieve, pressing really hard. This simplified crayfish butter will add a luxurious flavour to a fish sauce or soup.

At the end of summer or in the middle of autumn, when the basil starts to look straggly, we turn it into a highly concentrated basil butter. After thorough blending of the torn leaves and the butter (about 250 g of butter to 1 well-packed cup of leaves) in the food processor, we push it painstakingly through a drum sieve so that the flavour is concentrated but most of the fibrous stem is removed. The resultant butter is a lovely apple-green. The same method is used for our tarragon and chervil butters. Instead of mounting a demi-glace-based sauce with a knob of ordinary butter, you can now create tarragon, chervil or basil sauces. Do remember to label the herb butters, as they look remarkably similar.

I spent a day in the kitchens of Alain Dutournier at one of my favourite French restaurants in Paris, Au Trou Gascon, in 1982, and noticed that he too realises the value of the freezer. Crayfish tomalley or mustard – whatever name you use to denote the blackish, greenish matter in the uncooked head of a crayfish – is frozen, and a small amount whisked into his light emulsion sauces to give its unmistakable enrichment. All his filled ravioli and tortellini were dropped frozen into broths and sauces.

The next freezer compartment holds the bone marrow. Marrow bones are not always easy to get in quantity. If you love the taste of bone marrow, as I do, you will be tempted by recipes that instruct you to garnish your pot-au-feu or *filet à la ficelle* with beef marrow on croutons. Or you will love to serve *boeuf à la moelle* – that is, a thick fillet or other cut of steak garnished with a trembling slice of marrow and a fine, well-reduced, shining demi-glace. Not something you can always do as the mood takes you – unless you use your freezer. All you need do is to buy a marrow bone when you see one, crack it lengthwise with a hammer and chisel, carefully prise out the marrow, soak it in cold water overnight to extract all the blood, and then freeze the marrow in chunks. Take a piece whenever you need it, slice it with a knife dipped in hot water and poach it for about a minute in hot (not boiling) water until it is translucent.[+] If your demi-glace was also in the freezer, your

Lemon delicious pudding (page 153)

The classic flourless chocolate cake (page 143) with a rhubarb and raspberry sago sauce

dinner party could be given at only 1 hour's notice. Frozen stock will, of course, thaw overnight, but if you need it instantly, pour a little water into a pan and add your ice block of stock and let it thaw and heat together, very slowly.

I think everyone knows that egg whites freeze and thaw perfectly. Either freeze them individually or in measured quantity, remembering that 1 egg white equals 30 ml. Frozen egg whites are a great stand-by. They are ready to clarify a stock into an elegant consommé or an aspic, to build up a mousseline for a fish terrine, quenelles or a veal mousse to stuff a loin, to whip into a soufflé, or to make maca-roons, pavlovas, meringues and specialised cakes.

If you have one of those generous lemon trees and cannot find anyone who wants more lemons, juice them, measure the juice and freeze it. It will make *citrons pressés*, a wonderful summer drink of pure, juiced lemon stirred with powdered sugar, ice cubes and lots of water. It provides the makings for a lemon delicious pudding and, of course, it makes sorbets. You might like to wrap some of the spent rinds also so that you can spoon your lemon sorbet into a frozen shell of lemon rind.

If you have an ice-cream churn and love making fruit ices, your basic fruit juice and pulp can be frozen, ready to be adjusted with syrup whenever you feel like it. This is an excellent thing to do if your greengrocer ever has a tray of ripe fruit selling at a bargain price. A selection of fruit ices is a wonderful finale to a summer party. I have discussed such a selection presented in the frozen shells on pages 53–4. Another dramatic presentation is our croquembouche, where we pile balls of different coloured ices to echo the French celebration cake made from choux puffs laced together with toffee. If it were raspberries I might be tempted to make Melba sauce instead, such as the one I have described on page 227, and freeze it ready to sauce a melon ice-cream.

Many fruits will collapse on thawing, but this is not necessarily a disadvantage. There are times when nature's bounty is embarrassing. My sister has been known to creep out in the dark and wrench her distressingly fertile zucchini plants out by their roots and throw them onto the compost heap. My tomato bushes are somewhat similar. We tip whole tomatoes into shallow trays in the freezer. On thawing, these collapsed tomatoes make a lovely fresh-tasting soup, and after being cooked gently in a little butter, puréed and sieved, the soup is further enhanced by melting a pat of the frozen basil butter. Whole persimmons when fully ripened can also be frozen whole. They will be mushy after thawing,

✝ Nowadays a good butcher will supply marrow bones sawn into small pieces; there is no need to resort to a hammer and chisel! Soak them in salted water overnight and then either freeze them bone and all (labelled and dated), or push the marrow out firmly with your thumb and use it straight away or freeze it. Because small pieces or slices of marrow can get crushed in the freezer, I freeze them in a small lidded container half-full of water.

but the pulp can then be turned into a memorable fruit ice.

We also have one freezer devoted entirely to baked goods. Sheets of puff pastry are always rolled and cut ready to go, either as shapes for tarts, feuilletés or sugared palmiers. There is always at least one buttery tart shell ready for an emergency. Our frequently unannounced vegetarians can enjoy a mushroom tartlet thanks to our foresight, without the service being disturbed.[†]

Le Nôtre, one of the best-known French pastrycooks, with a training school and a chain of high-quality pastry shops, told me that he freezes his freshly baked croissants while they are still warm to the cheek. We don't often make croissants, but we make lots of brioche and frequently freeze the extra after baking.

If you have half a breadstick left after a meal and it has become dry, don't throw it away. Slice it thickly and make garlic croutons for a mussel soup as described on page 116, or slice it thinly, bag it and freeze it. These wafers will become golden Melba toast in 30 minutes in a moderate oven (watch them!) or 2 hours in a very slow oven. Bags of tiny croutons are also an asset for a quick garnish for soup, or they can be fried and tossed into a Caesar salad or a bacon and dandelion salad. And, of course, there are a million uses for breadcrumbs.

Last week we had a bowl of beautiful praline cream left over after filling lots of choux puffs. We experimented and put the cream in the freezer. It thawed perfectly with no loss of taste. It needed a whisk in the food processor and was ready to go. It is an excellent resource to have on hand for an emergency fruit tart or, with the help of some frozen egg white, a praline soufflé, perhaps served with a fruit sorbet created from frozen fruit pulp and accompanied by a caramelised, crisp puff pastry biscuit – all from the freezer and all top quality.

The three-course meal presented in this menu owes much to the freezer.

[†] Nowadays restaurants expect to cater for non-meat-eaters each day. And there are always suitable options on all of my menus.

Tomato soup with basil and croutons

1 onion, sliced
60 g butter
1.5 kg frozen tomatoes (or *very ripe fresh tomatoes, sliced*)
1 litre frozen chicken stock
2 tablespoons potato flour
salt, pepper
60 g frozen basil butter
½ cup frozen tiny croutons
oil/butter for frying

Put the sliced onion in a pan with the butter. Soften the onion for a minute or two. Add the tomatoes. If using frozen tomatoes, stir to prevent sticking until the tomatoes thaw and collapse. Cook gently until the tomatoes are quite soft, approximately 30 minutes. Pass the contents of the pan through the medium disc of a Mouli and return to the rinsed-out pan. Add the frozen chicken stock, allow it to thaw, and heat the contents of the pan to simmering point. Blend the potato flour with a little cold water. Stir in a ladleful of the hot soup and tip the mixture back into the pot. Whisk well until simmering. Taste for seasoning and simmer for 15 minutes. Whirl the soup in the blender if there are still fragments in it. It should be a good bright red in colour. Drop in the basil butter and stir to let it melt and blend.

Fry the croutons in a mix of oil and butter, then drain. Garnish each bowl of soup with them.

Fillet steak with bone marrow, Sauce bordelaise

butter/oil for sautéing
180 g fillet steak per person
pepper, sea salt
1 slice bone marrow per person, cut 1 cm thick

SAUCE BORDELAISE

2 shallots or *½ small onion, finely chopped*
1 bay leaf
1 sprig of thyme
crushed white peppercorns
½ bottle sound red wine
600 ml frozen demi-glace (page 241) or *well-reduced veal stock*
60 g unsalted butter
30 g frozen bone marrow

TO PREPARE THE SAUCE Place the shallots, bay leaf, thyme and crushed pepper-corns in a pan with the red wine. Heat to boiling point. Set light to the wine in the pan and let it flame until the flames die out. Adjust the heat so that the contents of the pan reduce rapidly by two-thirds. Add the frozen demi-glace and simmer very gently until the block of stock is completely thawed. Simmer together until the volume is reduced by half. The degree of reduction will depend on the strength of your veal stock or demi-glace. Strain the sauce through a conical strainer, pressing hard on the shallot debris. Bring to simmering point again, skimming off any impurities that collect at one side of the pan. Leave the sauce at this point until ready to serve.

In a food processor combine the unsalted butter with the frozen bone marrow until you have a smooth paste. Set aside.

TO COOK THE MEAT Heat the butter/oil in a heavy pan. Season each steak with a grind of pepper. When the butter in the pan has ceased to foam, put in the meat. Allow to sear and seal well, about 2 minutes. Turn the steak to the other side and sear it, still over high heat. Continue cooking to the requirements of each diner, about 3 minutes each side for rare meat, about 5 minutes for medium meat, and ages for well done! In each case, remove the steak to a warm place when it is cooked.

Season with sea salt. The meat will rest and relax while the sauce is finished and the marrow is poached.

TO SERVE Have ready a pan of lightly salted hot water. Slip the slices of marrow into the water and poach for about 1 minute until no longer pink.

Have the sauce at simmering point. Whisk the butter/marrow mixture into the sauce, whisking well. Push the pan to one side when the butter/marrow mixture has all been incorporated.

Place the steaks onto their hot serving plates. Spoon the sauce over and around, and top each serve with a slice of quivering marrow.

I would serve one special vegetable with this luscious steak. Any of the glazed vegetables mentioned on page 192 would be delicious, or, more simply, a bowl of lightly buttered and parsleyed tiny potatoes could be crushed into the sauce.

Lemon delicious pudding

This is a very old-fashioned pudding which deserves to be made more often. It is worthy of the name delicious and is very light. Underneath the golden sponge topping is a creamy lemon sauce. It can also be made with oranges or mandarins.

3 tablespoons butter
grated zest of 1 lemon
1½ cups castor sugar
3 eggs, separated

3 tablespoons self-raising flour
1½ cups milk
juice of 1½ lemons, fresh or frozen

In a food processor, cream the butter with the lemon zest and sugar. When thoroughly creamed, add the egg yolks. Add the flour and milk alternately to make a smooth batter. Scrape the mixture from the sides of the food processor and then blend in the lemon juice.

Beat the egg whites until a firm snow and delicately fold them into the batter. Pour into buttered individual moulds or a buttered 1 litre dish. Stand the moulds or dish in a deep baking dish and fill the baking dish up to the halfway mark with boiling water. Bake at 180°C in a non-fanforced oven for 35 minutes for the individual moulds, or 50 minutes for the larger pudding. Allow to cool a little in the baking dish before serving with pouring cream.

One family heirloom

MENU

ARTICHOKES BARIGOULE

SAUTÉ OF CALF'S LIVER WITH RASPBERRY VINEGAR

GRANDMOTHER'S BRAMBLE CAKE (BLACKBERRY PIE)

I have a near-addiction to artichokes. While these vegetables have their ardent admirers, there are many
people who do not share this passion of mine. When I
serve artichokes for lunch, there are frequently three or four
left. Almost always I eat them all.

It is well known that artichokes and wine make an
impossible combination. Just as well, I often think, as one
needs two hands to enjoy an artichoke. Two hands to pull
them apart, to dabble each leaf in calorie-loaded melted
butter or a mayonnaise, or a spicy *bagna cauda* mix of
anchovies, garlic and oil, or walnut oil with a few drops
of red-wine vinegar. I prefer them hot, warm or tepid.
I do not like them cold, when they become dank and
dark, nor so rubbed with lemon that one can taste only

lemon juice. They must be well drained upside-down to avoid the revolting experience of pressing an artichoke and realising that it is as full of water as a soaked sponge. The tender inner leaves can be dipped in melted butter and fine white crumbs and fried. Serve them with any of the sauces above or the salsa verde on page 85. The fleshy base of each leaf *could* be scraped off and beaten into a mayonnaise, but how impossibly tedious an operation! One starts to think of such esoteric ideas after watching the *mise-en-place* in a French-trained kitchen. My heart just about stopped when I first saw the junior cooks ruthlessly jettisoning every leaf save the very heart. Into the bin they went. It wasn't my kitchen, but if it had been I would have retrieved all the inner leaves to serve as an *amuse-gueule* delicacy.✢

The Italians prize the whole thistle and serve it with proper ceremony. *Large* fingerbowls (more reasonably a hand-bowl), capacious napkins, plates for debris – and often you are served two artichokes! French classic cuisine teems with dishes garnished with artichoke hearts stuffed with foie gras, peas, asparagus tips etc. Personally I find that these combinations do little for the taste of either vegetable, although it is true that the European varieties usually have large shallow hearts, which are inviting shapes for stuffing, while our local varieties do not. In the height of the artichoke season they are very reasonable in price, and one can perhaps contemplate a feast of hearts only. To me, part of the excitement of artichokes is the slow advance towards the exquisitely tender centre, and I do not often cook them minus leaves.✦

Both the pointed purple-leafed variety and the rounder green-leafed variety are excellent. Most of our artichokes do not have the thick inedible choke or *foin* (hay) always mentioned in European recipes. They do have a fibrous layer lining the heart, which can be inedible when the artichoke is old. In this case, remove it.✤

Never assume that all your guests are familiar with eating artichokes. It is helpful and friendly to ask, and offer reassurance or demonstrate the technique of scraping off the edible flesh from each leaf against the teeth. One restaurateur

---

✢ I learnt such a lot during the week I spent with Pierre and Jean Troisgros at their three-star restaurant in Roanne, not far from Lyon, in 1982. The generous staff/client ratio was also an eye-opener compared with what I was used to, and everyone seemed to have plenty to do! It was here that I watched in horror as the artichoke leaves were discarded. I had yet to learn the lesson that sometimes the gain does not justify the time spent. And there were no short cuts with preparation tolerated here. Precision and speed were equally prized, it seemed to me.

✦ I would not take such a purist stand concerning artichokes these days. I now frequently discard the outer leaves and sauté the trimmed sliced hearts to toss with pasta, or with peas and sage leaves for a very fancy vegetable garnish. And quickly sliced uncooked tender hearts seasoned and tossed with thin slices of young fennel and extra-virgin olive oil make a perfect side salad for a chunk of Parmigiano-Reggiano.

✤ And I find that almost all but the very youngest artichokes do have a choke that needs to be removed.

I know has a horror story of removing a totally empty plate from an obviously ignorant guest who had ordered an artichoke vinaigrette. Did he eat it all or did he stuff the leaves in his pocket? Someone should have noticed his distress or confusion and proffered advice.

The opening dish for this dinner is a whole artichoke stuffed and braised in olive oil. The dish is Mediterranean in origin, and versions vary. What I love to do is to thickly peel the stem and braise it alongside the artichokes and serve everyone their own miniature bouquet garni featuring a tender fresh leaf from my bay tree. The stem is delicious and tender and very similar to the heart. I have read about a vegetable called a cardoon in both *The Vegetable Book* of Jane Grigson and the works of Elizabeth David. It sounds as if it would be very similar in character to these peeled artichoke stalks, but so far I have never come across a cardoon.[+]

After the artichoke entrée I have described a simple sauté of calf's liver, where the pan is deglazed with a few drops of raspberry vinegar, whisked with a knob of either fresh butter or a compound butter and the liver is served on a bed of bright green leaves with the hot aromatic juices poured over to wilt and dress the dish. The technique is interesting in that it can be used to create a hot salad of duck liver on raw spinach or kidneys deglazed with sherry vinegar and mounted with a mustard butter, or a *soigné* little entrée of pigeon breasts deglazed with red-wine vinegar or plum vinegar, the scrapings built into a sauce with some tarragon butter, and so on and so on. I have spoken elsewhere about the benefits of a freezer stock of compound butters. Here it is worth dwelling on the humble origins of the currently fashionable raspberry vinegar.

When I was a small child, it was an obligatory part of every birthday party to drink glasses of diluted homemade raspberry vinegar. It was sweetly acid and a glorious rose-pink. I suppose it was before the era of carbonated soft drinks, although we could buy creaming soda and lemonade. (Always the way with nostalgia – the memory is selective. Perhaps these two soft drinks were the only ones my mother permitted.) The corner shop where I ate my lunch set places for the children with paper tablecloths, sandwiches on a plastic plate and in every place a glass of the favourite pink raspberry vinegar. I have revived the custom of producing bottles of this vinegar every year and have also made it with redcurrants and strawberries. I have found that my children absolutely baulk at the thought of drinking it, but they seem to enjoy dishes I have made using it. It is so simple![*]

A short step from raspberry vinegar to raspberry syrup. It is very common in France to see children drinking brilliantly coloured non-fizzy drinks in cafés. Think of the young girl in the movie *Diabolo Menthe (Peppermint Soda)* sipping her bright green drink. These are syrups made from fruits and aromatic oils, and they are mixed with either cold water or soda water or, for more sophisticated tastes, vermouth, champagne or white wine. A syrup made with blackcurrants (*cassis*) is perhaps the best known, but the same method can be used with fresh cherries, plums (either a red variety or greengage or mirabelle) or, as I have already mentioned, raspberries.

Nostalgia continues with the magnificent finale – my grandmother's bramble cake. 'Brambles' are blackberries. There are just a few weeks of the year when artichokes and blackberries are available together, and that is in autumn. Blackberries, of course, freeze well, and there is absolutely no better use for a small bowlful of frozen berries than this pie (which is called a cake). The tendency of frozen fruit to leak excessive amounts of juice when defrosting does not hurt this dish at all. It is meant to be juicy!

My grandmother came from Yorkshire, and this old family recipe for her bramble cake is a delicious example of English regional cookery. The pastry uses lard, a common feature of North Country cookery. Lard is also used to create the famous 'lardy cakes', which are rounds of hot pastry studded with currants and spread liberally with butter and treacle while hot. My grandfather ate lardy cake before the main meal every day of his adult life!✢ Going blackberrying used to be a popular family outing in autumn. Remember all those prickles, purple hands, unexpected ditches and snagged clothes? I'm sure we persevered by thinking of our blackberry pie for dinner. There was never a question in our family. Blackberry pie for one glorious meal rather than one lonely jar of jam!

Do not despair if you have no blackberries. Other fruits can be used, preferably those that give off plenty of juice and cook in a short time. Raspberries, mulberries or gooseberries are good. My own favourite substitute is finely sliced pink rhubarb tossed with currants.

The final luxury touch was to serve the pie with clotted cream, the milk poured into a wide enamel pan and left on the cast-iron top of our solid-fuel cooker overnight. The cream rose slowly and was skimmed off the next morning.

✢ I have now enjoyed cardoons occasionally in Australia and, more often, in Italy and France. There is a recipe for cardoon fritters in *Stephanie Alexander & Maggie Beer's Tuscan Cookbook*. They are still very rarely seen in our markets and fruit and vegetable shops. If you live near an Italian market, look for them in autumn and winter.

✦ The interest in fruit-flavoured vinegars seems to have been fleeting. I have not used any myself for many years, although speciality vinegars of other sorts are still very popular. Balsamic vinegar is the obvious example. I always have a very good Spanish sherry vinegar on hand (essential for a good gazpacho), and am very choosy about the maturity of the red-wine vinegars I buy for everyday use.

❖ Elizabeth David has lots to say about 'lardy cakes' and gives many recipes for them in her book *English Bread and Yeast Cookery*. She says, 'Based on bread dough, oozing with fat, sticky with sugar, often further enriched with dried fruit, lardy cakes are just about as undesirable, from a dietitian's point of view, as anything one can possibly think of.' But delicious!

Artichokes barigoule

6 large artichokes
1 tablespoon lemon juice
1 lemon, halved
200 ml fruity olive oil
1 large carrot, sliced
1 onion, sliced
6 whole cloves garlic, peeled
1 sprig of thyme
1 bay leaf
400 ml dry white wine

STUFFING

250 g mushrooms
6 fillets of anchovy
200 g chopped ham
pepper

GARNISH

1 small carrot
1 fresh bay leaf per artichoke
1 small sprig of thyme per artichoke
a generous amount of chopped parsley per artichoke

TO PREPARE THE ARTICHOKES   For each artichoke, snap off the stem, peel it thickly, dip in lemon juice and reserve. Snap off and discard the two outside rows of leaves. Slice away the top third of the artichoke and discard it. With kitchen scissors, snip off the pointed end of each leaf. Rub the artichoke with the cut half of the lemon and put it in a bowl of cold water with the squeezed other half of the lemon.

Lift out the artichokes one at a time, and with a sharp teaspoon dig out the centre cone of leaves and scrape free any tough fibrous material lining the heart. (This is not as tough or prominent as the choke in most European varieties, but it becomes more and more strawlike as the artichoke matures. The whole of very young, tiny artichokes can be eaten.)

TO PREPARE THE STUFFING   Chop the mushrooms finely and chop the anchovy fillets to a paste. Mix well with the ham and taste for seasoning. You will probably not need salt, but you will need a few grindings of black pepper. Divide the stuffing into 6 parts. Place a teaspoonful in the hollowed-out centre of each artichoke and divide the rest between the other rows of leaves.

TO PREPARE THE GARNISH   Cut slices from a small carrot and, with a fluted small cutter, stamp out 'flower' shapes. Simmer the slices in a little water for 5 minutes and set aside until needed.

TO COOK AND SERVE   Pour the olive oil into a non-enamelled baking dish of just the size to hold the artichokes and their stems firmly. Lightly colour the sliced carrot and onion in the hot oil. Place the stuffed artichokes and their stems into the baking dish with the carrot and onion. Add the garlic cloves, thyme and bay leaf. Pour over white wine to halfway up the sides of the artichokes.

Place a sheet of foil or oiled parchment over the artichokes. Bring the liquid to simmering point and adjust the heat to simmer gently. After 10 minutes, check the stems. If they are tender, remove them to a plate. After a further 10 minutes, test to see if a fine skewer will pierce the artichokes easily right to the centre. If not, continue to simmer gently for a further 5 minutes and check again. When the artichokes are cooked, remove the paper, return the stems to the pan and turn the heat to full so that the oil and the wine boil furiously and create an emulsified, rather syrupy sauce. Add the carrot 'flowers' to the braising juices for 2 minutes while the sauce is boiling furiously.

Serve each artichoke with its stem alongside in an old-fashioned soup plate, so that you can spoon over lots of the juices, a tender, cooked clove of garlic and some carrot 'flowers'. Garnish with a bay leaf, a sprig of thyme and some parsley.

TECHNIQUE FOR ARTICHOKE HEARTS COOKED IN BUTTER: Snap off all the leaves, exposing the pale yellow heart. Slice away the top third of the artichoke as before and also discard any pinkish/mauve pointed leaves from the centre of the artichoke. Trim the heart with a sharp knife and immediately rub with a cut lemon. Drop the trimmed bottoms into lightly salted simmering water into which you have whisked ½ a cup of plain flour, to lessen the discoloration.

Simmer the bottoms until barely tender and leave to cool in their murky-looking cooking blanc. When required, lift out the hearts with a slotted spoon, drain on paper and sauté in noisette butter until a golden-bronze colour. Scatter with parsley and serve at once.

After you have snapped off all the leaves, the most inner ones should be saved. Dip them in melted butter and very fine white breadcrumbs and fry them until golden.

Sauté of calf's liver with raspberry vinegar

~

1 kg calf's liver, pale and shiny
4 large potatoes
8 tablespoons melted pork fat or duck fat, flavoured with garlic (see pages 24–5)
12 thin slices smoked bacon
2 tablespoons raspberry vinegar (see page 162)
600 ml well-reduced chicken or veal stock
spiced cherries or spiced crab-apples or any other pickle you may have in your
store cupboard or fresh herbs, such as sage and oregano
100 g unsalted butter

SALAD GREENS

a selection from such varieties as: corn salad, rocket, mignonette, witlof, watercress,
baby spinach, oakleaf, radicchio, young dandelion leaves

2 frying pans, preferably of heavy cast-iron
1 tray of lightly seasoned flour
tongs, whisk, tasting spoon, wooden spoon
hot serving plates

TO PREPARE THE SALAD   Many of the salad varieties I have mentioned are very tender-leafed and must be handled with care. To me, a beautiful salad is a very special dish indeed, and I become quite pedantic about the methods of washing, drying and storing salad greens.[+]

Firstly, I cut them in the garden with a knife rather than tug them out of the ground. Oakleaf lettuce and some frisée varieties will re-shoot from the cut section, so there is a practical reason for this. Where the salad is a hearted variety, such as a mignonette, I first inspect it while holding it upside down, and discard any leaves that are torn, bruised or full of mud. Next I soak the whole lettuce in cold water, and after 2–3 minutes I can separate each leaf under the water without losing the shape of any. If the salads chosen are of the proper size, there will be no

[+] To put together a small salad of mixed leaves was a considerable challenge in 1985. We grew a few unusual salad vegetables, but many were simply unavailable. It took time before all the varieties we take for granted today passed through quarantine and the seeds were available for commercial use.

leaf so big as to look unsightly on the plate. When each leaf has been separated gently, I leave them all soaking for half an hour. I use a salad spinner to dry them, and believe that this method does not damage the leaves, providing one does not attempt to overload each batch and doesn't spin the basket too violently.

The greens are tipped lightly into a clean dry tub or basin and placed in the refrigerator to crisp until needed.✢ Your aim should be a bowl of leaves of different shapes and colours, all in absolutely perfect condition.

TO PREPARE THE LIVER AND POTATOES   Remove the skin of the liver and, using a sharp knife, cut slices on the bias about 1 cm thick. Avoid as much of the tubes and gristly material as you can. After slicing, inspect each slice on both sides and trim out any pieces of tube.

Place the slices of liver on a plastic-lined tray until you are ready to cook the dish. Before you prepare the potatoes, get everything ready for finishing off the dish as it should take only 5 minutes.

Peel and parboil the potatoes. Drain well. When cool, cut into chunks. In another frying pan, heat half the melted pork fat and when it is hot commence to sauté the potatoes. They will take longer than you think to develop a golden crust, probably 15 minutes. Toss frequently.

TO COOK AND ASSEMBLE THE DISH   Heat the 2 cast-iron frying pans. Fry the bacon until crisp in one of them. Remove the bacon and put it in the pan with the sauté of potatoes. Set aside.

Drop half the remaining pork fat into each frying pan. Let it get quite hot. Lightly flour the liver slices, shake off the excess and place the slices into the hot fat. Let them seal really well at high heat for 2 minutes. Turn and seal the other side for 1 minute. Press the liver with your finger. It should feel springy in the centre. Remove the slices of liver to a very hot plate. Tip off any pork fat from the pans and pour half the vinegar into each pan.✦ Let it hiss and sizzle. It will reduce to large bubbles in less than a minute. Pour half the stock into each pan. Stir and scrape to loosen any cooked-on scraps. As the stock commences to boil hard, combine it all in 1 pan. It should reduce really fast by half.

While the stock is reducing, arrange your salad greens in the centre of each hot serving plate. Place the liver slices on top of the greens.

✢ When drying salad greens for use at home now, I take them from the salad spinner and have a clean tea towel next to me lined with kitchen paper. I tip the leaves onto the paper and then fold the cloth around them. This delicate bundle goes into the refrigerator until I am ready to toss my salad.
✦ Alternatively, you could use balsamic vinegar, sherry vinegar or red-wine vinegar to deglaze the pans.

Throw some spiced crab-apples or cherries or a handful of chopped herbs into the sauce just before whisking in the butter. Taste for salt and pepper. Pour the sauce over and around the liver and spoon on the crispy potatoes and bacon. Serve at once.

NOTE: Like many of these quick sauté dishes, it takes much longer to describe than to do. As long as everything is ready and nearby and your plates are hot, these dishes should not be frightening to a competent cook as you will be away from your guests for less than 10 minutes.

Raspberry vinegar

500 g raspberries
2 cups white-wine vinegar or *red-wine vinegar*
2 cups castor sugar

Lightly crush the berries, pour the vinegar over them and let them stand overnight to extract the maximum juice. Strain the juice through a fine sieve into a heat-proof jar. Add the sugar. Stand the jar in a preserving pan or other pan and pour in water to come part-way up the sides of the jar. Stir with a clean metal spoon to help the sugar dissolve until the water comes to the boil. Simmer for 1 hour. Using a fine strainer lined with dampened muslin, strain into sterilised bottles with a screwcap. Keep in the refrigerator.

Using the same proportions of fruit to sugar and vinegar, you can also make redcurrant or strawberry vinegar.

Strawberry jam

This is my grandmother's strawberry conserve. It is very lightly set and the most glorious clear colour, with whole strawberries that float on the top. Apart from being delicious on your breakfast toast, it is ideal served with your own fresh cheese (page 193) or Italian mascarpone.

1 kg strawberries
1.5 kg sugar
½ teaspoon tartaric acid

Only wash the strawberries if they need it, and then very briefly. After washing, hull the strawberries and put them on to cook gently without any water. After 15 minutes add the sugar and tartaric acid, stirring until the sugar has dissolved. Increase the heat and boil rapidly for 10–15 minutes until the liquid tests 'set'. Bottle in sterilised jars (see method for sterilising jars in the following recipe).

Raspberry or redcurrant syrup

1 kg raspberries or *redcurrants*
800 g castor sugar

Briefly process the fruit and then press through a fine sieve. (Alternatively, if you have an electric juicer, pass the fruit through it.) Let the juice stand, lightly covered but at room temperature, for 24 hours. Stir once or twice.

Sterilise bottles or jars by simmering in boiling water for 10 minutes. Allow to cool still covered by the water.

Place the fruit juice in a pan with the sugar. Bring to the boil, then remove from the heat and let stand for 3 minutes. Return to the heat and slowly bring back to the boil, then pull off and stand for a further 3 minutes. Bring the syrup back to the boil again and skim off any froth. Pour the syrup into the sterilised bottles or jars and close with sterilised screwtops.

The syrup can be used at once, but will keep almost indefinitely. Store in a cool place, but not in the refrigerator.

Plum syrup

1.5 kg plums
500 g sugar
½ cup water
1 vanilla bean

Sterilise jars and/or bottles as for the previous recipe.

Wash the plums, drain and remove the stems. Cut the plums in half and remove the stones. With a heavy mallet, crush the stones and place them in a large, heavy saucepan with the plum halves, sugar, water and vanilla beans. Bring to the boil slowly.

Lower the heat and simmer for 12 minutes, stirring often to prevent scorching. Remove from the heat and cool thoroughly. Strain through a fine sieve into the jars or bottles and seal with sterilised lids. Store in a cool, dark place.

Grandmother's bramble cake (blackberry pie)

200 g plain flour
200 g self-raising flour
pinch of salt
200 g lard, at room temperature⁺
180 ml cold water to mix
egg wash (1 egg mixed with a pinch of salt)
⅓–½ cup sugar, depending on the type of fruit used and individual taste
60 g soft unsalted butter

FRUIT

2 cups blackberries, mulberries, raspberries or gooseberries, picked over and
    stems removed if necessary, but not washed
or
2 cups thinly sliced rhubarb mixed with ½ cup dried currants

Grandmother's bramble cake – blackberry pie bursting with berries and juice (page 164)

Orange cream with sugared jasmine flowers (page 172)

TO MAKE THE PASTRY   Sift the flours together with the salt. Rub the lard in quickly. Make a well in the centre and work in the cold water. Knead until you have a fairly soft, springy and elastic dough, 2–3 minutes. Form into a ball, cover and chill for 20 minutes.

TO ASSEMBLE THE PIE   Roll two-thirds of the pastry into a circle approximately 26 cm in diameter. Transfer this circle of dough onto a slightly larger buttered ovenproof plate. The pie must be assembled on the plate you intend to serve it on, as it is impossible to move.

Roll the remaining pastry into a circle 12 cm in diameter. The pastry should be rolled about 6 mm thick. Tip the prepared fruit onto the larger circle in a heap. Pleat the sides of the pastry around the pile of fruit so that it starts to resemble a mob-cap. The pleated edges should be leaning slightly inwards to the pile of fruit.

Rest the smaller pastry circle lightly on top of the fruit. The lid should extend just beyond the edge of the pleats. Do not seal the lid or press it down heavily, as it has to be removed after baking. As some juice may run in the baking, put a metal tray underneath the pie plate. Brush the pastry with the egg wash and put into a hot oven at 200°C for 25 minutes until the pastry is cooked and golden brown. Take the pie from the oven and carefully lift its lid, using a flexible spatula (loosen the edges of the lid first). Tip in the sugar, then the butter. Replace the lid and leave the pie in a warm place for at least 10 minutes before cutting into wedges and serving.

Be prepared. Use a spoon as well as a knife and lifter for serving. There will be plenty of delicious juice, which will flow into the pie plate as you cut. Do not waste a drop! Serve with clotted cream or pure, thick cream.

NOTE: The pastry should be flexible and elastic. The dough must not be rolled too thin. The sugar used could be brown, granulated or castor, depending on the flavour and degree of crunch preferred.

+ Lard (rendered pork fat) is becoming more difficult to find. Large supermarkets will have it in plastic tubs near the margarine and butter displays. It is also stocked by Asian supermarkets as some Chinese pastry is made with lard.

Edible fragrances

MENU

SMOKED QUAIL WITH
OYSTER MUSHROOMS

ROASTED LEG OF LAMB WITH
BASIL STUFFING

ORANGE CREAM WITH
SUGARED JASMINE FLOWERS

A love of food has a lot to do with smells and associ-
ations. I have only to hear the tinkling of an unseen
bicycle bell on a summer's evening to imagine myself
back in a dark street in Jakarta in 1962, and I swear I can
smell the satay. On a trip to Sydney in 1982 I was walk-
ing through the streets of Woollahra, and the heady smell
of the frangipani trees brought instant recall of Tahiti
experienced well over twenty years ago and no doubt
unrecognisable today. I smelt the frangipani then, too,
but it was my first taste of lime-'cooked' raw fish in the
Pacific manner that it reminded me of.

In the grip of the country's worst drought, in 1984,
I was musing about smells and their culinary association
as I hand-watered for my one permitted hour in my

precious herb garden. The herbs had endured yet another scorching day and seemed to release their breath-catching smells as the hose played on them. The spice of the basil leaves reminded me that the pesto season was still to be enjoyed, and perhaps I would bone and stuff that leg of lamb with basil tonight instead of painting it with a mustard glaze. The haunting lemony smell of the lemon verbena with its strange raspy leaves has a place in my largely practical selection of herbs, not only for its affinity with fish, but more particularly for its delicate and charming sprays of lavender flowers. I have a wall of scented geraniums, which all coexist happily and struggle in a good-natured way to stake increasing claims to the small space. My rose geranium is an often-mentioned favourite to steep in creams and custards, and its little miniature nosegay of pink flowers absolutely delights me. The slightest brush to the velvet leaves of the peppermint geranium releases its clean, sharp note – so far I have linked it in a sorbet based on tea. Curious and perhaps not altogether successful.

Other and more elusive aromas fascinate me. We once painstakingly painted the petals of white star jasmine with egg white and dusted them with sugar in an attempt to encapsulate the fragrance and served these little stars scattered over a creamy orange dessert. It looked lovely, but the perfume lasted only a few hours. It was more successful when we buried scented leaves in a jar of castor sugar as one does with a vanilla bean. The scented sugar was a revelation when used to make the crème anglaise to pour around a hot pudding.

Such musings awaken the appetite, the allotted hosing time is over – I am off to tackle the lamb!

I often serve a classic ratatouille with roast lamb, as I find that the mingle of juices from the vegetables enhances the simple *jus* from the lamb. Another option would be thickly sliced eggplant placed into the baking dish with the garlic halfway through the cooking time so that the flesh becomes pulp-soft and the purple skins are wrinkled and properly stewed.

Pesto is not normally made with bacon (see pages 170-1). As a sauce for pasta or to stir into the famous *soupe au pistou*, it is usually pounded basil and garlic mounted into a thick sauce with olive oil. Frequently pine nuts are added and frequently some sort of cheese: true Parmesan for preference.✝ One cannot stuff a leg of lamb with something that has a mayonnaise consistency, hence I use bacon to provide substance so that the paste clings to the meat.

✝ We are all much more attuned nowadays to the rich and powerful flavour and nutty texture of high-quality Parmigiano-Reggiano than was the case in 1985. It is always preferable to buy a chunk of cheese and keep it wrapped in a cloth to grate as needed. The only exception would be if you can buy your Parmigiano freshly grated from an Italian food store. Using a thin-bladed peeler one can also pare shavings of Parmigiano very quickly for draping over vegetables or pasta. Little containers of gratings are a poor substitute.

Once again, necessity is often the mother of invention. I have tasted one sauce made by a chef who substituted walnuts for pine nuts, hard ewe's milk cheese for Parmesan and parsley for basil, but retained the olive oil. It was a lovely sauce, and the chef merely mentioned to me in passing that this was his winter salute to pesto, until he could get basil again.

For some time I have been intrigued by a Chinese dish of smoked duck where tea-leaves and rice are burnt in a wok over direct heat to produce a dense but aromatic smoke. All recipes I have found stress the need for efficient ventilation and suggest lining the wok with foil in order to facilitate cleaning. Thus warned, but not put off, I decided to try it and to use quail, not duck, and my Japanese dome-shaped Kamado charcoal barbecue and smoker, not the wok. I made up a wonderfully spicy mix of roasted and pounded Szechuan pepper, salt, garlic, finely chopped spring onion and finely grated orange zest, massaged a dozen plump little quail and left them overnight.

Next day we made a small charcoal fire and let the coals reach smouldering point before throwing in two handfuls of a mix of tea, rice and dampened hickory chips and then closed the damper. *Dense* smoke instantly. We put in one little bird to test the system. Five minutes later it was beautifully golden all over and smelt delicious. The next batch took a little longer as the first flush of smoke had settled into a steady stream, but the whole experiment was voted most successful. The quail was thoroughly smoked, but not cooked, so with a brushing of oil or butter and into a very hot oven, and a crisp-skinned, juicy-breasted little delicacy was ready.[+]

I have often read of grilling over vine cuttings, said to give off a most aromatic smoke, but I haven't yet tried this.[♦] Elsewhere in this book I have reminisced about the delights of crayfish grilled over the snappy twigs of *herbes de Provence* at Eze on the Côte d'Azur. The humble sardine is a gastronome's delight. If you have

---

[+] Tea-smoking is now very well understood and I watched Christine Manfield, former teacher and owner-chef of Paramount restaurant in Sydney, demonstrate the technique at the 1995 Melbourne Food & Wine Festival Master Class. It is certainly less invasive if you can do the smoking somewhere outdoors.

[♦] By 1988 I had solved the problem of obtaining a supply of vine cuttings. I wrote in *Stephanie's Feasts and Stories*, 'As we increasingly become a nation of wine producers, more and more people have a friend who makes wine. If not, there are plenty of suburban grapevines that need a prune in the late autumn after the harvest. Cut the prunings into short lengths with strong secateurs and bundle them loosely into something where air can still circulate. I use string onion bags donated by the greengrocer.' And I went on to say that you can also feed vine prunings through a mulching machine and use the resultant bags of vine chips for hot-smoking or for fuelling a barbecue. A little goes a very long way. If using a wok or a covered roasting pan on top of the stove, half a cup of lightly dampened vine chips will satisfactorily smoke 3–4 pieces of fish or quail. The fish or birds should be rested on a rack, skin-side to the smoke.

the opportunity at a barbecue, gut some sardines, rub off the scales, salt and pepper the fish and wrap them in oiled grapevine leaves and grill them directly on the grill, or else oil and skewer them with a woody rosemary twig and toast them like marshmallows in front of the fire. A garlicky tomato sauce is a good strong accompaniment. Just dip your slightly charred fish – what wonderful aromas!

I cannot leave this eulogy to flavour and smell without mentioning garlic, yet again! Unpeeled, but with the tough outside skin rubbed off, and strewn around meat or poultry as it roasts, it is ambrosia to me. The garlic cloves transform into meltingly tender centres with crispy, papery skins. The skins are chewed for flavour and then discarded. Or one can create *tartines* of garlic. Oil-rubbed, slow-baked croutons of bread are spread with the purée of garlic obtained by pressing out the perfumed centre of each roasted clove. What a garnish! Or indeed it could be the central crunch of a *salade composée*. Similar roasting techniques yield equally wonderful results with small pickling onions or true pink shallots.

Smoked quail with oyster mushrooms

1 tablespoon Szechuan peppercorns
4 spring onions, finely chopped
5 slices fresh ginger, finely chopped
1 tablespoon finely chopped orange zest
1 tablespoon salt
1 tablespoon ground black pepper
6 plump quail

SMOKING MIXTURE

1 cup tea-leaves
½ cup hickory chips or mulched vine prunings, dampened

SALAD

choice salad greens
abalone (oyster) mushrooms
olive oil
12 slices kaiserfleisch bacon
sherry vinegar

Place the Szechuan peppercorns into a hot, heavy, dry frying pan and roast them until they start to jump. Grind them to a powder either in an electric coffee grinder or with a mortar and pestle. Whether you use the coffee grinder for coffee or not, be sure to wipe it out very thoroughly after this use. Do NOT wash it.

Combine the spring onion, ginger, orange zest, salt and the 2 peppers in a food processor and run for 1 minute until the marinade resembles a paste. Rub the mixture into the quail, inside and out. Leave, covered, for 24 hours.

TO COOK AND SERVE   On the following day light the barbecue and burn until you have hot coals. Throw on the tea-leaves and the damp hickory chips or vine prunings and smoke the quail for 5 minutes.

Preheat the oven to 220°C. Wash, dry and refrigerate the salad greens. Sauté the abalone mushrooms in a little oil in a hot pan until they are limp, about 1 minute. Brush the quail with a little melted butter or oil and put in the oven for 5 minutes. Meanwhile, fry the kaiserfleisch bacon until crisp.

Arrange the greens on a hot plate and add the sautéed mushrooms. Remove the quail from the oven. For each bird, pull off the legs, chop out the backbone with a quick thump of the knife and arrange the 4 pieces on one of the plates. Top with 2 slices of bacon. Add a few drops of sherry vinegar to the bacon fat in the pan and swirl to blend. Pour over the salad greens and serve immediately.

Roasted leg of lamb with basil stuffing

1 leg of lamb, tunnel-boned (see opposite)
olive oil
pepper, salt
12 unpeeled cloves garlic
3 medium-sized eggplants, sliced (optional)
1 glass dry red or white wine

STUFFING

100 g fat bacon, very finely chopped
15 basil leaves, torn into little pieces
3 cloves garlic, peeled and finely chopped
1 tablespoon chopped parsley
2 tablespoons roasted pine nuts

TO PREPARE THE STUFFING AND THE LAMB   Tunnel-boning results in a neat pocket for the stuffing. If you wish to carve the leg of lamb in the French manner, i.e. in long thin slices parallel to the bone, ask the butcher not to chop through the shank bone but to leave it straight to act as a convenient handle for the carver.

First prepare the stuffing by briefly combining the bacon, basil, garlic and parsley in a food processor or pounding together with a mortar and pestle. Combine with the pine nuts. Press this paste into the hollow of the lamb and skewer shut the opening with 1 or 2 poultry skewers. Rub the meat with a little olive oil, season with ground black pepper and a very little salt. Leave to stand for at least an hour at room temperature. If you have prepared the meat on the morning of your dinner, always bring it out of the refrigerator an hour before cooking so as not to distort the cooking time.

I find the most successful method of cooking lamb is to stand it directly on the oven rack in the top third of the oven and to place a baking dish on the rack underneath. This allows the hot air to circulate around the meat, thus sealing all sides and preventing the meat sitting in up to 3 cm of fat so that the bottom section stews. Any cut-up vegetables can be placed in the baking dish: carrots, potatoes, parsnips etc.

TO ROAST   Place the meat on the rack in a preheated oven at 220°C. After 20 minutes drop the unpeeled garlic and the eggplant slices into the dish. After a further 40 minutes test the meat by plunging a metal skewer into the centre at the thickest part, waiting for 30 seconds and then touching the point of the skewer to your top lip. If it is cold the meat is not yet cooked, so try again in 10 minutes. If the skewer is warm the meat is ready to rest, i.e. it is medium–rare but after 15 minutes' resting will carve as evenly pink, not red. If the skewer is hot, your meat is well cooked.

If this method seems too physical, try a meat thermometer. High-temperature roasting like this is very fast, so don't be surprised if a medium-sized leg of lamb is ready after 50 minutes. The internal temperature of the thickest part of the meat should read 60°C for medium rare or 65°C for medium. It will certainly not take longer than an hour. At the end of the cooking time turn the oven off, lift the meat and vegetables onto a platter and return them to the oven to rest. The resting time is critical. High-temperature roasting forces all the juices to the centre of the meat, and it needs the time in a warm place to relax and for the juices to seep evenly back through the meat, making it tender.

TO SERVE   Discard all fat from the baking dish and over very high heat deglaze the cooked-on scraps with a *generous* glass of wine, scraping and stirring. Add any juices that have seeped from the joint while it rested or during the carving. This simple juice is only enough to moisten the slices and is a far cry from the brown thickened gravy that even sophisticated cooks sometimes resort to automatically. Serve it in a jug alongside the meat.

Orange cream with sugared jasmine flowers

grated zest of 1 orange
¼ cup grenadine syrup
500 ml cream
2 eggs
2 egg yolks
125 g castor sugar
juice of 1 orange
1 tablespoon Cointreau or Grand Marnier

6 porcelain mousse pots or small soufflé dishes

GARNISH

white jasmine flowers or orange-blossom flowers
1 egg white
castor sugar
6 shiny orange-tree leaves

TO PREPARE THE ORANGE CREAM   Drop the orange zest into boiling water for 1 minute. Drain. Place the drained zest in a very small pan and barely cover with the grenadine syrup. Let it steep and simmer for 5 minutes. Drain again. Place the zest in the cream and *very* slowly bring to scalding point. Whirl the eggs, egg yolks, sugar, orange juice and alcohol in a food processor. Gradually add the hot cream. Pour carefully into pots and put the pots in a bain-marie, that is, cover the bottom of a baking dish with a wet cloth to prevent the pots moving and pour in boiling water to come halfway up the sides of the pots.

Cook at 160°C for 20–25 minutes. Test. They will still be *almost* liquid in the centre when done, and will get firmer as they cool. This cream is never turned out.

This recipe is based on the recipe for Orange Custards given in Jane Grigson's *Fruit Book*.

TO PREPARE THE GARNISH AND SERVE   Carefully paint both sides of star jasmine or orange blossom flowers with egg white. Drench them with castor sugar and then draw the stem of each painted flower through the grid of a fine cake rack so that the flower heads are not damaged, and allow to dry. Scatter these delicate flowers on the cream and serve with a shiny orange leaf.

East meets west

MENU

VEGETABLE CASSATA,
WATERCRESS SAUCE

SEAFOOD POACHED IN
LEMONGRASS BROTH

CHOCOLATE CASES WITH TWO FILLINGS –
COFFEE AND HAZELNUT CREAM

I have called the first dish on this menu a vegetable cassata as this best describes the studded effect of brightly coloured vegetables embedded in a creamy mousse, which is in turn encased in crisp puff pastry. It is a mousse filling, not a mousseline, as although the chicken flesh is raw, it is combined with very finely minced cooked ham and the airy effect is created by folded cream and beaten egg whites, rather than by using egg white to build the chicken paste into a mousseline.

'Mousse' in culinary parlance is an obligingly vague term that seems to refer to a spongy, foamy texture, whether it is found in confections set with or without gelatine but with whipped cream added, or used to describe various cakes and puddings and other savoury mixtures lightened with whipped cream, such as the ham mousse on page 44.

The choice of vegetables is open to individual preference, but roasted red pepper strips must be a part of this dish. It is their pungency that leaves the zing in the mouth. Choose others for their quality, compatibility and colour. In the recipe I have listed my favourites. I believe that when using a soft-textured food such as a mousse or a mousseline there is often a danger that the finished dish lacks strength. Too much mousse, froth and bubble is boring. A strong taste or a deliberate crunchy element will add excitement to the dish. Hence the red peppers.

We have frequently served a *sauce beurre blanc* with this entrée, but recently I have decided to serve a vegetable-based sauce. My first preference is for a water-cress sauce, which would be finished with a spoonful of chervil butter for a garden-fresh but sharp flavour. If watercress is unobtainable, try the same sauce based on parsley. Yet another choice would be a creamy purée of sweet garlic, lengthened with some chicken glaze and perhaps with the same nut of chervil butter added.

The main course was inspired by a trip to the Vietnamese market. I love fresh lemongrass, and now that it is available all year round, seven days a week, I find that it is increasingly becoming a staple of the shopping list.[†] Many years ago I feasted on *babi guling* (I think that was the name), a special dish of roasted young pig cooked at the roadside in Bali. It seemed to be a dish that just appeared, and as soon as it did, villagers came from everywhere and bought small portions, which were wrapped in banana leaves together with some sticky rice and a prized portion of the skin. I tried so hard to work out what was in this strange and marvellous spicing. Now I know that it included lots of lemongrass, probably turmeric, and lots of garlic, but I shall never know the secret. I have just finished reading *Traditional Recipes of Laos*, the manuscript recipe book of the chef at the royal palace at Luang Prabang, edited by Alan and Jennifer Davidson. Lemongrass appears in many of the recipes, and I like the repeated combinations of sour/hot in so many of the dishes and the subtle use of the salty fermented fish sauce, which takes the place of the soy used in other Asian cuisines.

I like broths and clear, strong tastes. This broth is served in a wide, hollowed dish. The dish should be shallow so that the pattern and colour of the white fish, pink prawns, pale green coriander and red tomato can be admired, but sufficiently

[†] The availability of all manner of Asian fruits, vegetables and flavourings has expanded exponentially since the mid-1980s. So has the popularity of eating the delicately flavoured dishes of South-East Asia, creating even more consumer demand. Former rarities, such as green papaya, green mango, immature coconut, fresh kaffir lime leaves, galangal, freshly made wheat and rice noodles, and greens of all shapes and sizes for poaching and stir-frying, are easily purchased. I should add that this availability is still restricted to capital cities and major regional towns.

hollowed so that the broth can be enjoyed with a spoon. The choice of which fish to poach should be made only after a trip to your fish market or a telephone call to a trusted fishmonger. A little extra substance is provided by serving large oven-dried slices of country-type bread spread with a slick of crushed anchovy with a garnish of a slice or two of lime. A scattering of fresh coriander adds extra piquancy as a final garnish.

After such a delicate and restrained main course, I have suggested a rich dessert. Paper cups are painted with melted chocolate and filled with a luscious mixture of powdered coffee and ricotta cheese. Do not use the drained ricotta cheese sold in supermarkets in unperforated plastic containers. You need to search out the moist, fresh variety, as traditionally made by the Italian community. The first-mentioned variety of ricotta is fine for filling pastries or for adding to a basic white-flour Vienna-type bread, and indeed for many cakes, but for this filling the desired texture is one of thick cream, not curds. The coffee must be pulverised Turkish coffee; instant coffee will not do.

For interest, I have given another filling – a hazelnut Bavarian cream. In either case, do choose SMALL waxed paper cases to paint with chocolate. Some people will leave the cases entirely, and only eat the middle. Others will nibble at the edges, but some will eat the lot and too much chocolate can be cloying. A small delectable taste will finish this meal superbly. As with all chocolate desserts, I believe that the coffee should be offered simultaneously.

Vegetable cassata, Watercress sauce

250 g puff pastry (see page 38)
1 egg
pinch of salt

MOUSSE

200 g chicken breast meat, free of all skin and tendon
200 g lean ham
200 ml unwhipped cream
200 ml cream, firmly whipped
2 egg whites, firmly whipped
salt, pepper

VEGETABLES

1 medium carrot
1 swede turnip
1 white turnip
4 stalks broccoli
1 large red pepper

WATERCRESS SAUCE

1 bunch young watercress
60 g butter
1 small onion, finely chopped
tiny shake of ground allspice
pepper, salt
300 ml chicken stock
100 ml cream
1 teaspoon chervil butter (optional)

TO PREPARE THE MOUSSE Purée the chicken flesh in a food processor or mincer, or push it through the medium disc of a Mouli. Press the purée through a drum sieve for perfect texture. Put it into a bowl. Purée the ham until you have a fine mince. Combine with the chicken mince and blend very well. Chill this mince for 1 hour. Return to the food processor and combine with the unwhipped cream. Transfer to a large bowl and fold in the whipped cream and then the whipped egg whites. Taste for seasoning. Leave aside in the refrigerator until assembly time.

TO PREPARE THE VEGETABLES   Peel the carrot and turnips. Cut into batons about 6 cm × 1 cm. Peel the broccoli stalks and trim into slender batons about the same size as the carrots and turnips. Blanch each vegetable separately in lightly salted water until barely tender. Refresh under cold water and pat very dry.

Roast the red pepper over an open flame, place in a paper bag or wrap in a clean cloth for 3–4 minutes, then rub off all charred skin. Wipe with a damp paper towel and cut into substantial strips about the same width as the other vegetables.

TO ASSEMBLE   Roll out the pastry into a narrow rectangle 40 cm × 16 cm and about 5 mm thick. Imagine you are making a long sausage roll. Spread one-third of the mousse on half of the rectangle, leaving a 1 cm border. Arrange half of the vegetable strips down the mousse, each strip end to end with another strip of the same colour so that you have stripes of colour on the pale mousse. Cover with half the remaining mousse. Make another layer of vegetable stripes in a different colour combination from before. Cover with the remaining mousse. Fold over the other half of the pastry and press the edges firmly together with a fork all along the long edge. Place the filled roll on a baking sheet and refrigerate until needed.

TO MAKE THE SAUCE   Pull off all the leaves and tender stems of the watercress and discard the tough woody stems. You should have 3 cups of well-packed leaves. Wash well and then drop into boiling water for 1 minute. Drain very well and then chop finely. Melt the butter in a cast-iron pan and soften the onion until yellow. Add the chopped watercress, cover the pan and sweat together over a very low heat for 5 minutes with the allspice, pepper and a very small amount of salt. Add the chicken stock and simmer gently, uncovered, for 10 minutes.

Blend the sauce in an electric blender and taste for seasoning. Put the cream into the rinsed-out pan and boil hard for 3 minutes. Add the watercress sauce and stir over a high heat until the sauce is of a light coating consistency. Stir in the chervil butter, if using.

TO COOK AND SERVE   Whisk together the egg with a small pinch of salt. Brush the pastry all over with the wash and place into a preheated oven at 220°C. Bake for about 15 minutes until deep gold and puffed. Let it rest for 1–2 minutes, then cut into slices with a sharp, serrated knife. Serve the slices on their side on each plate to show off the pretty pattern. Spoon the watercress sauce around or, better still, serve the sauce separately so that the pastry stays crisp.

Garlic cream sauce

⌁

2 tablespoons chicken glaze or 600 ml chicken stock
12 large cloves garlic, unpeeled
300 ml cream
1 tablespoon chervil, tarragon or basil butter from the freezer
salt, pepper

If there is no glaze on hand, reduce the chicken stock to 60 ml by rapid boiling in a wide pan.

Drop the cloves of garlic into a pan of lightly salted water and bring to the boil. Drain. Repeat twice more. Slip the tender cloves of garlic from their skins and cover with the cream. Simmer for 10 minutes. Add the chicken glaze and the herb butter. Simmer until the butter has melted. Blend to a smooth cream either in a blender or a food processor. Check for salt and pepper. If the sauce is too thick, add a few extra spoonfuls of cream.

Seafood poached in lemongrass broth

⌁

SEAFOOD PER SERVE (SELECT FROM)

prawns
green (i.e. uncooked) crayfish (rock lobster) meat
Balmain bugs
whole small fish
fish cutlets or fillets
scallops

LEMONGRASS BROTH

1.5 litres water
salt
3 stems lemongrass, chopped
4 large ripe tomatoes, halved
2 spring onions, chopped
10 sprigs of coriander

3 slices fresh ginger
2 cloves garlic, crushed
3 tablespoons fish sauce (nam pla), or to taste

CROUTONS

6 thick, angled slices of bread from a country-style loaf
olive oil
1 clove garlic, peeled and cut in half
3 fillets of anchovy, cut in half

GARNISH

2 limes, thinly sliced
a few coriander sprigs
6 tablespoons freshly diced tomato

TO MAKE THE CROUTONS Rub each slice of bread with olive oil and dry in a slow oven until pale gold. When thoroughly dried, rub with the garlic and spread each slice with half a fillet of anchovy.

TO MAKE THE BROTH Bring the water and salt to a boil, add the lemongrass and simmer for 30 minutes. Then add the tomatoes, spring onion, coriander, ginger and garlic and simmer for a further 30 minutes. Pass through a fine strainer, pressing well on the solids, and add fish sauce to taste.

TO PREPARE THE SEAFOOD Prawns should be shelled, beheaded and de-veined. If you like a soft finish to the prawn meat, after poaching you can use the Chinese technique of 'velveting', which is described on page 180.

Crayfish tails should be dipped into boiling water for 1 minute to enable the tail meat to be easily removed from the shell. Slice the meat into slanting medallions and leave, covered with plastic film, until needed. Check that the central intestinal thread has been removed.

Balmain bugs (or Moreton Bay bugs, or Spencer Gulf bugs, depending on your home state) can have the carapace cracked along each side so that the armoured shell can be lifted away from the meat. In this case, slit the underside of the flesh to extract the intestine. The more usual method of attack is to lean heavily on the shellfish with a cleaver and split the tail lengthwise, thus exposing the intestine for easy removal.

Either cut a whole fish into chunks or cutlets or else choose fillets to poach.

Refer to page 213 for instructions on how to clean scallops.

TO COOK THE SEAFOOD AND SERVE   Remember that all seafood poaches very quickly – scallops and thin fillets of fish in less than 2 minutes. When preparing to cook this dish, everything must be ready. The plates must be hot. All shellfish and fish should be assembled in order of cooking times. The garnishing croutons and other final touches must all be absolutely ready.

Heat the broth to boiling point. Do not use a receptacle so deep that the fish are lost from sight and you have to plunge skimmers and lifters around, thus breaking up the fish and risking overcooking. On the other hand, the cooking vessel should not be so wide that it cannot be maintained at a brisk simmer on your domestic stove. An Asian steamboat cooker can make this a fun participation dish, where each guest cooks his/her own meal at the table, probably poaching one sort of fish at a time. A more mundane but useful method is to use an electric frying pan.

When all the fish and shellfish have been poached, lift them into hollow serving bowls.✝ Pour over some broth, and for each serving add a crouton, a few slices of lime and some coriander leaves, and scatter over 1 tablespoon of diced tomato.

If the dish is being served 'steamboat-style', other cut-up vegetables could be poached in the stock. Perhaps even poach an egg or some rice noodles in the broth. Served in this manner, the oriental character of the dish becomes its main feature.

TO VELVET PRAWNS   For 500 g of prawns you will need:
2 teaspoons sherry or *rice wine*
½ teaspoon salt
1 large egg white
1½ tablespoons cornflour
1½ tablespoons light oil

This technique is described clearly and poetically in the definitive work on Chinese cooking, *The Key to Chinese Cooking* by Irene Kuo. She points out that the 'velveting' process preserves the texture of the prawns and prevents them from acquiring a woodiness that comes from cooking them in liquid without protection.

Place the prawns in a bowl and sprinkle over the wine and salt. Mix. Beat the egg white lightly and mix it through the prawns. Sieve over the cornflour and mix until smooth. (I find it easier to lift the prawns through the mixture with my fingers than to use a spoon or fork.) Add the oil and stir. Refrigerate the shellfish until needed.

The prawns can now be simmered in either broth or water. Simply tip them in and move them around to prevent any tendency to stick. When they float to the surface, they are cooked. Remove from the liquid immediately.

✝ The French describe these bowls as *assiettes creuses*, literally 'hollow plates'. We would probably describe them as old-fashioned soup plates or large pasta plates.

Chocolate cases with two fillings – coffee and hazelnut cream

CHOCOLATE CASES

300 g best couverture chocolate
150 g unsalted butter
6–8 waxed-paper cake cups – not too big

COFFEE FILLING

2 tablespoons powdered Turkish coffee
100 ml rum
400 g ricotta cheese
100 g castor sugar
softly whipped cream
chocolate-coated coffee beans

HAZELNUT CREAM FILLING

70 g hazelnuts
2 eggs
6 tablespoons sugar
1½ cups milk
3 leaves (5 g) Dr Oetker gelatine
2 tablespoons Frangelico (Italian hazelnut liqueur)
⅔ cup cream

TO MAKE THE CHOCOLATE CASES   Buy superfine dark chocolate from a name manufacturer, such as Valrhona or Lindt. Beware packages of cooking chocolate or chocolate bits sold in supermarkets where the word 'compound' occurs. It will not have the same shine or flavour as the more expensive varieties (see footnote on page 137).

Melt the chocolate and butter over a gentle heat. Stir when melted, allow to cool and then pour through a strainer into a bowl.

Arrange the paper cups on a lightly oiled baking tray. (Buy a bottle of sweet almond oil from the chemist for this sort of oiling. It has no taste of salad oil, and a little goes a long way.) If you have bought foil baking cups that have their own paper liners, spoon some chocolate mixture into each paper lining and coat the inside quickly with the back of a spoon. Drop each lining immediately inside its foil cup and place the tray of filled cups in the freezer for 10 minutes.

If you cannot find these double cups, you will need to invert the paper cups after painting them with chocolate or they will spread out like a flower under the effect of the warm chocolate.

When all the cups have been filled, move any inverted cases very delicately to ensure that you have not overfilled them, which would result in them setting with an overflow edge that will be hard to chip off after the chocolate is set. Place in the refrigerator to set.

When the cases are set, take one at a time from the refrigerator and peel off the paper, being extra careful around the edges. If it is a warm day, have a bowl of iced water nearby and continually dabble your fingers in the water and dry them before proceeding. At the restaurant we do this job standing in a very cold refrigerated room, but we are often making 30 cases, not 6 or 8, as with this amount of ingredients.

TO MAKE THE COFFEE FILLING   Dissolve the coffee in the rum. Combine all ingredients in a food processor and process until smooth and shiny. Spoon or pipe the filling into 3 or 4 of the chocolate cases and top with a little whipped cream. At Stephanie's we scatter a few 'coffee bean' chocolates around the place.

TO MAKE THE HAZELNUT FILLING   We use only leaf gelatine, which is very much superior to the powdered form. It is first soaked to soften it and then dropped into a small quantity of hot liquid, where it instantly dissolves leaving no trace or taste of its presence, except its foolproof setting capacity. It is not always easy to find, so I have included figures for conversion purposes on page 14. Always remember that both leaf and powdered gelatine can be substituted if the quantity given in a recipe is specified by weight: 30 g of powdered equals 30 g of leaf gelatine. Most recipes are less helpful, and specify gelatine by number of teaspoons (1 metric teaspoon equals 3.3 g).

Toast the hazelnuts in a hot oven until golden. Tip into a clean cloth and rub hard to remove the skins. Shake through a very coarse sieve or colander to separate the nuts from the flakes of skin. Reserve 1 nut to decorate each chocolate case and pulverise the rest in a nut mill or food processor.

Beat the eggs with the sugar until pale and thick. Bring the milk to boiling point. Pour it onto the egg mixture, return the mixture to the heat and stir until it coats the back of a spoon thickly. Immediately strain this thickened custard (crème anglaise) into a metal bowl that you have ready resting inside a large bowl half-filled with ice.[+]

[+] For those unaccustomed to cooking stirred custards, the degree of thickening can cause anxiety. It may be helpful to know that between 84°C and 86°C is the moment of maximum thickening, and the custard should be removed from the heat immediately.

Soften the leaves of gelatine in cold water for 5 minutes. Squeeze the sheets of gelatine and drop them into the hot custard. Stir until there is no trace left, then add the liqueur to the cooling custard.

When the custard is cold and saucelike in consistency, fold in the cream, whipped until firm but not stiff, and the crushed nuts. This has now become a bavarois. Spoon the bavarois into the remaining chocolate cases and decorate with the reserved whole hazelnuts.

PETIT FOURS: As an absolute labour of love, and if you have nothing else to do on a cold day, make a tray of really tiny chocolate cases and fill them with one or other or both fillings and serve them as superb petits fours.

A game pie

MENU

❧

Tomato Flan with a Ragoût
of Vegetables

Hare Tourte, Sauce Poivrade
Glazed Vegetables

Coeur à la crème

❧

I first cooked this tomato flan in autumn, when the
tomatoes were still red and bursting and the tarragon
was just starting to straggle. I served it with a little 'stew'
of vegetables, cooked in the manner often described as
à la grecque with the addition of a few sultanas. It is good
menu planning in any restaurant these days to provide at
least one dish suitable for vegetarians. It must be depress-
ing if you are a non-meat eater to be forever offered
a plate of assorted vegetables as the only choice. It is also
not in the chef's interests. I pride myself on the care I take
in combining textures and flavours, and it is a bit hard to
create a masterpiece or even a good dish when the request
for a special dish arrives at 8.30 on a Saturday night. Courteous and twice-shy vegetarians always ring the day before.[+]

Definitions seem to me to have become blurred. When is a vegetarian a vegetarian? I had always believed that a vegetarian is someone who eats vegetables and derives their proteins from nuts, pulses and, usually, cheese. We often have self-styled vegetarians who eat fish, many who eat no dairy produce at all, some who don't eat meat but who have no objection to, say, wild rice cooked with meat stock. Recently one customer rang to say she ate no wheat flour, no dairy products and no fish. We prepared her a walnut-oil-dressed salad of exotic fungus and crudités on rocket leaves with fried walnuts for an entrée. The main dish centred on a plate of steamed vegetables with bean curd and a sauce of oriental rice wine and toasted nori seaweed and ginger. To our astonishment, she then ordered a quince Bavarian cream for dessert and was quite hostile when she was reminded of its cream content.

I am digressing. The tomato flan with its red–gold vegetable ragoût is a light and lovely beginning to a meal for anyone at all. The timbales will hold their heat for at least 30 minutes if left covered with foil in their water bath in a warm place. Unless you have a second oven, you will have to remove them from the oven, as the main dish – a rich hare tourte✦ – requires a hot oven to bake and crisp the puff pastry.

There is a classic and well-known French tart known as a pithiviers. It has a double crust of puff pastry filled with a rich almond cream made from fresh, unblanched almonds. The top crust is traditionally scored in sweeping arcs across the top and scalloped around the edge. The hare tourte is moulded in the same design. In the restaurant we make individual pies, so that they can be baked to order, but in a way the larger assembly is a better dish as the amount of puff pastry per diner is reduced. I had a wedge of a duck pie made in this manner on one visit to Alain Chapel's restaurant at Mionnay in the early 1980s, and very delicious it was too.

This recipe uses the technique of mixing meats to create a rich *farce* with some of the ingredients left in larger pieces to vary the texture. This is a technique similar to the one used for making a pâté or terrine. The differences in proportions are required because the tourte will be served hot with a sauce. It is not a good idea simply to use the mix that goes into your favourite pork-and-game pâté. Because a pâté or terrine will be served in a thin slice, which must hold together, the proportion of fat to lean is quite high. What is delicious and chewy cold can be unpleasant when hot and with all the pork fat flowing! My *farce* is bound with

---

✢ I have already commented on the increased popularity of vegetable dishes (see footnote on page 150). As a cook I want to cook vegetables so that they have the same sensual appeal and the same excitement as any other dish. I find that I turn to Italian cuisine, where the repertoire of fritters, gratins, salads and blended vegetable stews offers infinite choice.

✦ Tourte is a French word denoting a double-crust pie, as opposed to a *tarte*.

cream, not eggs, and is flavoured with some madeira and, for superb subtlety, truffle juice. Truffle juice is not usually readily obtainable in small quantities, and the large tins are wasteful in a small domestic situation as the flavour diminishes rapidly after the tin is opened and the juice should be used fast. The best alternative, and I cannot deny the expense involved, is to buy one of the very small tins of truffles and decant the truffle and any liquid into a clean screwtop jar and cover it with madeira overnight. The truffle will not have much flavour (but mince it up into the *farce* even so), but the juice will be highly perfumed.[+]

The *farce* cannot be so liquid as to run and ruin the bottom crust. Pigeon could be substituted for the hare, or wild duck, or venison. When buying the pork fat, specify back fat to your butcher. If you have to buy it from a delicatessen (often sold as 'speck'), ask for unsmoked fat. Smoked fat will completely alter and drown out the other flavours. Smoked speck is fine for lining or enclosing a country-style pâté or terrine, although I would always prefer the prettiness, strength and neutral flavour of a piece of caul.

The hare sauce is the sauce that I have described on page 34. As I mentioned in the recipe for the roasted saddle of hare, all scraps, carved carcasses and any juices should have been bagged, labelled and frozen. Now is the time to bring them out and add to the bones for this sauce. Madeira could be substituted for the cognac in the deglazing process to reinforce the flavour in the tourte itself.

Sauce-making is a very soothing occupation. I enjoy the whole procedure, from the making of the first veal stock through the roasting of bones, trimmings and vegetables, to the further reduction of wines, the straining, the blending of mixture A with mixture B, the skimming, and the final adjustments of seasoning or enriching with butter or cream. A sensible cook will spread all these processes out over a number of days. I find it very satisfying to work alongside a gently simmering stockpot. I rest a ladle in an old pot nearby, and from time to time give the stock a careful skim. In between times, I build up neat piles of fresh vegetables for the next process.

With such an elaborate main course, I would serve a vegetable as a separate course. Avoid starchy vegetables because of the pastry, and serve instead a dish of perfect green beans or whole witlof braised in a little stock until coated with a golden glaze.

Coeur à la crème means very different desserts, I have discovered. Its literal

[+] In *Cooking & Travelling in South-West France* I describe finding out all about first-cooking and second-cooking truffles. It is quite complex. You either buy truffle juice canned on its own at considerable expense, or a second-cooking truffle, which will have little flavour and a few drops of juice, or you may be able to buy a first-cooking truffle which will have no weight marked on the tin but will have its original juice still inside. Try a specialist restaurant supplier.

meaning is 'creamy heart', a suitably vague concept, so I suppose it is legitimate for various cooks to interpret it in their own way. There is another word in French, *crémet*, which specifically refers to a dish of fresh cheese sweetened and lightened with egg whites and sometimes extra cream as well. These little *crémets* are usually spooned into muslin-lined pierced moulds, and these moulds are usually hearts. The dish is turned out and eaten as it is, accompanied by raspberries or wild strawberries. Frequently one is served a *crémet* under the name of *coeur à la crème*. Some versions of the sweetened, lightened cheese heart are more successful than others. I have tasted one made from processed cream cheese, which was quite horrible, and the texture all wrong. It was pasty rather than a moist, spoonable sweet. Fresh ricotta cheese gives a much better texture. It is good made with the luscious Italian full-cream cheese mascarpone. But to my taste this is not the best way to appreciate mascarpone. Try it with a few Armagnac-soaked sultanas folded through it, or eat it just as it is with a fresh pear.

My version of *coeur à la crème* belongs to another French tradition. A freshly made cheese is moulded briefly to allow the whey to drain, and is then covered with thick cream and sprinkled with castor sugar or vanilla sugar. This is also eaten with fresh berries. In Paris one would buy a *petit-suisse*. Years ago, when I lived in France, *petits-suisses* were sold six to a waxed box, each cylinder dripping and circled with a band of paper. Nowadays they come in a plastic box with six sealed compartments, rather like the similarly unaesthetic plastic egg-containers.

Fresh *fromage fermier* is sold in French markets, dripping and sometimes still warm, by rose-cheeked farmers' wives exactly as has happened for generations. The cheeses vary both in fat content (*matière grasse*) and in composition and are always clearly labelled 45 per cent *matière grasse* or up to 60 per cent, and if labelled *mi-chèvre* are made of half goat's milk and half cow's milk.[+]

So, back to the *coeur à la crème*. First we make our cheese and drain it in a muslin bag, and later we line our hearts with more damp muslin and spoon in the very soft cheese. It is left to drain and firm up for just a few hours, and is served while still soft and creamy in the middle. This cheese is very good to eat plain with fruit, and is even more memorable if made from whole, unpasteurised milk.[◆]

[+] *Petit-suisse* is the name of a fresh cheese made from cow's milk, universally available in French fromageries and supermarkets. Its pre-portioned presentation is especially appealing to children. *Fromage fermier* is the same simple curd (cow's or goat's), but instead of being made in a factory it comes to market direct from the farm.

[◆] I cannot imagine what made me write about unpasteurised milk. It is not legal to make cheese from unpasteurised milk in Australia, although I have many delicious taste memories of cheeses made in just that manner in France.

This same simple white cheese, when seasoned with herbs, drops of matured wine vinegar and judicious amounts of shallots and garlic, becomes the Lyonnais speciality *cervelle de canut*, which translates as 'silkworker's brains'! (Lyon has been a centre of the silk industry for many centuries.) A successful commercial version of this cheese is sold as Boursin.

Tomato flan[+] with a ragoût of vegetables

1 kg ripe tomatoes
250 g carrots, peeled and sliced
60 g butter
1 large sprig of tarragon or *fresh basil* or *even parsley, finely chopped*
salt
1 teaspoon sugar
4 eggs
4 egg yolks
white pepper
1 extra tablespoon finely chopped tarragon (optional)

VEGETABLE SAUCE

60 ml virgin olive oil
1 onion, finely diced
1 teaspoon lightly crushed coriander seeds
1 bay leaf
2 tomatoes, peeled, seeded and cut into very fine concassé dice
2 medium unpeeled zucchini, cut into 1 cm dice
1 medium unpeeled eggplant, cut into 1 cm dice
1 large red pepper, cut into thin strips
pepper
2 tablespoons sultanas
60 ml dry white wine
salt

TO MAKE THE VEGETABLE SAUCE   Heat the oil in a cast-iron enamelled pan and tip in the onion, coriander seeds and bay leaf. Cook gently until the onion is soft and pale gold. Add the tomato and continue to cook for 1 minute longer until the tomato practically melts into a sauce. Tip in the rest of the vegetables, add some pepper and then the sultanas and wine. Cook, covered, for 5 minutes. Remove the lid, stir gently to mix and prevent sticking, and adjust the salt. Simmer for a few more minutes until all the flavours are well blended but the vegetables still have texture.

The sauce will be very moist, but will not have a great deal of liquid. It can be made hours beforehand and is best reheated for 1–2 minutes in a steamer.

TO MAKE THE FLAN   Roughly chop the tomatoes and place in a pan with the carrot, butter, tarragon, salt and sugar. Cover the pan and simmer gently until the carrot is quite soft. Remove the lid and cook over moderate heat until the mixture has reduced by one-third. It should not be cooked until all the moisture has evaporated. Press the contents through the medium disc of a Mouli. You should have 3 cups of purée.

Whisk the eggs and egg yolks well and combine with the tomato purée. Taste for seasoning. It should be delicately seasoned, and if the tarragon flavour is not definite add the extra tablespoon of leaves. You will have enough mixture for 6–8 portions. Butter 8 timbale moulds, or teacups if you have no special moulds. Fill with the flan mixture and place the timbales in a baking dish, resting on a folded wet cloth to stop them moving about. Half-fill the dish with boiling water. Cover the dish with aluminium foil.

Cook at 160°C in a non-fanforced oven for approximately 25 minutes. Press the centre of a mould with your fingertip. It should feel just firm. If the timbales are left to rest for 20–30 minutes, they will firm up a little more before the unmoulding.

TO SERVE   Unmould the tomato flans onto hot plates and spoon the hot sauce over and around. Garnish with a few leaves of the herb used in the flan.

VARIATIONS: Use the sauce with fried eggs, grilled sausages, hamburgers or lamb cutlets, or serve it cold as part of a mixed hors-d'oeuvre with some sort of crisp toast to spread it on. It can also be tossed quickly through hot pasta.

✝ A 'flan' in French means a firm baked custard. It does not mean a pastry tart. (One of my favourite French snacks is simply called *flan*, a generous wedge of vanilla-flavoured custard with a crinkled, almost burnt, top skin. It does not usually have any pastry.) I have had great success with vegetable custards over the years. This tomato custard was followed by an asparagus custard, a leek custard, a mushroom custard, a green pea custard and a garlic and goat's cheese custard. Many of the recipes have reappeared in *The Cook's Companion*. The portions should be quite small as the eggs and cream result in a rich mixture.

Hare tourte, Sauce poivrade

sauce poivrade (see page 33)
500 g puff pastry (see page 38)
egg wash (1 egg with 1 pinch of salt)
cold unsalted butter
salt, pepper

FARCE

1 hare
125 g lean pork
150 g lean veal
100 g pork back fat
salt, pepper
60 g duck livers
60 g rabbit fillet
120 g duck breast or 60 g rabbit
    fillet and 60 g duck breast
1 tinned truffle
100 ml madeira
3 cloves garlic
100 ml cream

MARINADE 1

60 ml cognac
30 ml olive oil
freshly ground pepper

MARINADE 2

60 ml red-wine vinegar
60 ml olive oil
1 sprig of thyme, leaves stripped
1 bay leaf, roughly crumbled
1 pinch of salt

DAY 1: PREPARING THE FARCE AND THE SAUCE   Prepare marinade 1 and marinade 2 in separate bowls. Set aside.

Using a boning knife and a cleaver, separate the forelegs and hindlegs of the hare. Remove the kidneys and liver and any fat attached to the belly. With a flexible sharp knife, remove the silver-greyish membrane from the saddle (back) of the hare and from the hind legs. Remove the choice fillets from each side of the backbone. Weigh them. Cut one fillet into neat, narrow strips about 1 cm wide and 5 cm in length. Place 60 g of these strips to one side. Cut off the rest of the meat from the hind legs, scraping it free of all skin and tendon. You will need altogether 150 g of hare meat for the *farce* as well as the 60 g of hare fillet. Keep the two types of meat separate. All the remaining carcass and meat scraps will be used for the sauce. Break up the bones etc. into smaller pieces. Place them in a bowl and refrigerate.

Cut the pork, veal and pork fat into cubes and mix with the 150 g of hare meat. Sprinkle with salt and pepper, cover with plastic film and refrigerate overnight.

Check the duck livers to ensure that there are no green spots or bile ducts present. Even one speck of green will make the dish bitter. Gently hold the two lobes in one hand and pull away from the network of veins, trying to keep the livers as whole and shapely as possible. Place the livers in a small glass or stainless steel bowl with marinade 1. Leave refrigerated overnight.

Remove the membrane from the rabbit fillet and/or remove the skin from the duck breast. Cut the meat into narrow strips the same size as the hare strips. You should have 120 g of these strips. Combine with the hare strips and pour over marinade 2. Refrigerate overnight.

Prepare the sauce poivrade (page 33) and leave overnight.

Open the tin of truffle. Place the truffle and the liquid in a clean jar and pour the madeira over. Close the jar tightly and leave in the refrigerator overnight.

DAY 2: PREPARATION CONTINUED Peel the cloves of garlic, put in cold water and bring to the boil. Drain and repeat this procedure twice more, until the garlic is quite tender. Drain the strips of meat and reserve the marinade. Discard the pieces of bay leaf. Drain the duck livers and reserve the marinade. Tip both marinade liquids over the bowl of pork, veal, pork fat and hare cubes. Throw the cloves of garlic into the bowl. Roughly chop the truffle and pour on the truffle-flavoured madeira. Mix all this together roughly and then pass through a medium disc of a meat mincer. If you don't have a good mincer, use your food processor but process the meats in small batches as you are aiming at a chopped texture, not a purée. Place the mince in a large bowl and, with either your hands or a large wooden spoon, mix in the cream.

Fry a ball of this mixture lightly to test for salt and pepper. Adjust the seasoning. Cover the bowl of *farce* and chill until needed.

TO ASSEMBLE AND COOK THE DISH Using a round pie plate of about 24 cm diameter as a guide, cut 2 circles of pastry each 25 cm in diameter and 6 mm thick. Place 1 circle on a baking sheet and press it out a little with your fingers to slightly increase its diameter. Using a pastry roller or fork, prick it very thoroughly all over to prevent the surface rising too much. Brush lightly with egg wash all over, but do not let any wash trickle over the edges.

Place a third of the *farce* in the centre of the pastry circle, forming an inner circle and leaving a clear border of 4 cm. Arrange half the reserved strips of meat and several pieces of duck liver over the *farce* like spokes in a wheel. Cover with half the remaining *farce* and the rest of the strips and livers. Place the remaining *farce* and mould the filling a little like an upturned basin, although flattish rather than very domed in shape. Immediately place the second circle of dough over the *farce*, stretching it as necessary and pressing down on the unfilled border to make a good seal. Cut a small airhole in the dough to let the steam escape, then place the tourte in the refrigerator for the dough to firm up before you trim and decorate it.

After 30 minutes remove the tourte from the refrigerator and place an upturned basin (slightly smaller than the tourte) over it. Using a very sharp knife so as not to crush the pastry layers together, cut the edge into a scalloped design, separating the scallops with little nicks in the pastry every 4 cm. Remove the basin and brush generously with egg wash, tracing arcs on the top crust if you wish. These arcs may decide your portions or they may be purely decorative.

Set the oven to 220°C. Place the tourte in the middle of the oven for 20 minutes until it has puffed and is looking golden. Reduce the temperature to 200°C and continue to bake for a further 25 minutes. Check during this time, and if the pastry is browning too much, cover it with foil and reduce the temperature again to 180°C. Let it settle for at least 5 minutes after coming from the oven, then cut and serve.

As it looks most dramatic, it is perhaps worth baking the tourte on, say, an unglazed terracotta bread slide or something that can be brought to the table. You can then plunge in the knife in front of your lucky friends.

While the tourte is baking, remove any particles of fat from the sauce poivrade and bring it back to a rolling boil. Let it reduce by one-third. You should have between 350 and 500 ml of sauce. Whisk in a few pieces of cold unsalted butter and have a final taste for salt and pepper.

Ladle some of the sauce onto each plate before placing a wedge of tourte, and serve the remaining sauce in a heated sauce boat.

Glazed vegetables – basic recipe

INGREDIENTS PER PERSON

30 g butter
1 tablespoon sugar
1 witlof or 2 small peeled turnips or 2–3 peeled carrots or 1–2 whole onions
salt, pepper
light veal or chicken stock
1 thin slice frozen herb butter (optional)

OTHER GARNISH IDEAS

tiny croutons, fried crisp
smoked bacon, fried crisp
freshly chopped herbs
toasted slivered almonds

Select an appropriately sized, heavy-based pan. Put in the butter to melt, add the sugar and let it dissolve. Cook this syrup until pale gold in colour and then add the peeled and trimmed vegetables. Roll them to coat well with the glaze. Season lightly.

The skill in cooking vegetables by this technique is to judge correctly the amount of liquid needed to just cook them, and to evaporate to a glowing glaze precisely at the time the vegetables are ready. Vegetables have different cooking times, so check after 10 minutes. Add hot stock to come halfway up the vegetables. (If you have no stock, water can be used. The butter, sugar and natural flavour of the vegetables will still create a delicious glaze, possibly with less colour.) Cover the pan and shake it gently after a few minutes. After 10 minutes remove the cover and start to increase the heat as the vegetables become nearly cooked. Shake gently more often to even the glaze. As the last few spoonfuls of stock evaporate, throw in the slice of herb butter and any other garnish, and serve.

Coeur à la crème

3 plain junket tablets
1 litre milk
400 ml pure cream at 45 per cent milk fat
fresh berries
thick cream
castor sugar

butter muslin
6 porcelain heart moulds

To make this lovely sweet, it is necessary to first make the fresh cheese. Crush the junket tablets very well with a spoonful of water. Stir the milk and cream together very thoroughly. Heat the milk and cream in a scrupulously clean pan to 30°C. The temperature is most important and must be measured with a thermometer. As soon as the temperature is reached, pull the pan off the heat, stir in the crushed junket tablets and let stand at room temperature for 3 hours.

Line a large, fine strainer with a very large, doubled piece of butter muslin. Suspend the strainer over a clean bucket or bowl and strain the cheese. Tie the ends of the muslin to form a large bag and hang it from a hook in the refrigerator to drip into the bucket overnight.

Next day, tip and scrape the cheese from the muslin into a basin. Whisk well, and if there is a great difference in the texture of the cheese from the middle of the bag and the cheese that was pressed against the muslin, process briefly in a food processor to even up the texture. This is sure to be the case if you have doubled the quantities in the recipe, as the ball of cheese will be much larger.

Next, prepare the heart moulds. Cut squares of muslin, wring them out in water and line the moulds. Spoon in the cheese, filling the moulds well as they will settle a little when more whey drains from the cheese. Fold over the dangling ends of muslin and stand the moulds on a tray with a rim. Refrigerate for up to 12 hours before serving. If you do not wish to serve the cheese within this time, leave it, covered, in the basin and delay the moulding process. Otherwise too much whey will drain from the cheese and it can be dry.

Unmould the *coeurs* and serve in a straw basket lined with strawberry leaves, with a pile of berries, thick pure cream and castor sugar.

Cervelle de canut (speciality of Lyon)

400 g fresh cheese (see page 193)
100 ml fresh cream
1 tablespoon red-wine vinegar
2 tablespoons walnut oil (optional)
1 tablespoon chopped parsley
1 tablespoon chervil
1 teaspoon chopped chives
1 teaspoon very finely chopped shallot
salt, pepper

Combine all the ingredients except the salt and pepper in a bowl or food processor and season to taste. A little garlic could be added if you like. Serve with a basket of crunchy toast.

Crowd pleasers

MENU

CHEESE SOUFFLÉ IN A CHOU PUFF,
ONION SAUCE

MARINATED ROAST PORTERHOUSE,
SOUR BREAD SAUCE
MUSHROOMS IN VINE LEAVES

A TRIO OF CHOCOLATE DELIGHTS . . .
MOCHA CREAM, CHOCOLATE CREAM LOG AND
CHOCOLATE SORBET

This menu links three dishes that are traditional in
their appeal – a savoury soufflé, a roast of beef and
a dessert of chocolate. Each dish has been given increased
élan by preparing it in an unexpected manner. The cheese
soufflé comes to the table wobbling inside a delicate chou
puff.[+] The prime piece of porterhouse has been briefly
marinated as for the German *sauerbraten* and the marinade is used to create the 'sour' in the wonderful sauce.
For the dessert, a trio of chocolate tastes and textures are
served together to delight the most ardent chocolate
lover. There is a super-dense chocolate 'cake', which isn't
really a cake and isn't really a custard, a luscious mocha
cream in its porcelain pot, and a smooth, slippery chocolate sorbet.

Chou pastry is a versatile and easy dough to master, and the food processor has made it much easier to incorporate the eggs properly. The Burgundy region of France produces *la gougère*, a cheese chou pastry crown that splendidly accompanies the famous cheeses and wines of the area. There is no reason why this cheese version of chou paste cannot be used to create dishes other than the traditional loaf. Small spoonfuls baked quickly are perfect appetisers served well puffed and straight from the oven. Larger puffs can be split and filled with a savoury filling, such as a ragoût of mushrooms or just-cooked asparagus. The basic dough can have some crisply fried smoked bacon added to it as well as the miniature cubes of Gruyère cheese. It is important to buy good Gruyère cheese, as it alone has the pungent and nutty flavour. Locally produced Gruyère-type cheeses melt to a rubbery consistency and do not give the correct taste.✦

Soubise refers to onions. There are many possible ways of making a *sauce soubise*. Often such sauces are thickened with rice. The sauce for this soufflé is made with the onions melted very slowly in some butter until quite soft. The mixture is then puréed and lightened with a little stock. If the dish is intended for non-meat eaters who do not under any circumstances eat stocks made from bones, lighten the purée with some hot milk and perhaps a tablespoon of cream. The same sauce could be made with leeks or bulb fennel.

The idea for the sauce to accompany the beef came from my enjoyment of Madeleine Kamman's book *When French Women Cook*. I love her recipe for bread soup, and it recalled a similar but forgotten German peasant dish of sausage and lentils, where pieces of dark bread were dropped into the soup tureen to add nourishment and thickening. Another echo was my mother's preferred garnish for her *sauerbraten*. She crumbled black bread and raisins and scattered them around the braised meat shortly before dishing it up. All of these threads came together as I decided to make a smooth, deep-tasting sour sauce that would complement the tangy quality imparted to the meat by the marinade. The marinade I used was quite high in its proportion of best-quality vinegar to other ingredients, but the meat rested in its bath only overnight. It was just the flavour I was after, not wishing to 'cook' the porterhouse, and nor did it need the tenderising effect of a long marinade as would, say, a piece of venison.

✢ I would not contemplate making a soufflé inside a chou puff today – I can hardly credit that I did it in 1984. I could have removed this recipe from the book but decided to leave it to make the point that amongst all the creative energy and rethinking that characterised cooking in the mid-1980s, there were a few silly moments!

✦ The outstanding exception is Frank Marchand's memorable Heidi Farm cheeses, both his Gruyère and Emmenthal. Lactos in Tasmania now owns Heidi Farm Cheese but Frank is still there making the cheese and passing on his skills. His Matured Gruyère has twice won Best Specialist Cheese in the annual Specialist Cheese Awards, held in Sydney each year since 1995.

The first autumn nights are always a surprise. Dark so early and suddenly so crisply cold. The vine leaves also start to crisp and fall and I rush to use the last of them. This wonderful dish of mushrooms in vine leaves was inspired by a recipe of Elizabeth David's in her book *Italian Food*. I like to serve it in individual brown earthenware dishes, lifting the lid only at the table as the aroma is magnificent. It is a dish that is good with tinned, rinsed vine leaves, cultivated mushrooms and a light blended oil, but it is sublime when made with black field mushrooms, your own gathered vine leaves and a full, fruity olive oil. The mushrooms shrink alarmingly in the pots, so pack them really hard and have bread available and soup spoons to enjoy the plentiful black juices.[✢]

Resist any temptation to serve noodles, potatoes or dumplings with the main course. The meat and sauce are intense flavours, as is the crockful of mushrooms. Most importantly, one wants the guests to lust for their chocolate dessert and certainly not feel that they are unable to do justice to it.

Serve the chocolate log in a thin slice cut with a knife dipped in hot water. I would probably offer a bowl of whipped cream. For the mocha cream I would choose small mousse pots; the quantities given will fill 8 × 100 ml pots. The sorbet is refreshing and cleansing, and the three desserts are an excellent combination. The sorbet should be churned not more than several hours before the dinner, as it can get quite hard. All sorbets when served should permit the spoon to slide easily through them.

A suggestion of melted liquid around the scoop of sorbet on one's plate is, to me, more than acceptable – it is desirable. One has the certainty that this icy delight is just at the right consistency to enjoy. If your spoon bounces off the sorbet or fruit ice it will never yield the same pleasure.

Any one of the three desserts could be served singly in slightly larger portions.

[✢] Field mushrooms are rarely seen in cities any more. I hope this is not the case in the country. Given this fact, large, fully opened cultivated mushrooms (sold as 'flats') or, even better, the variety sold as Swiss Browns or portobello mushrooms, give the best flavour.

SPECIAL NOTE: It may seem that with this menu I have proposed an impossible combination of dishes to be cooked in one oven. Organisation is all-important, but there is really no cause for alarm. This is how I would do it.

The day before I would:
1. Make the chocolate log.
2. Make the mocha cream.
3. Make the sorbet mixture, but leave it liquid.
4. Make the chou puffs.
5. Put the beef in the marinade.

In the morning I would:
1. Drain the beef.
2. Make the beef sauce.
3. Assemble the mushroom pots.
4. Make the onion sauce for the soufflé *en croûte*.
5. Make the soufflé sauce base.
6. Split the chou puffs.

Early afternoon I would:
1. Churn the sorbet.
2. Set the table, arrange the flowers.
3. Whip cream, set up coffee apparatus etc.

Evening of the party:
7.30 p.m.   Set the oven to 220°C.
7.45 p.m.   Seal the beef and put into the oven – middle shelf.
            Mushroom pots in – bottom shelf.
8.00 p.m.   Set up a bain-marie for my three sauces (soufflé base, onion sauce, beef sauce) – a deep baking dish half-full of boiling water over a low flame. Sauces placed hot into jugs will stay hot for hours.
8.25 p.m.   Beef out.
            Reduce the oven temperature to 200°C.
            Wrap the beef.
8.40 p.m.   Finish the soufflés and into the oven.
9.00 p.m.   Serve the soufflés.
            Plates in to heat for the beef.
9.30 p.m.   Serve beef and mushrooms.

Chou pastry

250 ml water
100 g butter
pinch of salt
140 g plain flour, sifted
4 eggs

Place the water, butter and salt in a pan and slowly bring to the boil so that the butter has melted by the time the water is boiling. Take the pan from the heat and tip in all the flour, mixing vigorously with a wooden spoon to fully blend it in. Return the pan to the heat and continue mixing until the mixture is smooth and does not stick to the sides of the pan.

Cool until you can comfortably rest your hand on the mixture for a few seconds before adding the eggs. Either beat in the eggs by hand one at a time, ensuring that each egg is thoroughly incorporated before adding the next one, or, using a food processor or the heavy beater attached to your electric mixer, add the eggs one at a time.

Pipe puffs in whatever size you wish on a lightly greased baking sheet. Smooth the tops with the back of a teaspoon moistened with water if your piping isn't perfect. Allow plenty of room between puffs.[+]

Bake at 220°C for 15 minutes and then reduce the heat to 200°C for a further 5–10 minutes until crisp and dry. Unless you have a forced-air oven, you will need to move the trays around halfway through the cooking time.[*]

Extra puffs can be frozen when cool. Return them to a hot oven for 1–2 minutes after thawing to recrisp them, then fill and serve.

CHEESE CHOU PASTRY: Fold in ½ a cup of really tiny cubes of top-quality Gruyère (or Swiss Emmenthal) cheese after the eggs. Pipe to whatever size you wish.

[+] Once you are comfortable making chou pastry it is one of the very best treats to offer with a drink. Freeze the piped dough and, when really firm, transfer the balls to a plastic container, seal with a lid and leave the container in the freezer. Thirty minutes before your guests arrive, set out the required number of balls on an oven tray lined with baking paper, brush the tops with a little beaten egg, press on a scattering of grated Gruyère and bake at 180°C for about 30 minutes until golden and crisp.
[*] After making chou pastry dozens of times I have decided that the results are better when small puffs are cooked at 180°C for 30–40 minutes until crisp and golden.

Cheese soufflé in a chou puff, Onion sauce

1 quantity chou pastry (see page 199)

CHEESE SOUFFLÉ

butter
25 g Parmesan from a quality cheese supplier, finely grated
4½ tablespoons sifted plain flour
375 ml hot milk
salt, pepper
6 eggs, separated
2 egg whites
100 g grated Gruyère or Swiss Emmenthal cheese

ONION SAUCE

4 large onions
60 g butter
100 ml hot, well-reduced stock, preferably chicken or veal
salt, pepper
1 tablespoon cream
1 teaspoon finely snipped chives

TO START THE SOUFFLÉ Assemble all the ingredients and preheat the oven to 200°C. If you are making this soufflé in a classic soufflé dish or dishes, rub the inside of the dishes with butter and sprinkle with some of the finely grated Parmesan. There is no need to tie on elaborate paper collars. Your soufflé will rise without them, and it only delays the serving when you are wrestling with removing string and paper.

Melt 60 g of butter in a pan, stir in the flour with a wooden spoon and cook over a moderate heat for 2 minutes without allowing the roux to colour. Remove the pan from the heat and gradually whisk in the hot milk. Whisk well and return to the heat, whisking until the sauce boils. Add salt and pepper. Whisk in the egg yolks one at a time. This is the basic 'sauce'. This far can be prepared hours ahead of time. Skim the surface with a piece of butter to prevent a skin forming, press on a piece of plastic film and leave until needed.

TO MAKE THE ONION SAUCE   Slice the onions into rings. Melt the butter in a wide sauté pan and add the onion. Place the sauté pan over a simmer mat to prevent the onion catching in the centre, cover and cook very slowly for about 20 minutes until the onion is golden and quite soft. Stir once or twice during the cooking process. Purée in a blender and add the stock. Taste for seasoning, but keep the sauce delicate. Do not add salt and pepper until after the stock. The sauce should have the consistency of cream. Stir in the cream and chives and keep hot in a bain-marie while the cheese soufflés *en croûte* are cooking.

TO CONTINUE THE SOUFFLÉ   The basic soufflé should be warm when the cheese and egg whites are added, so either reheat gently, stirring well, over a very low flame, or else place the bowl of sauce in a steamer for a few minutes. If making the soufflé within an hour, keep the base warm by placing it in a basin in a pan half-full of warm water – the classic bain-marie.

Whisk the 8 egg whites until they are satiny and very firm, but not rocky. Stir a spoonful of egg white into the warm soufflé base to lighten it and make it easier to fold in the rest. Tip the rest of the beaten egg white onto the sauce and sprinkle over the grated cheese. Fold in rapidly with deep, sweeping strokes. I prefer a large metal spoon for folding and find myself always rotating the bowl as I fold.

TO BAKE IN CHOU PUFFS[+]   Pipe or spoon chou puffs into rounds of 6 cm diameter. Keep the puffs as round and as high as you can to allow maximum space for the soufflé mixture.

Split the chou puffs about two-thirds from the bottom. Settle the hollow bases on a preheated oven slide. Spoon in the soufflé mix, keeping it as high as possible. Quickly transfer the filled bases to the 200°C oven and cook for approximately 12 minutes.

Transfer the cooked soufflés to a hot serving plate, spoon a little onion sauce around and serve at once.

TO BAKE IN A TRADITIONAL SOUFFLÉ DISH   Spoon the soufflé mixture into its prepared dish or dishes. Run your thumb firmly around the edge of the soufflé dish, creating a flat rim about 5 mm in width.

Place the soufflé in the oven and immediately lower the heat to 180°C. In my

---

[+] I recommend that cooks ignore the instruction to cook the soufflés in a chou case. Instead, serve the cheesy puffs with a pre-dinner drink and proceed to the classic cheese soufflé in its traditional straight-sided dish. A soufflé baked in the traditional way will have a creamy middle with a well-cooked outside section. Each person can then enjoy the contrast. And there would really be no need to make the onion sauce!

oven this soufflé baked in one dish takes 35 minutes to cook. Individual ones cook in about 20–25 minutes. Check at the end of these cooking times. The soufflé should be well risen and golden brown on the top. If not, let it cook for a further 5 minutes before checking again.

Sauce Variations: Substitute well-washed leeks for the onions or use a mixture of onion and leek; or substitute sliced fennel for the onions or use a mixture of onion and fennel; or dilute the purée with hot milk instead of stock for a Lenten meal or for non-meat eaters.

Marinated roast porterhouse, Sour bread sauce

2 kg piece of aged porterhouse
olive oil

MARINADE

350 ml cider vinegar or white-wine vinegar
100 ml red wine
250 ml water
1 tablespoon whole peppercorns
2 tablespoons sugar
2 onions, sliced
1 carrot, sliced
2 bay leaves
12 whole cloves
1 teaspoon yellow mustard seeds
2 teaspoons salt

SOUR BREAD SAUCE

reserved marinade (see above)
1 litre well-reduced veal stock or demi-glace (see page 241)
100 g sour black rye bread
1 cup hot milk
salt, pepper

TO MARINATE THE BEEF AND MAKE THE SAUCE   Tie the porterhouse firmly into a good shape and place in a glass, stainless steel or pottery dish. Combine all the marinade ingredients in a pan, simmer together for 10 minutes and cool. Pour the cooled marinade over the meat and leave for 10–12 hours. If you are not cooking the beef at this stage, remove it anyway and let it drain on a rack in the refrigerator. It should not stay in the marinade for longer than this time. Proceed with the sauce.

Strain the marinade, pressing hard on all the solids to extract the maximum liquid. Combine the liquid in a pan with the reduced stock and simmer together, skimming off any scum that rises. Let simmer together for 30 minutes. Slice the bread into small cubes and pour over the boiling milk. Allow to soak for 30 minutes. Blend this bread paste to a smooth purée. Add the bread purée to the sauce and once again bring to the boil. Taste for seasoning. It should be smooth in texture with a deep, mellow flavour. Strain once more and reheat at serving time. Adjust the flavour, if necessary, with a few drops of vinegar or a spoonful of meat glaze if you have any. I once made this sauce using the ruby pickling vinegar left after I had finished some spiced cherries. It was different and delicious.

TO COOK THE BEEF   Pat the meat dry with kitchen paper. In a baking dish heat a film of oil to smoking. Seal the meat really well on all sides and then pour off any liquid that has oozed into the pan. Transfer the meat in the drained pan to a preheated oven at 220°C. Cook for 25 minutes and then test to see if the meat is ready. To test the meat, plunge a metal skewer into the centre of the beef, wait 1 minute and then touch the skewer to your top lip. If the skewer feels faintly warm, the meat is rare. If it is cold, continue to cook and test again after 5 minutes. If the skewer feels quite warm, the meat is medium. (If you prefer, test the beef with a meat thermometer. It should register 60°C in the thickest part of the joint.) Reduce the oven to 200°C. Do not cook the beef more than medium, as it will rest wrapped in aluminium foil while you are folding and spooning your little soufflés, readying them for their quick cooking.

Remove the beef, wrap in a generous double fold of foil, and place in a warm place. It will happily hold its heat for at least 30 minutes.

Mushrooms in vine leaves

3 vine leaves
3 large field mushrooms or *an equivalent quantity of other mushrooms*
2 tablespoons virgin olive oil
1 clove garlic
pepper, salt
small pottery pot with lid

Wash and dry the vine leaves. Wash and peel the mushrooms or, if you have to use cultivated mushrooms, just wipe them. Halve them if really huge. (Near where I live we can find wonderful bright orange pine forest mushrooms, which are great added to this dish. They are usually very dirty and come with bits of grass and twig still attached. They need to be wiped with a damp cloth and brushed with a soft brush to loosen all the extra bits of vegetation.[+])

Cut off the stalks of the mushrooms, discard the sandy end bits and slice the rest of the stems. Then pour most of the oil into the small pot. Line the pot with half the vine leaves. Pack in the mushrooms, interspersed with slivers of garlic and chopped mushroom stems. Grind over some pepper and a little salt and cover the mushrooms with the rest of the vine leaves. Trickle over the last of the oil.

Put the lid on the pot and let it cook on the bottom shelf of the oven for at least 45 minutes. For the last 10 minutes you can remove the lids to let the leaves crisp a little, but it is more dramatic to serve the pot closed up so as to trap all the aroma.

If I were serving these mushrooms as an entrée or on their own I would cook them for 1 hour at 180°C, but in this case the oven is a little hotter to cook the beef and the soufflés, hence the shorter cooking time.

[+] The habitat for pine forest mushrooms (*Suillus granulatus*) is not restricted to pine plantations. They can be gathered in open bushland in the autumn and have become the most commonly accepted wild mushroom. They are very firm-textured and, although a few slices could be added to this dish, I think they are too dense to be the only variety. I like them best sliced and sautéed in oil with garlic and parsley, with a small amount of cream added for the last quick toss.

A trio of chocolate delights . . . mocha cream, chocolate cream log and chocolate sorbet

～

Mocha cream

1 teaspoon instant coffee powder
30 g coffee beans, freshly ground
500 ml milk
1 split vanilla bean
100 g best-quality dark chocolate
100 g castor sugar
2 tablespoons cold water
3 tablespoons boiling water
2 egg yolks
2 eggs

muslin
porcelain mousse pots

Put the instant coffee, ground coffee, milk and vanilla bean into a non-stick pan and slowly bring to simmering point, stirring frequently. Simmer for 10 minutes very slowly. Strain through a double piece of muslin to extract all the coffee grains. Return the coffee-milk to a clean pan with the chocolate and heat until the chocolate has completely melted and the mixture is quite smooth. Strain again through a fine strainer.

Dissolve the sugar in the cold water and cook until it is a deep-golden caramel. Taking care to stand well back, pour the boiling water onto the caramel and allow to dissolve into a smooth caramel syrup. Pour the caramel syrup into the chocolate/coffee-milk and stir. Set aside until the mixture has cooled a little.

Whisk the egg yolks and eggs and pour onto the chocolate mixture. Strain again. Pour the mixture into individual pots and place them on a wet, folded cloth in the bottom of a baking dish. Fill the dish up to the halfway mark with boiling water and bake at 150°C for 40–50 minutes or until the centre feels just firm when touched with your fingertip. Chill before serving in the pots.

Chocolate cream log

250 g best-quality dark chocolate
250 g unsalted butter
250 g castor sugar
1 tablespoon plain flour
5 eggs

In a double boiler, melt the chocolate with the butter. Stir and strain to ensure that there are no lumps. Add the sugar and stir to mix. Whisk the flour and eggs together and add to the chocolate mixture. Mix lightly to combine.

Brush a cast-iron terrine pan (1 litre capacity) with tasteless oil (sweet almond oil is the best for this and is available at chemists) and line with a long, folded strip of aluminium foil. Have the foil strip long enough so that the ends extend at least 5 cm over the ends to assist in unmoulding of the cake. Pour the mixture in, cover and stand the terrine in a deep baking dish. Fill the dish up to the halfway mark with boiling water and bake at 180°C for 1¼–1½ hours until it has formed a crust and feels firm in the centre. It will firm up more as it cools. Leave to get completely cold, preferably overnight, before unmoulding.

Run a knife dipped in hot water around the edge of the terrine. Loosen the log by wiggling the protruding foil ends, then invert onto a flat platter. Wrap the terrine pan in a hot cloth if the log is reluctant to move.

As I have mentioned in the introduction, this is extremely rich, so serve small slices. You will have leftovers.

Chocolate sorbet

250 g castor sugar
60 g Dutch cocoa powder
1 tablespoon instant coffee powder
pinch of powdered cinnamon
750 ml water

Mix all the dry ingredients in a bowl. Gradually mix to a smooth paste with some of the water. Add the balance of the water and bring the mixture to boiling point, stirring until all the sugar is dissolved. Simmer for 5 minutes and then strain into a jug to cool. Churn when required.

Fudgy chocolate mousse

This seems an appropriate place to include my favourite recipe for chocolate mousse. Once mandatory on any restaurant menu, it was then shunned for years. It is about to be rediscovered, I suspect, as the very considerable number of chocolate lovers refuse to allow such a lush and easy dessert to be ignored.

200 g best-quality dark chocolate
4 eggs, separated
100 g soft unsalted butter
2 teaspoons castor sugar

Melt the chocolate gently in a double boiler or in a basin set over a pan of simmering water. When the chocolate has melted, remove the basin or the top of the double boiler and beat in the egg yolks one at a time. Add the soft butter, beating well until the mix is glossy and quite smooth.

Whip the egg whites to soft peaks. Sprinkle over the sugar and continue to whip until you have a firm snow. Tip the whites onto the chocolate. Mix thoroughly and quickly. Do not be afraid – it takes a few minutes to ensure a perfect blend.

Chill the mousse but allow to return to room temperature before serving. The consistency of this mousse is such that you can shape small servings with 2 spoons dipped in warm water and offer a little mousse with a little sorbet (see page 206) and chocolate log (page 206; or any other chocolate cake) as an alternative to the mocha cream (page 205).

It is of course perfectly possible to serve the mousse on its own. It is very rich, so small helpings only. It will keep, covered, in the refrigerator for several days without any change of flavour or texture.[+]

[+] On its own, a scoop of chocolate mousse thickly dusted with best cocoa and surrounded by a coffee custard or a raspberry sauce with a slice or two of almond bread is a very simple and delicious extravagance.

In praise of tarragon

MENU

GRILLED SCALLOPS WITH SAFFRON NOODLES
AND SAUCE BEURRE BLANC

ROAST POUSSIN WITH TARRAGON,
CHINESE BROCCOLI

CHOCOLATE-DIPPED PRUNES IN
BRANDY CREAM SAUCE

As the beginning of this meal I have chosen grilled scallops with Pernod and saffron pasta and a *beurre blanc* sauce. This recipe is one that I demonstrated on morning television in 1984 and I had a great response to it. Part of its appeal, I feel sure, was that the microphone was dangled low over the grilling plate and every hiss, sputter and crackle of the scallops was communicated loud and clear.

The Victorian and Tasmanian scallop industry has progressed apace over the last few years, and many cooks are now quite familiar with these decorative molluscs.[+] We are fortunate in that our scallops are always sold with roe intact, which is not the case in the USA. The roe of the scallop changes in colour and size as the reproductive cycle progresses.[+]

A great advance has been that good suppliers now sell 'dry' scallops, that is, shellfish direct from the markets, unwashed. There is a fairly widespread and quite nefarious practice of washing scallops and leaving them to soak in cold water. Not only do the scallops present as pearly-white rather than creamy, they also have no odour as opposed to the distinctive fishy smell of a fresh scallop, and they are plastic and damp to touch instead of firm and sticky. They also gain weight in their water bath so that there is a greater return for the retailer, who is selling you quite a bit of water with your kilo of scallops. These cosmetically treated scallops do not handle as 'proper' scallops should. Sauté them, and they eject a milky fluid in the pan and shrink into tough little balls. Attempt a mousse, and your proportion of egg white and cream must be altered as the extra liquid released will result in a watery product. So point number one when considering this dish is to buy unwashed scallops.✤

Reverting briefly to one of my much-repeated statements that a simple dish often needs care in the execution, scallops must be cleaned. Some time ago I ordered a scallop salad in one of our best-known hotel dining rooms. The dish was presented to me with each scallop nestling in a green leaf and each black intestinal thread intact and staring at me! The second point about a scallop dish, then, is to slice off the dark thread on each scallop and nick off any wispy fibrous beard attached to the roe.

Everybody loves pasta. The current interest in home pasta-making has included many variations on the basic theme. I find that often the additions result in pretty colours but not much change of flavour. Tomato pasta is a pretty orangey-pink but doesn't really taste like tomatoes; spinach pasta can be bright green and have absorbed quite surprising amounts of puréed spinach, and yet still doesn't taste like

✢ When I originally wrote this, the scallop industry was just recovering from shameful dredging of the seabed and overfishing. Nowadays the majority of scallops in the market come from net-fishing in Queensland and Western Australia. A positive initiative has been the development of scallop farms, principally in Tasmania. Phillip Lamb of Spring Bay Seafoods sees the future as very positive for the company. They have previously relied mainly on wild spat collection methods but have recently been sourcing juvenile scallops from a local hatchery. They supply two markets – live and half-shell. Scallops sold on the half-shell provide the perfect container for scallops and sauce. Up until now most of these have been collected by divers in remote locations such as South Australia's Eyre Peninsula, but there are tentative plans for other locations at the time of writing. In 1984, if you wanted to serve scallops in the shell, you had to buy the shells separately.

✦ Scallops intended for export, especially the saucer scallops caught in Western Australia, Queensland and the Northern Territory, always have the roe discarded.

✤ It can still happen that you are offered soaked scallops as described here, but it is less likely. And hopefully the scallop-loving consumer is now more aware and chooses more carefully.

spinach. Beetroot purée results in shocking-pink pasta, enabling a sort of Zandra Rhodes or Jenny Kee effect on the plate if combined with other vividly coloured noodles, but it doesn't taste like beetroot. This recipe does manage to capture the musky flavour of the saffron and the aniseed of the Pernod.

I also find that the orange pasta I have used in the offal salad described in the section on *salades composées* (page 233) is another winner. The tang of the zest is very apparent in the final noodle.

So, to the main course. I love chicken and would like to see it reinstated as special food rather than continue to be regarded as a quick takeaway.[+] I remember the large roasted fowl we used to enjoy for Sunday lunch when I was young. There was always plenty for the six of us, its breast yielding seemingly endless slices. And I would like to briefly toast the perfection of the combination of French tarragon (*Artemisia dracunculus*) and chicken.

A couple of years ago the public was still unsure about what was 'real' tarragon and what was Russian. They look very different. French tarragon is a lower and more spreading plant with a much finer and softer leaf. Russian tarragon grows quite tall and is more woody, and its leaves are quite tough. However, if faced with two tiny plants in pots, the best criterion is taste. French tarragon tastes delicately of aniseed; Russian tarragon tastes rank and like grass. There can be no mistake. I then hasten to note that I have noticed considerable variation in intensity between plants of French tarragon grown in different locations, but the aniseed taste must be there. It is not nearly as likely to happen now as then that one is sold as the other.[+]

Tarragon is one of the classic herbs in the French *fines herbes* – the others are parsley, chervil and, sometimes, chives. A *fines herbes* omelette, properly runny and skimmed with a point of butter, is a delectable supper dish when the cupboard is otherwise bare. If you have a healthy tarragon plant in the garden, divide

[+] I did my best to convince the specialist poultry farmers that their best chance for market success was to differentiate their product with visible labelling and packaging and to make very proud claims for it, just as I had seen over and over again in French markets where the *poulet de Bresse* or the *poulet fermier* was highly priced and highly valued by knowing consumers. Nearly two decades later, there has been a marked improvement in the availability of these superior birds as the demand has increased.

[+] You should also be wary of buying Mexican tarragon (*Tagetes lucida*). It has a common name of sweet Mexican marigold and its tiny yellow flower does vaguely remind you of a marigold. It is strongly flavoured and frankly nasty, and is sometimes supplied to restaurants during the winter months. Here we have an excellent example of the problems that can arise as a result of expecting everything to be available all the time. True French tarragon dies down in the autumn and shoots again in the springtime. You should not expect to see or use tarragon in the intervening months. Because so many culinary herbs are grown in hothouses, supply is maintained artificially and this has created an unreal expectation from chefs who ought to know better.

it in autumn before it vanishes completely, as sometimes it mysteriously doesn't reappear in the springtime. A rooted division of tarragon in a small pot is one of the nicest presents anyone can give a friend moving into a new house.

Chinese broccoli has been suggested to accompany the chicken. It is such an elegant vegetable. Trimmed of excess leaves but with one or two left to frame the delicate head, the stem peeled and the whole washed and quickly steamed and buttered, it is delicious. A friend in Hong Kong sent me two publications by Martha Dahlen and Karen Phillips, *A Guide to Chinese Market Vegetables* and *A Further Guide to Chinese Market Vegetables*. In the first publication, Chinese broccoli is illustrated and called Chinese kale or *gaai laan*. The authors comment that it has a stout stem like a small broccoli stalk and suggest that in western cookery it should be treated like broccoli, but that the Chinese more commonly stir-fry it, either alone or with shredded pork. Both publications feature exquisite paintings of these fascinating and usually exotic vegetables. Not only are the pictures superb for accurate identification, but they go much further than a formally accurate botanical drawing and communicate a truly sensual response to each vegetable. Snake beans sinuously slide across the page, the lotus root is drawn whole and sliced into cross-section to display its improbable design, and the various sorts of Chinese spinach look slithery, wet and bright, bright green.✢

Now that we have seven-day Asian markets, such books take on new relevance. They not only identify but suggest suitable cooking methods and flavour combinations, both western and Asian.

In my generation, some childhood complaints brought forth the automatic remedy of castor oil. I still become very angry at the Anglo-Saxon notion of forcing one to eat abominably prepared concoctions because they are supposedly 'good for you'. Some delicious foods were frequently ruined in this manner. Prunes, for example. To a European, prunes are rightfully seen as a lush dessert fruit, something to be glorified in a tart with Armagnac, for example. Put prunes on the menu in Australia and you are sure to get sniggers and 'nudge, nudge' jokes. So I do it often, to show that soaked, marinated prunes are sensual and velvety, and if soaked in wine and cognac they are very heady indeed. These chocolate-dipped prunes are delicious. The wine and cognac could be replaced by strong, strained tea and liqueur muscat or tokay. Similarly dipped plump dried figs make good petits fours – especially if halved to display the decorative seeds.

An alternative way of serving prunes is to ignore the chocolate and just serve them after a week in their alcoholic bath with a little of the liquid and perhaps a

✢ These little paperbacks are out of print, although I believe they were reissued as hardbacks, which I do not own. Nowadays I look for reliable information either in *Oriental Vegetables* by Joy Larkcom or the *Encyclopedia of Asian Ingredients* by Charmaine Solomon.

few shreds of blanched orange zest, or some roasted almonds or pine nuts.

The Troisgros brothers, in their book *Cuisiniers at Roanne*, have another excellent recipe where the prunes are soaked in raspberry juice as well as red wine and are left for two weeks. After all the prunes have gone, any remaining liqueur is a rich haul. It can be beaten into a vanilla ice-cream mixture or a crème anglaise or a soufflé base, drunk in tiny glasses with coffee, drizzled over a poached pear or quince, and so on.

Such delicious juices and drops come from a good kitchen!

Grilled scallops with saffron noodles and sauce beurre blanc

1 kg dry scallops
pepper, salt
olive oil

SAFFRON NOODLES

2 envelopes pure powdered saffron
1 pinch saffron stamens
60 ml Pernod
300 g plain flour
2 teaspoons salt
1 tablespoon finely chopped parsley
2 teaspoons olive oil
3 eggs
extra flour for dusting the pasta

BEURRE BLANC SAUCE

½ mild onion or 3 shallots, very finely chopped
white pepper
1 glass dry white wine
1 tablespoon cream
250 g cold unsalted butter, cut into 6 pieces
salt (optional)

1 pasta machine

Grilled scallops with saffron noodles and caramelised carrot (page 212)

Coulibiac – poached salmon wrapped in dill crêpes and then in brioche –
with melted butter sauce (page 223)

1 large stockpot with salted boiling water and 1 tablespoon oil
1 colander ready in the sink to strain the noodles
1 tray
1 small enamelled saucepan
1 whisk
1 solid hotplate or *heavy cast-iron frying pan*
1 steamer or *small colander that fits into a tall saucepan of*
boiling water, to reheat the noodles
tongs
1 folded clean cloth on a warm plate

TO PREPARE THE SCALLOPS   Slice off the dark thread of each scallop and snip off any wispy fibrous beard attached to the meat. When all the scallops have been cleaned, place them in a large strainer, flush quickly with cold water and shake and tap the strainer to drain quickly. Tip onto lots of kitchen paper and pat dry. Transfer to a large bowl, grind over a little pepper and a shake of salt and about 1 tablespoon of olive oil. Mix thoroughly, cover and refrigerate until needed.

TO MAKE THE NOODLES   When making pasta, remember that egg sizes vary and some flours are more absorbent than others, so you need to be sensitive to the texture.

Sprinkle the powdered saffron and saffron stamens over the Pernod in a small bowl. Leave to soak for 5 minutes. Then place the flour, salt, parsley, oil and soaked saffron and Pernod into the bowl of a food processor. Break the eggs into a bowl, keeping 1 egg white separate. With the motor running, feed in the rest of the eggs. Operate the machine with the pulse button for a few seconds until the dough gathers together. Stop the machine and feel the dough. If it is still like crumbs, you can add the reserved egg white and process again until well combined. If the dough feels springy and is clinging together, there is no need for the last egg white. Tip the dough mix onto plastic film. Knead into a roll and wrap up. Leave to rest for 1 hour in the refrigerator.

Set up the pasta machine and divide the dough into 2 or 3 pieces. Have ready a pot of salted water with a little olive oil in it at a good rolling boil. If the first roll of the dough through the widest setting of the rollers is a little raggy, fold the strip in 3, turn it 90 degrees and reroll on the same notch. If the dough ever feels really sticky, smooth both sides of the piece with a little flour. Continue rolling until all the dough has been rolled to the thinnest setting. Drape each strip over the back of a chair.

Set the machine to its cutting rollers. Dust each strip with flour before cutting. Cut the strips of dough into 2 if they are more than 20 cm long, as longer strips are more difficult to pick up and divide neatly into portions when serving. When all the dough has been cut, drop the strips into the boiling water, stir once and leave to come to the boil again. This will take only 1–2 minutes. Boil for 2 minutes only and immediately tip the contents of the pot into the colander already in position in the sink. Run cold water to stop the cooking. Lift and agitate the noodles to drain and to ensure that they will all be well chilled. After *careful* draining, shake over a few drops of oil, lift and mix through. Coil the noodles in portions onto an oiled tray, cover with plastic film and refrigerate until needed.

TO MAKE THE SAUCE   Make a reduction by gently simmering the onion and some pepper with the wine in the small enamelled saucepan, until the liquid has practically evaporated and the onion looks moist. (The French term used to describe the moment when the reduction has adequately reduced is a *marmelade*.) Add the cream and boil vigorously for 1 minute. With care, whisk in the butter one piece at a time, adding the next piece just as the previous one has been fully absorbed. The butter should be added quickly enough so that the sauce does not overheat and turn the butter to oil. Remove the saucepan from the heat to incorporate the first piece of butter, and then you will need to return the pan to the heat to ensure that there is no reluctance on the part of the butter to melt into a creamy consistency. Once all the butter has been incorporated, taste for salt. Keep the sauce in a warm spot or in a bain-marie over hot, but not boiling, water.

TO COOK AND SERVE   Heat the grill plate or heavy cast-iron frying pan to very hot. Have ready the steamer or saucepan of boiling water. Place the pasta in a buttered dish into the steamer or colander and plunge into the water.

Pour a little oil onto the grilling surface. Quickly spread it with a metal spatula and throw one oiled scallop onto the plate to check the temperature. It should sizzle and sear to a golden colour instantly. If the temperature is correct, scatter over as many scallops as will easily fit. It is better to grill the scallops in two batches if your pan is small. They mustn't stew or steam. Turn the scallops quickly and systematically to grill the other side. Remove to a hot plate lined with baking paper. Do the second batch, if necessary. All this takes perhaps 2 minutes to achieve.

Spoon the sauce onto hot serving plates. Tip a small pile of noodles onto each plate and tumble on the scallops. Because I enjoy the strange sweetness of scallops, in this case emphasised by the saffron note in the noodles, I sometimes garnish the dish with thin slivers of oriental mixed pickles.[†]

[†] It is mind-boggling for a non-Asian shopper to survey the rows and rows of pickled vegetables in Asian supermarkets. The best idea is to go there with a knowledgeable Asian friend, as I do. The mixed pickles I have tried include turnip and ginger and lots of other things I cannot really identify, all in a slightly sweet and hot sauce that seems to marry well with this dish.

Roast poussin with tarragon, Chinese broccoli†

6 × 500 g poussins, wingtips folded under to hold the neck skin in place
salt, pepper
6 cloves garlic, peeled and smashed
6 thin slices lemon or *lime or orange*
6 large sprigs of tarragon (say 15–20 leaves)
180 g soft butter
trussing string
18 more fat cloves garlic, unpeeled
baking dish of appropriate size (i.e. not so big that the butter will burn,
    but big enough not to crowd the poussins)
12 tiny new potatoes, washed but not peeled
12 small pickling onions, washed but not peeled
12 heads Chinese broccoli, stems peeled and excess leaves removed
200 ml white wine
2 tablespoons pure cream at 45 per cent milk fat
lemon juice (optional)
1 tablespoon finely chopped tarragon

Preheat the oven to 220°C. Wipe the birds with kitchen paper. Season inside and out. Inside each bird place 1 smashed clove of garlic, 1 slice of lemon, 1 tarragon sprig and 1 dessertspoon of soft butter. Truss to hold the thighs neatly by looping a string around each drumstick, crossing the string and pulling tight. Bring the string up the back of the bird, cross it again, loop around the wings and tie. Melt the rest of the butter. Roll the unpeeled garlic cloves in some of the butter and paint the outside of the chickens with the remainder. Settle the birds in the baking dish with the garlic, potatoes and onions around.

Put the dish in the preheated oven. After 15 minutes, baste with the buttery juices and bring a large pot of water to a boil for the broccoli. Check the birds

---

† This way of cooking a small bird, nowadays sold as a 'poussin' (weighing 350–500 g), has become an all-time favourite. In the last few years I have sat each bird on a thickish slice of baguette during the cooking process. The juices ooze into the bread and it becomes crunchy at the edges and quite magnificent. In the past, this size chicken was sometimes erroneously marketed as a spatchcock, which is actually a small chicken or game bird that has been split down the back and opened out for grilling.

after 10 more minutes and prick the thighs. The juices should run practically clear. If they are still red, leave for a further 5 minutes and then recheck. Once the poussins are ready, remove the birds and the garlic, onions and potatoes to a hot plate and keep warm. Tip off the extra butter from the pan and drop the broccoli into the pot of salted water, which is boiling away vigorously.

TO FINISH THE SAUCE AND SERVE   Place the baking dish over a direct flame and deglaze with the white wine. Stir and scrape over high heat to loosen all the delicious little morsels. After a minute or so, add the cream. Scrape, stir and bubble your little sauce and then strain it into a hot small pot or jug.

Drain the broccoli and pile it on a hot serving dish. Season and add a few drops of lemon juice if you like. Do not add butter as the birds and sauce are sufficiently buttery. Place 1 poussin on each plate with some garlic, onions and potatoes. Spoon over a little of the sauce and scatter over the chopped tarragon.

Don't forget fingerbowls with warm water, perhaps with a sprig of tarragon and a lemon slice floating in each.

Chocolate-dipped prunes in brandy cream sauce

24 large, fancy-grade pitted prunes
½ bottle good red wine
60 ml cognac
300 g couverture chocolate (Valrhona plain dark is very good)
100 g unsalted butter

BRANDY CREAM SAUCE

2 egg yolks
25 g castor sugar
60 ml cognac
300 ml cream

TO PREPARE THE PRUNES   Soak the prunes in the wine and cognac, ensuring that they are completely immersed in the liquid. Leave overnight at the very least, or up to 1 month (they only improve). On the morning of the dinner, lift out the prunes and drain well on a cake rack set over a tray to catch the drips. Melt the chocolate and butter gently over hot water and remove from the heat. Have ready a plastic-lined tray and, using a skewer (I use the wooden satay type), impale each prune, dip it in the chocolate, allow any excess to run back into the bowl and slip the prune carefully onto the tray. Continue until all the prunes have been dipped, then refrigerate the tray.

TO MAKE THE BRANDY CREAM SAUCE   Beat the egg yolks and sugar until fluffy and lemon-coloured. Whisk in the cognac. Lightly whip the cream in a separate bowl and gently fold it into the egg mixture, giving a few firm whisks to combine. It is best to prepare the sauce just before dinner as the cognac tends to sink to the bottom. If this happens, give the sauce a quick rewhisk.

TO SERVE   Pour the sauce onto the serving plates and arrange the prunes on the sauce rather like floating islands. Don't forget to use the wonderful liqueur left in the bowl after all the prunes have been enjoyed!

You will probably have coating chocolate left over. These chestnut truffles (see below) make delicious petits fours. Don't serve them after this chocolate-dipped dessert, but they will keep well, covered with plastic in the refrigerator, for 2–3 days.

Chestnut truffles

4 tablespoons brandy
1 × 440 g tin natural chestnut purée without sugar
125 g crushed macaroons or *Italian amaretti* or *granita biscuits*
coating chocolate (see above)

Combine all the ingredients in a food processor and mix until they form a sticky paste. Roll into 'sausages' about 10 cm long and let them harden in the refrigerator. Place on a rack over a tray and pour the leftover chocolate (see above) over the logs. When the chocolate has set, cut the logs into slanting pieces, like little logs, with a sharp knife.

If you are feeling particularly artistic, run a fork lightly along the logs before the chocolate sets. They will then resemble miniature *bûches de Noël* (the French Christmas cakes).

When is a turkey a ham?

Menu

❦

Salad of Turkey Ham

Coulibiac of Salmon,
Melted Butter Sauce

Canteloupe Ice-cream
Melba Sauce

❦

Recently a customer took exception to us serving an
entrée that we styled 'Salad of turkey ham'. A ham,
he objected, is a leg of pork. Strictly speaking a ham *is* a
leg of pork, salted and frequently smoked. So where does
that leave a salted and air-dried duck breast, goose breast
or, as in our case, turkey breast?

I find it hard to endorse some of the nomenclature
used in modern French restaurants, where a dish of
poached scallops and other fish in a *beurre blanc* sauce can
be styled a *blanquette* or a pot-au-feu. But I would claim that
the error in these examples is not only that the ingredients
have changed completely from the original, but that the
titles are misleading. A *blanquette* is a dish, usually of
blanched veal, cooked in a light liquid that is subsequently

thickened with cream and eggs and sharpened with lemon juice. A pot-au-feu implies by its very nature ingredients that have simmered together for a long time so that all flavours meld and enrich each other – a total impossibility when cooking fish.[+]

If the name of a particular dish has come to mean the technique as much as the type of raw material used, I think it could be argued that there is nothing untoward in the concept of a turkey ham. Certainly Michel Guérard has popularised the idea with his salad of duck-breast ham. I ate a plate of lovely goose-breast ham in Paris in 1983, and a plate of rich and unusual goose-breast pastrami at Jo Goldenberg's famous Jewish delicatessen in the Marais *quartier* of Paris. Both examples seemed legitimate to me. The goose-breast ham was unmistakably 'ham' as much as it was goose, and the pastrami was unmistakably pastrami.

So our salad of turkey ham has been a great success and most versatile. We have served it with slivers of melon as a complimentary appetiser to friends or late-comers if the hot *amuse-gueule* has run out, assembled it with peeled baby broad beans and hot fried walnuts, wrapped it around slim salted breadsticks, served it with salty fetta cheese and olives, and so on. The salad I have described here is a joint celebration of the beautiful ham and the short season of juicy, purple figs.

If the curing and drying of the hams is being done in the heat of the summer, it is imperative to provide protection from flies and other flying insects. The traditional Australian Coolgardie safe seems the answer. I searched army disposal stores, camping stores and other unusual and eccentric shops, but to this day I have not found one. We constructed a sort of internal shade-house for our hams using gardeners' shadecloth tacked onto heavy wood, which dropped down like a roller blind and could be fastened in front of a recessed, sealed-off chimney. The little hams, all festooned with muslin, hung from hooks rather like bandaged limbs, I thought. Not a totally appealing image, so up until now I have kept that thought to myself.

One final word about hams. Drawing attention to the process of ham-making enables the cook to experiment with all sorts of hams. The Spanish frequently rub their drying hams with hot chilli pepper. One could do that.[+] Some Italian country hams

[+] My severe pronouncement on naming dishes sent me rushing back to Michel Guérard's masterpiece, *Cuisine Gourmande*. First published in 1977, this book became an essential reference work for all those restaurateurs influenced and excited by the changes happening in France. It still stands today as an extraordinary collection of lovely dishes, any one of which would be exclaimed over today. Guérard includes a recipe for a 'pot-au-feu of foie gras'. It is true that the fattened liver only cooks for a short time (compared with the usual shin beef etc.), but he is faithful to the technique of a pot-au-feu, building a savoury broth with many vegetables.

[+] I wonder if the Spanish habit of rubbing drying hams with pork fat and hot chilli pepper is to discourage insects as well as to add flavour?

are rubbed with black pepper and aniseed – one could try those flavours. The air-dried beef of the mountainous regions of Italy and Switzerland is usually served with a small jug of excellent olive oil and lemon juice – thus suggesting another way of enjoying the product.

To follow the light but stimulating salad I have suggested a coulibiac. It is known to have originated as a Russian dish, but is equally well known in the French repertoire. A coulibiac is a buttery, fluffy loaf. The dish combines poached fillets of salmon with a special stuffing, rolled in dill-flavoured pancakes, the whole encased in brioche dough and served in thick slices with a butter sauce.

Coulibiac is ideal for home entertaining as its rather long and complex preparation is finished early. It presents as a most impressive dish and, most importantly, it tastes good. The grain was originally cracked wheat. Cracked wheat can be used, but in this recipe I have used long-grain rice. Brown rice would be successful also, but takes much longer to cook. Coulibiac is also a good introduction to wrapping food in brioche and becoming relaxed when using this most versatile dough. The assembly sounds terrifying, but it is quite easy. Read it through before starting and make sure you have all the ingredients ready. And when you serve it (at the table for maximum effect), have on hand a really sharp serrated knife and a wide fish slice.

The ice-cream recipe made with our luscious canteloupe melons is another from the works of Elizabeth David. My contribution is the mode of service, the Melba sauce to accompany it and the suggestion that it can also be made with a really ripe honeydew melon. The texture of this ice-cream is like velvet, and it is a curious fact that the flesh of melon, once cooked either in a custard as here or in a tart, seems to transmute completely. One recognises that it is melon, but it has changed remarkably.

Salad of turkey ham

Nowadays it is possible to buy one turkey breast and many other small joints of poultry. This makes the preparation of this ham much easier and less expensive. It is, however, worth noting that the hams, once cured and dried, will keep for months in the refrigerator. They become a little drier as the months pass by, but this is a natural maturing process and the ham is none the worse for it. It is so satisfying and so impressive to be able to put together a plate of such superior charcuterie at a moment's notice that it is worth making more than one ham at a time, or even buying a whole turkey and using the thighs in a pâté or braised dish and the carcass for some poultry stock. In the recipe I have assumed a boned turkey breast weighing around 600–800 g. The skin is left on.[+]

> 4 sprigs of fresh thyme (you could use caraway thyme or
>   lemon thyme for a special flavour)
> 2 bay leaves
> 1 teaspoon lightly crushed coriander seeds
> ½ cup coarse salt
> 1 twist of dried orange zest (optional)
> 1 teaspoon lightly crushed peppercorns
> 1 × 600–800 g turkey breast, skin on, bone removed
>
> 1 metre butter muslin

TO CURE AND DRY THE HAM Mix together the thyme, bay leaves, coriander seeds, salt, orange zest and peppercorns. (Try to cadge a small branch from a bay tree if you know someone who has a huge one. The flavour is superior by far to the dried-out packets available from supermarkets. Bay ought to have a very strong and distinctive fragrance.) Lightly massage this into the breast of turkey and leave in the refrigerator in a glass, stainless steel or enamel dish for 12 hours or overnight if the ham weighs around 600 g. If it weighs 800 g or more, leave it in the mixture for 24 hours, turning it over after 12 hours.

Remove the ham from the salt mixture, drain on a rack for an hour or so and

[+] In later years we decided to bone, cure, tie and dry the legs as well. This was very successful and we used the legs rather as one uses pancetta, thin slices sautéed before adding other vegetables. It was ideal used with dried beans, lentils or rice. The skin remains very tough and has to be cut away before slicing.

brush off any pieces of salt still adhering. Wrap very tightly in the muslin and truss at intervals to form the ham into a small, fat sausage. Make a loop with the string and hang in a cool, draughty place protected from all insects.

The drying time is not very precise. It depends on the weather, the draught, the size of the ham and how it 'feels'. In our experience a small ham feels right in about 5–7 days and the bigger ones take up to 2 weeks. It should feel quite firm but supple when pressed with your finger. When you have judged it to be ready, remove the ham to the refrigerator and use as required.

TO SLICE THE HAM   Remove the muslin and, with a very sharp knife or an electric slicer, cut the thinnest possible slices on a bias. You will probably need to remove the skin, which is very tough to cut. Do not be alarmed at the whitish powdery look that the ham gradually acquires. As it dries out in the refrigerator, the salt is drawn out to the surface.

In winter, or if you live in a very cold climate, the ham could hang in a cool room without need of refrigeration. Cellar temperature is ideal.

SUGGESTIONS FOR USE OF THE HAM   I have given many suggestions in the introduction (page 219). With the right sort of crusty bread – grilled rather than toasted – and unsalted butter, it makes a fantastic sandwich or supper dish. When you get to the very end of the ham and it is no longer possible to carve elegant slices, it can flavour a pilaf of rice or enhance a paella or a dish of fresh pasta. There are endless ways of enjoying it.

Exactly the same method is used for duck breasts or goose breasts. The flavour is, of course, different, and they will both have a trim of fat to each slice, which is missing on the turkey breast. They will not need to marinate longer than overnight in the salt and would be sufficiently dry in 5 days.

Coulibiac of salmon, Melted butter sauce[+]

butter
6 spring onions, finely chopped
200 g button mushrooms, sliced
1 × 700 g fillet salmon, pin bones
    removed
salt, pepper
2 sprigs of parsley
1 sprig of dill
100 ml dry vermouth
200 ml dry white wine
1 egg for glazing
chopped dill

FISH SAUCE

liquid from cooking the fish
    (see above)
150 ml fish stock or water
60 g butter
60 g plain flour
3 egg yolks
60 ml pure cream
salt, white pepper
few drops of lemon juice

DILL CRÊPES

75 g plain flour
1 tablespoon chopped dill
1 tablespoon chopped parsley
1 egg
1 egg yolk
salt, pepper
300 ml milk
30 g melted butter
clarified butter for frying the crêpes

RICE AND EGGS

30 g butter
1 tablespoon finely chopped onion
125 g long-grain rice or cracked wheat
450 ml stock (either a light fish stock
    or a light chicken stock)
salt, pepper
3 eggs
2 tablespoons chopped parsley

SIMPLE BRIOCHE DOUGH

30 g sugar
250 ml milk
2 teaspoons dried yeast
6 egg yolks
500 g plain flour
1 teaspoon salt
150 g soft unsalted butter

[+] This recipe is sure to terrify most people by its length alone, but making brioche and making pancakes are pretty basic skills, and poaching fish, cooking rice and boiling eggs are not very challenging, either. As is often the case, a multi-step recipe looks more daunting than it is. This is sure to establish your reputation as an impressive and serious cook! There is no reason why the sauce for the coulibiac could not be a classic *beurre blanc* (page 214). Or save a little of the salmon cooking liquid and substitute it for all or part of the white wine in the basic recipe.

All preparation can be completed the day before the dinner except the making of the brioche. The assembly should be completed about 1 hour before dinner. If you must assemble several hours before the party, place the assembled loaf in the refrigerator to retard the working of the yeast, but remember to bring the coulibiac out a good hour before you wish to cook it. The dough will need this time to recover and to puff – otherwise your laborious filling will be encased in an unappetising, hard crust.

TO COOK THE FISH Butter a baking dish that will hold the salmon comfortably. Scatter over the spring onion and mushroom. Lay the fillet in the pan, season and sprinkle with the herbs. Pour over the vermouth and white wine. Cover the dish with well-buttered foil and put into a preheated oven at 180°C for 10 minutes. The salmon is only partly cooked at this stage. Lift the fish out with a slice onto a tray, and as soon as you can handle it remove and discard the skin, lift off the fillets and leave to cool. Cover with plastic film.

Strain the liquid in the pan, pressing hard on the mushrooms and onions. Reserve the liquid.

TO MAKE THE FISH SAUCE Measure the liquid saved from the cooking of the fish and make it up to 600 ml with the fish stock. Heat it to simmering point. Make a blond roux with the butter and flour, stirring well and cooking for 3–4 minutes. Gradually whisk in the hot stock, whisk well and bring to simmering point. Simmer for 10 minutes over a low flame to mature the sauce without reducing it, then take it off the heat. Beat the egg yolks with the cream, ladle in a little hot sauce, whisk well, then pour this mixture back into the pan and return to the stove. Stir for 2–3 minutes to enrich and slightly thicken the sauce, but do not allow it to boil. Taste the sauce for salt and pepper and adjust it with drops of lemon juice. It should be quite thick, smooth and mellow in flavour. Press plastic wrap down on the surface to prevent a skin forming, and reserve for the final assembly.

TO PREPARE THE DILL CRÊPES Put the flour and herbs into a bowl and make a well in the centre. Drop in the lightly beaten egg and egg yolk and season with salt and pepper. Add half the milk. Gradually mix from the centre of the well, drawing the flour in gradually to avoid lumps. Add the balance of the milk and whisk well. Leave the batter to rest for 2 hours.

Add the melted butter and mix well. Heat a well-seasoned 16 cm crêpe pan and grease with a very light brushing of clarified butter. Tip in some pancake batter, swirl to spread, tip off the excess and cook for 1–2 minutes. Turn and cook the other side quickly. Transfer each crêpe to a plate as you go, separating them with waxed paper or bands or aluminium foil. This mix makes 12 thin crêpes. Reserve for final assembly. (If the pancakes have adhered to each other, warm them in a low oven for a few minutes so that they will separate without risk of tearing.)

TO PREPARE THE RICE AND EGGS   Melt the butter and simmer the onion until soft and yellow. Add the rice and stir until each grain is shiny. Add the heated stock, cover and bring slowly to the boil. Stir in salt and pepper to taste, cover the rice with a clean, folded towel or a wad of kitchen paper and replace the lid. Turn the heat to the lowest possible setting, slip a simmer mat under the pan and continue to cook until the rice is quite tender and all the stock has been absorbed, about 12 minutes. Turn into a bowl and leave for the final assembly.

Hard-boil the eggs. Press through a sieve and mix while warm with the parsley, and salt and pepper to taste. Set aside for the assembly.

NOW FOR THE BRIOCHE   Start the dough 3½ hours before cooking the coulibiac. Warm the sugar and milk in a pan until just lukewarm. Sprinkle over the yeast and leave to froth. Beat the egg yolks lightly and add to the warm yeast/milk mixture. Sift the flour and salt, form a well in the centre and pour in the liquid. Transfer to an electric mixer with a dough hook and beat the dough well. Add the softened butter in several lots, beating well after each addition. Continue to beat the dough until it is shiny and smooth and comes away cleanly from the sides of the bowl.

Lightly butter a bowl and put the dough in it. Cover with a damp cloth and leave to rise in a warm place for approximately 2–2½ hours. When well risen, knock the dough down and proceed to the final assembly of the coulibiac.

THE FINAL ASSEMBLY   Have ready the brioche dough, cooked fish fillets, fish sauce, dill crêpes, rice and eggs, 1 beaten whole egg as a glaze, and a large, buttered baking sheet.

Flour a board well. Put the brioche dough on this and pat it into a 30 cm × 15 cm rectangle 1 cm thick. Transfer the rectangle to the buttered baking sheet. Down the centre of the brioche assemble layers in the following order:
1.   a row of 4 overlapping crêpes
2.   half the rice and egg mixture
3.   half the sauce
4.   half the fish fillets
5.   an additional 4 overlapping crêpes
6.   the rest of the rice and egg mixture
7.   the rest of the sauce
8.   the rest of the fish fillets
9.   the last 4 crêpes.

Brush all exposed brioche with the beaten egg. Fold the ends up over the crêpes and bring the sides up to overlap slightly. Pinch and press the edges firmly together. Carefully turn the roll over so that the seam is underneath. Brush the whole surface with egg. Leave in a warm place in the kitchen for about 20 minutes to recover from the working and to puff a little. (Remember, it will need longer than this if it has been assembled some hours previously and has been refrigerated.)

Put into a preheated 200°C oven. After 10 minutes, lower the heat to 180°C and cook for a further 15–20 minutes until the coulibiac looks puffed and golden brown. Let it rest for 10 minutes to settle before serving.

Slide the coulibiac onto a serving tray. Cut thick slices with a serrated knife and hand around separately a jug of melted butter with additional chopped dill.

SIMPLE MELTED BUTTER SAUCE   The principle is much the same as for the sophisticated *beurre blanc*. Butter is whisked into a warm base and kept in a creamy suspension by carefully regulating the heat. In this case, the liquid is water.

In a small cast-iron or enamelled pan of approximately 16 cm diameter, bring 1 cm of water to a fast boil. Have ready about 200 g of unsalted butter cut into 6 equal chunks. Whisk the butter into the boiling liquid one chunk at a time, lifting the pan and moving it away from the heat for the first piece or two. Then, as the butter takes longer to melt in the lowered temperature, you can finish adding it over the direct flame – but do not stop whisking. Remove from the heat and sharpen with a few drops of lemon juice. Season to taste.

Canteloupe ice-cream

1 canteloupe
125 g castor sugar
4 egg yolks
few drops of kirsch
juice of ½ lemon
300 ml cream

Cut a lid from the top of the melon. Scoop out the seeds and discard. Scoop out all the pulp. Place the hollow shell in a freezer bag and place in the freezer overnight.[+] Purée the melon flesh with the sugar in a food processor or blender. Cook this pulp over low heat until the sugar has dissolved. Strain. Beat the egg yolks until pale. Pour over the hot melon purée, return to the heat and cook until lightly thickened.

Pour the thickened custard into a metal bowl sitting on another one that is half-full of crushed ice. Stir in the kirsch and lemon juice. When the mixture is quite cold add the cream, whisking lightly to combine. Pour into an ice-cream churn and churn the mixture.

Pack the ice-cream into the rigid, frozen shell and return to the freezer to get quite hard. When ready to serve, *carefully* cut wedges and serve them with raspberry (Melba) sauce (see below).

Melba sauce

500 g fresh or *frozen raspberries*
250 g castor sugar
2 tablespoons framboise liqueur

In a food processor, whirl the raspberries and sugar together. Press through a nylon or stainless steel strainer to extract all the seeds. If you wish to freeze the sauce for later use, label it and freeze now. Add the liqueur to the sauce after you have thawed it. If you are making the sauce to use straight away, add the liqueur after the sieving process.

A berry coulis such as this one is wonderful with many pastries as well as ice-creams. It can be made successfully using a mix of berry fruit. With some fruit you may need less sugar, so it is a good idea to taste the fruit before starting to blend it.✦

⸸ This ice-cream is still a favourite. An easier way to proceed is to first halve the melons crosswise, scoop out the seeds, then the flesh, and freeze each half-shell in a plastic bag. It is easier to cut a filled half-melon accurately than a whole one, and there is less risk of the knife skidding on the frozen shell.
✦ The word *coulis* came into the language with nouvelle cuisine in the early 1980s. It is now widely understood to mean a puréed sauce with some texture, often made with fruit.

A palette of salads

Menu

─◦─

Sweetbread Salade composée

Ear, Tongue and Trotter Salad with Orange-zest Pasta

Hot Salad of Pigeon Breast and Duck Livers

Autumn Salad

─◦─

We don't hear a lot in the west about the texture of food. In Asian cuisine there are many ingredients that have little or no taste but which are valued because of their slipperiness, crunch or cartilage. I think immediately of jellyfish, cloud-ear and silver tree fungus, shark's fin, and so on.

With the popularity of what is most reasonably known as modern French cookery,[+] more and more restaurants are serving composed salads. They can be a delight to eat, light but inventive, and provide perhaps the best and most accessible way to blend textures and flavours. In this section I have included recipes for four of my favourite composed salads.

I like to compose my salads with a definite artist's

Sweetbread salad with pistachios, orange zest and Jerusalem artichokes (page 231)

Autumn salad – buckwheat noodles, roasted chestnuts, spinach,
red pepper and wild and gathered mushrooms (page 237)

eye. I decide on my background first. Will it be radicchio, curly endive, water-cress, home-grown dandelions or corn salad, or hearts of mignonette? Or will the background come from quite a different direction? It could be warm, marinated pasta, warm, just-cooked green beans, wild rice or cracked wheat, or spicy lentils. Or the availability of one magnificent ingredient may provide not only the back-ground but the whole inspiration for the salad. A prolific crop of sun-ripened tomatoes, sliced and scattered with a fine dice of red onions, torn basil leaves and wet slices of fresh little bocconcini cheeses, all drizzled with the very greenest olive oil, is a delicious composed salad, the very embodiment of summer.✦

I next decide on the crunch. My mind ranges over the possibilities: dry-sautéed kaiserfleisch cut paper-thin so that it curls as it crisps; croutons rubbed with oil and garlic and baked until golden; toasted pumpkin seeds, pine nuts or almonds; or thin slices of potato dipped in clarified butter and baked until they are golden and crispy. Restaurant kitchens often yield quantities of sautéed duck skins from the popular duck-breast dishes. One can sliver these reserved skins and fry them crisply in a little oil, deglaze the pan with a few drops of vinegar and pour it all – fat, vinegar and the *grattons* of duck – over a bowl of slightly bitter salad leaves, such as dandelion or curly endive, or soaked cockscombs poached until tender in light stock and then sautéed in butter. And, even more exotically, one could borrow from another culture and sauté Chinese duck sausage, soak and sauté cloud-ear fungus, or even deep-fry prawn crackers.

The next important element is the 'fat' in the salad. The range is infinite. Is this salad to be about the sea? I would think of prawns or chunks of rock lobster, and shellfish ranging through oysters, mussels, scallops, crabs and pipis. Or do I want to excite people about innards and feature gently simmered ears or ox tongue, or braised sweetbreads or brains? Sometimes the 'crunch' and the 'fat' can be combined in one ingredient. By breading the brains one adds a crunchy exterior to the soft, creamy middle. I have included a recipe in this section for a tongue and ear salad, which is absolutely delicious and should be tried before being dismissed as an outrageous idea. Of course, what may seem outlandish to one person or culture will be perfectly understood and received by another. I guess that is what makes travelling such a great gastronomic stimulus. My salad of cold marinated duck's tongues on shredded jellyfish was a quite extraordinary dish that I encountered in 1984 in Hong Kong when I was a judge at a food festival, with a strangely numbing dressing, which I attribute to the use of Szechuan pepper. Other 'fat' tastes are matjes herrings soaked overnight in milk, spicy Portuguese sardines, smoked trout or eel, smoked gypsy ham, and so on and so on.

I then move on to consider the 'juices', or the dressing or sauce. Some ingredients contribute their own marvellous juices. The brine of a freshly opened oyster, the bacon fat from kaiserfleisch, the golden and sweet liquid trapped inside a roasted red pepper, or the flavourful juices resulting from braising sweetbreads with vegetables, herbs and good stock. But the whole field of oils, seasonings and vinegars has changed very dramatically in recent years. One can choose from green extra-virgin olive oil (Australian or imported), the roasted flavours of walnut oil or almond oil, and the somewhat lighter note of hazelnut oil. Fresh orange juice can be used in many dressings instead of vinegar or lemon juice. Always add them drop by drop, tasting as you go. The liquid from a jar of pickled plums can be used, and nowadays you can choose from dozens of different mustards, not to mention the special notes of tarragon and other herb vinegars and the even more exotic sherry, raspberry, strawberry or old-matured vinegars.✝ Use the best there is – you do not need large quantities. Mix your sauce separately.

The central parts of my picture are now assembled. It is a bit like arranging flowers in a vase. The shape or skeleton must come first and then the delicate touches. Similarly with the delicate touches that still remain to be added to your salad. The tarragon leaves need not be chopped; don't destroy the shape of the little *pluches* of chervil; don't try to snip your chives too small. Remember to blanch any delicate wisps of orange zest to avoid bitterness, rub off the skins of pistachios if they are very salty, and scrupulously remove the strings of your snow peas. If you are planning to scatter a few marigold or violet petals over a salad, be sure that the flowers have not been sprayed. (This means that you should have grown them yourself.) Pat dry any pickled fruits so that the coloured vinegar doesn't stain your salad, and scatter a julienne of beetroot at the very last minute for the same reason.

A composed salad must be just that. It is not put together until the last minute

✝ I have commented on vinegar elsewhere (see footnote on page 157). Nowadays the verjuice made by Maggie Beer in the Barossa Valley in South Australia, and by others around the country, offers another possibility. Its gentle acidity and 'grapey' taste makes it wonderful in salad dressings.

(for home entertaining) and in the ideal restaurant situation it is not composed until it is ordered. All components should be at room temperature, or a steamer should be at the ready if some parts are to be briefly warmed.

A final note. I think that lightness and a certain air of spontaneity should characterise this most delightful way to commence a meal. The next time you are offered a sliced avocado and prawn salad, think about the millions of options available and be sad about the lack of interest and imagination this suggests.

Sweetbread salade composée

½ orange
½ cup shelled, unsalted pistachio nuts
6 handfuls corn salad

SWEETBREADS

1 kg veal sweetbreads (ask your butcher well in advance for export quality)
1 carrot
1 small onion
1 leek
butter/oil
1 litre veal or chicken stock
1 bay leaf
parsley stalks
1 sprig of thyme

DRESSING

¼ cup orange juice (approximately)
¼ cup walnut oil (approximately)
¼ cup extra-virgin olive oil
salt, pepper

TO PREPARE THE SWEETBREADS Soak the sweetbreads overnight in cold water with some salt to draw out as much blood as possible. The next day drain the sweetbreads, place in a pan with cold water and bring to the boil. Drain, rinse in cold water and then pull off as much as possible of the loose membrane and pieces of fatty tissue attached. Roughly chop the washed vegetables and sauté in a little butter and oil until a good colour. Pour on the stock and add the herbs and then the sweetbreads.

Bring to simmering point, reduce the heat and cook gently, covered, until the sweetbreads are quite tender, 20–25 minutes. Leave to get cold in the stock.

TO PREPARE THE ORANGE ZEST, PISTACHIOS AND DRESSING   Use a potato peeler to pare off strips of orange zest. Check that there is no pith attached. With a very sharp knife, cut the strips into a fine julienne. Drop into a little cold water, bring to the boil and simmer for 5 minutes. Drain and pat dry on kitchen paper.

Rub the pistachio nuts in a dry cloth to remove as much loose skin as possible, and any excess salt if the nuts are salted. It is preferable to do this and leave on some fragments of skin than to blanch the nuts in water, as they will then have to be thoroughly dried in the oven.

Prepare the dressing by whisking the orange juice into the walnut and olive oils and tasting carefully. Season.

TO ASSEMBLE THE SALAD   I have suggested corn salad, known in French as *mâche*. This grows very easily from seed and is one of the most commonly seen salads in Europe in the autumn and winter. It grows in flat little rosettes, and each plant has a number of small, rounded leaves with a mild yet peppery taste. If you can't find corn salad, use any other special greenery, or choose some quite different background for the salad.[†]

On different occasions I have surrounded the sweetbreads with sliced turnip cooked until barely tender in a little butter, sugar and water, or Jerusalem artichokes prepared in the same manner, or wild rice.

Take each piece of sweetbread from the stock and, with your fingers or a small knife, remove any remaining pieces of gristle. If the pieces are large, slice them into 2 or 3 escalopes and drop immediately into a bowl containing a little of the strained stock. If the pieces are small, leave them whole or divide them further into their natural sections. In either case, drop each piece directly into the bowl with the small quantity of stock as the exposed surfaces will dry out if they are not bathed in some liquid. When all the sweetbreads have been cleaned and sliced or sectioned, stir them around, drain and transfer to a clean bowl. Add the nuts and the orange rind. Whisk up the dressing and pour over just enough so that the sweetbreads are quite moist but not wet.

Arrange a handful of washed and dried greens on each plate and spoon some sweetbread salad into the middle. There is no need to dress the corn salad as there is enough flavour and moisture in the sweetbreads.

[†] Rocket or its cousin, wild rocket, would now be a favourite for such a salad. Corn salad is still hard to find. It is also very perishable so is not a favourite with greengrocers.

Ear, tongue and trotter salad with orange-zest pasta

4 pig's ears[+]
juice of 2 lemons
6 fresh pig's trotters
1 pickled ox tongue
2 tablespoons chopped parsley
1 tablespoon chopped chives
2 tablespoons walnut oil
1 tablespoon sherry vinegar
salt, pepper
cornichons or *capers for garnishing*

6 pieces muslin, string

STOCK FOR POACHING THE EARS
AND TROTTERS

1 onion stuck with 3 whole cloves
1 carrot, sliced
1 leek, washed and sliced
6 unpeeled cloves garlic
1 bay leaf
1 sprig of thyme
3 parsley stalks
200 ml dry white wine
1 teaspoon rock salt

STOCK FOR POACHING THE
TONGUE

1 onion stuck with 3 whole cloves
1 carrot, sliced
1 leek, washed and sliced
1 bay leaf
1 sprig of thyme
3 parsley stalks
200 ml port or *madeira*

ORANGE-ZEST PASTA

200 g plain flour
2 teaspoons salt
3 teaspoons olive oil
finely grated zest of 2 bright oranges
2 eggs

TO PREPARE THE EARS Using a small knife, scrape off any remaining hairs on the ears. Wash the ears very well under cold water, using a small brush. Inspect closely

[+] According to Jonathan Gianfreda, the well-known Melbourne butcher and food lover, pig's ears are available in Vietnamese stores because they are the last retailers who can still get their pig carcasses from 'local abattoirs', i.e. abattoirs that are not export-registered and as such are permitted to sell their carcasses with ears on the head. Pig abattoirs are decreasing by the month in Victoria, and the majority that are left are all designated 'export' and sell their pigs headless due to health regulations.

to make sure they are quite clean. Put into a pan of cold water and bring to the boil. Simmer for 2 minutes, drain and rinse well. Drop into a bowl of water to which you have added the juice of 1 lemon.

TO PREPARE THE TROTTERS   Scrape off any hairs remaining on the trotters. If they are stubborn they will have to be singed off over a flame. Drop into a bowl of water to which you have added the juice of 1 lemon. When all the trotters have been prepared, roll each one tightly in muslin and tie each parcel with string.

TO PREPARE THE TONGUE   Soak the tongue in cold water for a few hours before poaching to remove any excess salt. Put it in a pan of cold water and bring to the boil. Pour off the water. The tongue is now ready for poaching.

TO POACH THE EARS AND TROTTERS   Because trotters are particularly rich in gelatine, the lengthy poaching they require will result in very gelatinous stock. Both the ears and trotters will be poached in the same stock. The trotters will take about 4 hours to be really tender, while the ears will be ready after 2 hours.

Place the trotter parcels in a pan and cover them with cold water. Add all the poaching-stock ingredients, bring to the boil and skim off any scum that rises. Partially cover and time to simmer for 4 hours. After 2 hours add the ears to the stock and continue to simmer. After a total of 4 hours has elapsed, test. To test the trotters, pierce the parcels with a fine skewer; there should be no resistance. If tender, remove the trotters and ears (reserve the stock), unwrap the trotters and leave until cool enough to handle.

Slice the ears into thin strips and place in a bowl. Split the trotters with a knife and, with your fingers, remove all the bones. Cut up the trotter meat and put it in the same bowl as the sliced ears. Press a piece of plastic film over the bowl to stop any discoloration or drying out of the meat. If there will be a long delay before adding the tongue and dressing the salad, cover with stock (you can drain it off later).

TO POACH THE TONGUE   Although the poaching ingredients are practically identical for the tongue as for the ears and trotters, the tongue is poached separately because it has been salted and there is a possibility that its stock might still be a little salty at the end of the cooking process. If this stock were then to be reduced to increase its 'set', it would be far too salty.

Place the tongue in a pan with all its stock ingredients and simmer for approximately 2 hours until quite tender. Test with a skewer; there should be no resistance. Lift the tongue out of the pan (reserve the stock) and rinse with cold water until it can be handled comfortably, then peel off the skin. Trim any gristly pieces from the root end. Cut into 1 cm slices and then cut each slice into 5 mm julienne.

TO MAKE AND COOK THE PASTA   The method of pasta-making and cutting has been fully described on page 213, and this is identical. I prefer to cut the noodles for this dish on the finest setting, resulting in fine, linguine-like pasta. Once cooked, drained, oiled and coiled, all the components of the dish are ready.

USING THE POACHING STOCKS   Taste both poaching stocks. If the tongue stock is not salty, combine the two, test the 'set', and if satisfactory proceed to clarify the stock or refrigerate it and clarify the next day (see page 68). The clarified jelly can be used to set eggs or indeed to set the boned trotters themselves, as a different presentation. Before clarifying the jelly, taste it and decide whether to add a little extra flavouring, such as port or madeira, and for seasoning. Also test the 'set' by placing a little liquid in a saucer and putting it in the refrigerator. If it doesn't set firmly, it will need to be strengthened by rapid reduction before the clarifying process, or if it is already as salty as it can stand, you will have to add a little gelatine.

TO ASSEMBLE THE DISH   Mix the tongue strips with the pieces of ear and trotter and toss with the parsley and chives. Mix the walnut oil and sherry vinegar together and mix into the meats. Taste and adjust with salt and pepper. Add 1–2 spoonfuls of poaching stock to the meats. They can be quite wet at this stage as the pasta is still to be added.

Toss the pasta with the sliced meats, mixing thoroughly but lightly. Taste again for seasoning. It should taste highly seasoned and a little on the sharp side. Add a few more drops of sherry vinegar if necessary.

Heat the salad in small glass bowls in a steamer, so that it is warm to hot. Tip onto plates in a mound and scatter with a few finely chopped cornichons or a few very small, best-quality capers.

This seems an appropriate place to record here how delighted I am with the Time-Life series *The Good Cook*, edited by Richard Olney, for a long time one of my favourite cookbook authors. The volume *Offal* gives a wonderful introduction to the gastronomic possibilities of all sorts of innards.✢

VARIATIONS: These poaching methods are basic techniques, and either the tongue or the trotters could be separately set in clarified jelly and served as an entrée or as part of a cold buffet. The ears, after being poached, could be stuffed and fried with a coating of egg and breadcrumbs.

✢ Richard Olney, who was one of my very favourite food writers, died in 2000. He will always be remembered for the important series *The Good Cook*. He is less well known for some of his truly visionary books, such as *Simple French Food, The French Menu Cookbook* and *Lulu's Provençal Table*.

There is also a classic preparation called Sainte-Ménéhould, whereby the poached trotters can be rolled twice in clarified butter and fresh crumbs and then grilled and served with mustard and chopped pickled cornichons and capers. As I have already said, the resultant jelly, once clarified, can make perfect eggs in jelly, or the aspic can be used to set a ham mousse as described on page 44. You may need to use some gelatine (see page 14) if the stock is not very firm. These are just a few possibilities.[†]

Hot salad of pigeon breast and duck livers

6 small pigeons, approximately 350 g each
1 cup stock made from pigeon bones (see page 23)
washed inner leaves of 1 bunch spinach
washed inner leaves of 1 red radicchio lettuce
2 tablespoons sultanas
1 cup late-picked dessert wine
oil, butter
6 duck livers
60 ml red wine or vinegar
pepper
unsalted butter

This whole dish takes far longer to describe than to do. It is essential that everything is ready before you start, so read through the recipe carefully first.

On the day before you want to serve the salad, bone the pigeons, reserving the breasts and thighs for the salad. Season these. The carcasses, heads and feet are used to prepare the stock and reduced to 1 cup, following the method given for quail stock on page 68.

Wash the spinach and radicchio well, dry carefully, wrap in a clean cloth and place in the refrigerator. Soak the sultanas in the dessert wine as long as overnight, but for no less than 3 hours.

[†] Michel Guérard offers a recipe for an apéritif crouton using small pieces of cooked pig's ear. He dips them in a mixture of beaten egg, parsley, Dijon mustard, salt, pepper and a few drops of olive oil, then in fine breadcrumbs. The ears are then fried in browned butter and served on hot grilled croutons that have been spread with Dijon mustard.

Have ready a carving board, a sharp knife, heated plates and, in a warm place, a roomy resting dish with a cover. Strain the sultanas and reserve the liquid. Add the liquid to the stock and bring to simmering point. Keep it on a very low flame to stay hot but not to reduce any further.

Heat some oil in a heavy frying pan of an appropriate size to hold all the pigeon pieces and the duck livers. When the oil is hot add a nut of butter, and when the butter has stopped foaming put in the pigeon breasts, skin-side down, and thighs. Reduce the heat a little and cook for 2–3 minutes. Add the duck livers and cook for 2 minutes each side. Remove the livers to the warm resting dish. Turn the breasts and just seal the other side, so as not to toughen the delicate flesh. Remove to the resting dish. Check the thighs with the point of a small knife. If there is any resistance, transfer them to a little pan in a hot (220°C) oven for 2–3 minutes while you make the sauce.

Tip out all the fat in the frying pan. Increase the heat to full. Let the residue 'grip' on the pan for 1 minute to caramelise, and then tip in the red wine or vinegar. Swish it around, scraping well. Tip in the wine/stock mixture and boil vigorously for 1 minute. Add the sultanas. Taste for seasoning. Probably it will need a grind of pepper, but no salt because of the natural reduction of the sauce. Remove the sauce from the heat. Retrieve the legs from the oven and place them in the resting dish.

Divide the spinach and radicchio between 6 plates. Slice the breasts and the livers and arrange on the salad. Boil the sauce once more, drop in a small piece of unsalted butter, swirl to blend and pour over the salads.

Autumn salad

This salad is one of my favourite dishes, and when I designed it I was thinking of a forest floor on a clear autumn day. One thinks of the damp brown leaves, here a yellow leaf, there a bit of green lichen, perhaps a mushroom pushing through the leaves, and perhaps some fallen chestnuts or acorns. It is an important element in Japanese cookery to present ingredients that not only typify a season but are also arranged on the plate in a way to give a visual impression of the season or of a natural geographic feature. This salad, then, uses several Japanese ingredients and techniques. Considerable knife skill is involved with the turnip chrysanthemum, but the idea of the salad is presented with the hope that a clever and interested cook can think of his/her own way of celebrating autumn – or indeed any other season.

1 bunch spinach
6 pieces cloud-ear fungus
6 pieces silver tree fungus
3 large dried shiitake mushrooms
6 yellow pine forest mushrooms
6 even-sized flat field mushrooms[+]
salt, pepper
2 small turnips
rice vinegar
½ cup hazelnuts or *peeled roasted chestnuts*
225 g buckwheat (soba) noodles
1 red pepper, chopped

SPINACH SOUSE

1 cup light, fat-free chicken stock
1 teaspoon mirin or *dry sherry*
1 tablespoon light soy sauce

SAUCE

2 tablespoons light soy sauce
4 tablespoons rice vinegar
1 tablespoon sesame oil
1 tablespoon mirin or *dry sherry*
½ teaspoon finely chopped ginger
½ teaspoon finely chopped garlic
¼ teaspoon finely chopped fresh hot chilli

TO PREPARE THE VEGETABLES, FUNGI AND NUTS Remove the stalks and stems from the spinach. Wash the leaves well. Drop the spinach into a large pot of unsalted boiling water. Swish around and allow to wilt for 1 minute. Drain, then run cold water on the spinach to stop the cooking. Squeeze dry.

Mix together the sousing ingredients and bring them to the boil. Remove from the heat. When the sousing mix is cold, add the spinach and allow to marinate for at least 5 hours. The spinach keeps well for 2–3 days. Silverbeet leaves or any soft green vegetable from the Asian markets can be used instead of spinach.

Soak the cloud-ear and silver tree fungi in separate bowls for a minimum

[+] I would use Swiss brown mushrooms for this salad. The largest Swiss browns are often marketed as portobello mushrooms.

of 20 minutes. When fully reconstituted, they can sit in the soaking water for 2–3 days without harm.

Shiitake mushrooms are brownish mushrooms beloved by all Asian cuisines. They are widely available and are sold in packages of various sizes.[+] These mushrooms are quite expensive. They should be soaked in warm water for 3–5 hours. Before use, slice off any tough parts of the stems. The soaking liquid, once strained, can be added to stocks and soups, or could replace the chicken stock in the souse for the spinach (ideal if the salad is to be served to non-meat eaters). For this salad, after the preliminary soaking slice the mushrooms about 5 mm thick. Reserve until assembly time.

Remove the stalks of the fresh mushrooms and season the caps lightly with salt and pepper. In separate frying pans sauté the field mushrooms and the pine forest mushrooms in a little oil. Drain the mushrooms skin-side down on some kitchen paper and reserve until assembly.

The preparation of the turnips is splendidly described in Shizuo Tsuji's book (see below). The essential method is to peel the turnips and slice off the tops to expose the maximum surface area. With a very sharp knife, cross-score the turnips, ensuring that each cut does not go right through. Leave to soak in salted water for 20 minutes and then remove each turnip and squeeze out the liquid. Place the squeezed turnips in a bowl and cover with rice vinegar. Refrigerate and leave for at least 1 day before using. They will keep for a week.

Roast the hazelnuts in a hot oven until golden. Rub off the skins in a clean cloth. Reserve.

TO COOK THE NOODLES   Buckwheat noodles, which are brownish or café-au-lait in colour, are available in Japanese marts and other speciality food shops. They are very popular in Japan and are eaten either in soup or chilled and marinated. Given the current popularity of cold pasta salads, I find it interesting to expand the range of noodles one works with. The magnificent work on Japanese cookery *Japanese Cooking: A Simple Art*, by Shizuo Tsuji, gives a recipe for making one's own soba, but I have found the commercial variety quite satisfactory.[+]

Bring a large pot of unsalted water to the boil and drop in the buckwheat noodles. Stir to prevent them sticking and taste after 4 minutes' boiling. They should be cooked a little more than the usual *al dente* recommended for European pasta. Rinse under cold running water, swishing the noodles well to remove any surface starch, then drain in a colander. Set aside until assembly time.

[+] Shiitake mushrooms are grown both in Australia and in New Zealand and are fairly widely available fresh. However, the flavour and aroma of the fresh variety do not compare with the very best dried mushrooms, still imported from Hong Kong. The bigger the better. Once soaked and cooked, these mushrooms are extremely meaty and very substantial. Each mushroom will yield 6–8 slices.

TO ASSEMBLE THE SALAD   Choose large, plain plates. Be as artistic as you like in arranging the various ingredients. I would coil some buckwheat noodles on the plate, place the cold sautéed field mushrooms and pine forest mushrooms next, then tuck small pieces of the soaked cloud-ear and silver tree fungus around. Squeeze the spinach from its sousing mixture and divide into small mounds for each salad, rather like moss. Take out a marinated and cross-scored turnip, cut into 3 or 4 pieces and then press open the 'petals' and place a small piece of red pepper in the centre of each flower. Scatter the slivered shiitake mushrooms over and roll on some hazelnuts to look like fallen acorns. At the very last minute, mix the sauce ingredients well and ladle some sauce over all. The sauce should be very spicy, so taste it and add more chilli and ginger if it is not sufficiently piquant.

✦ Buckwheat for making soba noodles has been grown in Australia since the 1970s. New South Wales is the largest buckwheat-producing state in Australia. Buckwheat growing commenced in Tasmania in 1991, and Tasmania's entire crop is exported to Japan so that Japanese noodle lovers can enjoy freshly made soba even when the crop is out of season there. There is also a noodle factory near Ballarat, Victoria, called Hakubaku, which has been in operation for a few years. They make Japanese-style dried noodles (soba, udon, somen, hiyamugi) from organic buckwheat sourced from around Australia, and sell to both the local and export markets.

Demi-glace

Throughout the book I have mentioned stocks, and frequently I have specified demi-glace, or reduced veal stock. Demi-glace is an indispensable resource in a good restaurant kitchen. However, it is difficult to create at home without quite a bit of planning. Basically, it is a well-made stock that is reduced in order to concentrate its flavour. The need to reduce the stock by at least eight times means that to achieve 1 litre you must begin with at least 8 litres of strained, fat-free stock. It should be stressed at once that, because of its concentration, only small amounts of demi-glace are needed in recipes. It is always combined with something – either a lump of butter or butter blended with herbs or bone marrow, or with a separately made reduction of red or white wine and shallots, or shallots, mustard and cognac – used to enrich and strengthen pan glazings, braising juices or any number of other more specific additions. In a domestic situation one would never need to use more than 200 ml or a scant cup for any meal for six people.

Demi-glace is the one thing above all else that deserves prime space in your freezer. If you are serious about your cooking and have managed to organise pots of sufficient size, and good meaty bones and knuckles, make as much as you can. Not a drop should ever be wasted.

The following is the method we use, with two differences. As we make really enormous quantities that commence in a 50-litre stainless steel boiler and that we reduce by at least fifteen times, we do not roast the bones. The concentration by reduction gives us all the colour we need. The other difference is that after we draw off the first stock and commence its reduction, we make a *remouillage* in the initial stockpot. We refill the pot with clean water and add fresh vegetables. I learnt this trick during my week at Restaurant Troisgros in Roanne, France, in 1982. This second stock is not as good as the first, but is quite satisfactory for such tasks as an initial poaching of tripe before it is stuffed, or to use in place of water to make a richer beefsteak and kidney pie, or indeed to incorporate into many different dinners for the staff. (We all eat together at six o'clock before service.)

I have avoided being specific about quantities. Remember! Start as large as you can. Simmer overnight if you can trust your simmer plate to keep the liquid just murmuring. If not, simmer for at least six hours, preferably eight to ten. Skim well before adding the vegetables.

Cool the final reduction as rapidly as possible. When cold, divide into cupfuls and pour into containers, leaving a little room for expansion. Label, date and freeze.

To thaw, either place the container on a plate in the refrigerator overnight or, as mentioned in 'To freeze or not to freeze' (page 146), if it is needed urgently, place the frozen demi-glace directly in a pan with a little water and heat gently until the iceblock melts. Give it a good boil and a final skim of any impurities.

SPECIAL NOTE: You will be unable to lift the pot once it has its liquid and bones in it. Therefore, it must be in position on the stove before you add the liquid and you will have to decant or, rather, ladle the stock into your next receptacle to commence the reduction as the hot stockpot will similarly be far too heavy for you to try and pour the liquid through a strainer.

BONES

veal shin bones, cracked and sawn
beef shin bones, cracked and sawn (save the bones after you have extracted
    marrow on another occasion)
any other veal bones

You will need enough bones to come halfway up your stockpot when rammed down hard. If your butcher has no extra veal bones, sigh and purchase 3 veal knuckles and have them sawn into pieces. Believe it or not, butchers often find bones a nuisance and have waste-management companies come to remove them in large quantities. If you are planning to build stock-making into your life, place a weekly or fortnightly order for bones.

MEAT SCRAPS

pieces of skin, gristle, sinew etc. (saved from trimming meat for a stew or braise)
skinny ends of oxtail

GELATINOUS INGREDIENTS (SELECT FROM)

a veal knuckle
3–4 fresh pig's trotters
a piece of pork rind
chicken feet, washed thoroughly

onions, unpeeled and quartered
carrots, washed and sliced
celery (not too much), washed and sliced
leeks, washed and sliced
mushroom trimmings
onion peelings (collected during the day or the day before)

AROMATICS

1 whole head of garlic, sliced in half crosswise (optional, or use less garlic)
1 bay leaf
parsley stalks
fresh thyme

EXTRAS

white wine or *vinegar to deglaze the roasting pan*
several spoonfuls of tomato paste (optional)
a few juicy tomatoes (optional)

Roast the bones, turning to prevent any from catching. Tip away any fat and put the bones into the stockpot. Deglaze the roasting dish with a little wine or vinegar and tip the juices into the pot. Place the pot on the stove. Add cold water to cover the bones and bring slowly to the boil. Skim off all scum. When boiling point is reached, skim again and add 2 cups of cold water. This will cause more scum to be released. Skim this and wait for boiling point again. Adjust the heat to a medium simmer. Tip in all the meat scraps, vegetables and aromatics and your choice of gelatinous ingredients, plus the tomato paste and tomatoes, if using. Push down firmly. There should be sufficient to fill the pot to three-quarters full. Add extra water to fill the stockpot to just below the rim. When the stock reboils, skim and adjust the heat to the lowest possible simmer.

After 6 hours minimum and preferably 8–10 hours, ladle off the stock through a strainer into a clean pan that is already in position on the stovetop, alongside the stockpot. After you have ladled all the stock you can easily retrieve, bucket out the larger bits of debris until the pot is light enough for you to lift.

Have a strainer placed over a bucket. Tip the stockpot to retrieve the rest of the stock and add it to the reduction pan. At this point you have created a good veal stock that can be used without any reduction to braise dishes, make a velouté sauce, replace water in any stew or soup, cook a pilaf of rice, or hundreds of other uses. To form an adequate base on an unthickened sauce, you must now reduce the veal stock to demi-glace.

Bring the strained stock to the boil, then skim. Adjust the heat to achieve a strong simmer, but not so strong that the stock will boil over. Leave until reduced by three-quarters, i.e. if you have 4 litres of strained stock you will stop the process when you have 1 litre of demi-glace. Skim from time to time while the stock is reducing. Strain the final sauce through a fine strainer, cool it quickly and then store it.

The actual attention needed is minimal, but the time taken is considerable, and there should be lots of ingredients. A fine demi-glace is a very costly sauce.

Breads

At Stephanie's we make all the breads served. We offer diners a choice of three varieties of bread roll, variously twisted, plaited or rolled and made from a variety of flours and seeds. In addition to the dinner rolls, from time to time there are dishes that seem to need some special bread.

We make crusty sourdough loaves with floured tops to slice into big oval slices that are brushed with butter and grilled to accompany our salad of raw fish petals (page 31) or a rich pigeon mousse. The very special flavour of our Finnish pumpernickel is excellent with a salad of smoked fish or a platter of golden sprats. By adding finely ground sesame seeds to a simple basic dough made from unbleached baker's flour, we add a subtle nuttiness to the bread cases that we fill with an assortment of fresh mushrooms.

We also make a walnut bread to accompany the cheese; and a recent appetiser was a tiny pot of smoked and potted tongue accompanied by a toasted slice of bacon bread that had been baked in small loaf tins.

We always use instant dried yeast, which has the advantage that it can be mixed directly into the dry ingredients. This, of course, means that the basic mixes can be weighed out early in the day and the liquid added much later in order to time the rising to suit kitchen logistics of space and staff. We use an electric mixer fitted with a dough hook.

Our flour bin contains strong plain flour (sold as pizza flour), unbleached baker's flour, stone-ground rye flour, stone-ground wholemeal flour, unprocessed bran, buckwheat flour and cornmeal. Smaller containers hold poppyseeds, sesame seeds, cracked wheat, linseed, caraway seeds, brown rice and sea-salt flakes.

Other frequently used ingredients are buttermilk, ricotta cheese, unsalted butter and milk. Nuts, dried fruits and other special ingredients are ordered as required for special festive breads.

Sourdough starter

350 g unbleached baker's flour
1½ teaspoons instant dried yeast
1½ teaspoons salt
3 teaspoons olive oil
200 ml water

Mix the first 4 ingredients together. Add the water and knead until smooth and elastic. Place the dough in a bowl and cover loosely with a damp cloth. Place in a warm spot and leave for 3 days. Redampen the cloth each day. At the end of this time the dough should have a sourish smell rather like beer. This is the starter dough. Simply use this to bake your bread as in the following recipe.

Each time you make a batch of bread, divide the dough into 3 parts. Return 1 part to a bowl, cover with a damp cloth that is changed each day, and allow the dough to ripen further. If you don't wish to use the dough after 3 days, give it a quick knead and refrigerate it. Let the starter dough stand at room temperature for 12 hours before you use it.

Country-style crusty bread

800 g unbleached baker's flour
200 g wholemeal flour
1 tablespoon instant dried yeast
1 tablespoon salt
2 tablespoons olive oil
2 tablespoons unprocessed bran
600 ml water
sourdough starter (see above)

Using an electric mixer with a dough hook, mix all the ingredients and knead in the machine until the dough is smooth and not sticky. Divide into 3 parts. Return 1 part to the bowl as the starter dough for a new batch of bread in 3 days' time. Allow the rest of the dough to rise until double in size. Knock down and knead for 1–2 minutes. Let the dough rise again, about 45 minutes.

Form into 2 loaves like fat cigars. Place each loaf on a liberally floured clean cloth. Preheat the oven to 220°C. Allow the loaves to rise for 30 minutes, when they should have doubled in size again. Roll gently from the cloths onto a preheated heavy oven tray. Bake for about 20 minutes. Turn over for the last 4–5 minutes. Tap the base of each loaf and remove if it sounds hollow. Cool the loaves on their tray.

If the loaves are to make crusty toast, they are best used when 1 day old.

You can substitute different flours for different flavours and textures. For example, if you use a portion of rye flour, the recipe will make an ideal bread to serve with oysters.

Finnish pumpernickel[+]

¾ cup dark corn syrup
3 teaspoons finely grated orange zest
1 tablespoon salt
650 ml buttermilk
150 ml water
700 g rye flour
700 g unbleached baker's flour
1 tablespoon instant dried yeast
extra 2 tablespoons corn syrup for glaze

Warm the ¾ cup of corn syrup with the orange zest and salt, then combine with the buttermilk and water and allow to cool. Mix the flours with the yeast. Add the buttermilk/corn syrup mixture to the flours and knead until a smooth dough. Shape into a ball and place in a lightly greased bowl to double in size, approximately 1½ hours.

Punch the bread down and shape into 2 loaves about 25 cm long. Allow to rise again until nearly double in size. Preheat the oven to 200°C.

Mix the extra corn syrup with 3 tablespoons of warm water and brush this glaze over the bread. Bake for approximately 20–25 minutes, brushing with the glaze every 10 minutes. Cool on a rack.

This bread should be made a day ahead or at least the morning of the party, not that afternoon. It is best sliced thinly.

[+] This is a lovely bread that I had almost forgotten until I came back to this book. If your supermarket does not stock buttermilk, you can use the same quantity of regular milk and add the juice of 1 lemon.

Bacon bread

250 g bacon
1½ cups milk
¾ cup water
⅓ cup reserved bacon fat
900 g unbleached baker's flour
2 tablespoons sugar
1 tablespoon instant dried yeast
2 teaspoons salt
1 egg
egg wash (1 egg mixed with a pinch of salt)

Chop the bacon and fry gently until crisp. Reserve all the fat. Heat the milk, water and ⅓ cup of reserved bacon fat to lukewarm. (If the bacon was very lean, make up the quantity of fat with a little extra water.)

Mix together the flour, sugar, yeast and salt. Chop the bacon finely and add to the flour mixture. Pour in the warm liquid and beat for 2–4 minutes to a smooth batter. Add the egg and, if necessary, a little extra flour to make a soft dough. Knead well, place into a floured bowl and allow to double in size.

Knock down and divide into greased bread tins. Cover with a cloth and allow to rise to fill the tins. (This quantity will make enough for 3 × 500 g tins.)

When the bread has risen to the top of the tins, brush lightly with egg wash and bake in a preheated oven for approximately 25 minutes at 200°C. Carefully turn the loaves out of the tins and return the bread to the oven for a few minutes to brown all sides and further crisp the crust. Cool on a rack.

Stephanie's walnut bread

350 g unbleached baker's flour
150 g rye flour
3 teaspoons instant dried yeast
3 teaspoons salt
2 eggs
250 ml water
125 g walnuts, roughly chopped
1 egg yolk beaten with 1 tablespoon water and a pinch of salt, as a glaze

Mix the flours, yeast, salt and eggs. Add the water and knead well. Place in an oiled bowl and let rise until double in size. Punch down and spread the dough on your workbench. Scatter over the chopped nuts and work them into the dough. Divide the dough in half and let it rise again until double in size.

Shape into 2 round loaves and place on greased baking sheets. Preheat the oven to 200°C. Allow the loaves to rise well. Brush with the glaze and bake for 30–35 minutes. Cool on a rack.

Glossary

ABALONE MUSHROOM (OYSTER MUSHROOM)   Variety of cultivated mushroom that resembles *pleurottes* in France.

AMUSE-GUEULE   An appetiser, to tickle your fancy.

BAGNA CAUDA   Hot anchovy dip for vegetables; an Italian dish of oil, butter, garlic and chopped anchovies.

BOCCONCINI   Literally 'a small mouthful' – here it refers to a fresh, small mozzarella cheese sold dripping and stored in its whey.

BOUILLON   Broth; a clear, savoury liquid obtained from meat, bones and vegetables, properly seasoned and unclarified. Used as the base of dishes without significant reduction, e.g. pot-au-feu.

CAUL FAT   Lacy fat that lines the stomach of a pig. Used as a self-basting wrapping for roasts, to line terrines or for small parcels of stuffing to be fried or grilled (crépinettes).

CEVICHE   South American dish of raw fish cured with lime or lemon.

COCKSCOMBS   Available if you ask nicely from a poultry processor (you risk receiving heads and all). Soak overnight to remove blood, simmer in light stock until tender and then sauté. They spit when cooking.

CONCASSÉ   From the French *concasser*, meaning to break or crush. Traditional tomato preparation: peel, squeeze gently to remove the seeds and chop the flesh into small pieces. Helps tomatoes melt evenly into a sauce.

CORIANDER   A herb whose leaves are used a lot in Asian cooking. They are very powerful and not enjoyed by everyone. The dried seeds have a quite different, spicy flavour – a little like dried citrus peel.[+]

CORN SALAD   Also known as *mâche* and lamb's lettuce. Grows in autumn and winter. There are several varieties. It grows in a flat rosette shape with dark green, soft, rounded leaves.

[+] This herb, important in Middle Eastern, Mexican and Asian cookery, has become mainstream and is now to be found in almost every fruit and vegetable shop.

CLOUD-EAR FUNGUS   Chinese dried fungus that swells to enormous proportions when soaked. Has practically no taste, but is a texture food. Silver tree fungus (q.v.) is much more enjoyable, in my opinion.

CRÉPINE   *see* caul fat

DAIKON   The Japanese name for white radish.

FEUILLETÉ   Means 'layered'. *Millefeuille* means 'a thousand layers'. A popular way to describe a dish presented between two pieces of cooked puff pastry.

FRISÉE   Common name in France for a wide variety of salads that have frizzy, curled edges to their leaves. They tend to be rather bitter.

FROMAGE FERMIER   Farm cheese. Implies a fresh, unprocessed cheese made from cow's, goat's or ewe's milk.

FUMET   Means 'essence', 'scent'. In culinary terms it usually refers to *fumet de poisson*, or fish stock.

GLACE DE VOLAILLE   Poultry stock heavily reduced until it becomes a dark, gluey paste. Tiny quantities are added to stews, soups or sauces. Keeps indefinitely under refrigeration.

HOG CASINGS   Sausage skins; obtainable from your butcher. They are often sold salted and need to be soaked in cold water before use.

JUS   Means 'juice'. A sauce obtained from cooking juices, perhaps boosted with a little wine or flavouring; not a complex, separately made sauce.

KASSERI   Hard Greek cheese, cream in colour, made from ewe's milk.

KOMBU   Japanese dried seaweed. Needs to be soaked for 30 minutes in warm water before use. Cut into pieces with scissors.

MARMELADE   French term to denote the correct degree of reduction before building a sauce with butter or reduced stock. The shallot/onion and vinegar or wine is moist but no longer liquid.

MENU DÉGUSTATION   Common in starred restaurants in France. The chef offers a selection of small courses ideally designed to present the diner with a balanced meal, but also to enable him/her to sample the widest variety of specialities. Often such meals are unbalanced and one eats too much.

MOREL MUSHROOMS   Cone-shaped, with a honeycomb texture. The French variety arrives dried and is very expensive but has a marvellous aroma and texture. Our own morel mushrooms have to be gathered from secret places by a few knowing enthusiasts. They have an excellent flavour, but lack perfume. They have a very short season in Victoria: the first three weeks of September.

NAM PLA   Fermented fish sauce used in South-East Asian cookery as universally as soy sauce is used in Chinese cookery.

NORI   Japanese dried and pressed seaweed, sold in sheets. Nori is passed over a flame quickly to toast and crisp it, and is either crumbled onto a salad or used as a wrapper for vinegared rice to make sushi.

PANCETTA   Italian pork product; pork belly that is salted (and sometimes has hot chilli added) and sometimes rolled.

PINE FOREST MUSHROOMS   Abundant in Victoria in autumn. Until very recently, no one bothered to cook them. They are closely related to the *sanguines* of the south of France. Magnificent when sautéed with oil, garlic and parsley.

PLUCHES   Each little leaf of a herb, such as parsley or chervil, where the head of each stem is made up of lots of individual little pieces.

RADICCHIO   Italian red-leafed lettuce. It is sometimes quite bitter. There are many varieties, and not all have red leaves.

REMOUILLAGE   Means 'to remoisten' and refers to the practice of remoistening bones and vegetables in the stockpot, adding some fresh vegetables and proceeding to a second, lighter stock.

RENNET   Substance obtained from the lining of calves' stomachs, used as the curdling agent in much cheesemaking. Can be obtained as plain junket tablets or from a cheese manufacturer in a far more concentrated liquid form.

ROCKET   Peppery salad vegetable that grows easily. Best picked when quite young, when the leaves are tender and not too strong. This salad is best used in combination with others or as a garnish. Also known as arugula and roquette.

SALMIS   Usually applied to game birds, but can be equally used for ducks etc. The meat is part-roasted and then finished in a special, separately made sauce. Frequently the legs of a game bird are cooked in this manner while the breast is removed and served rare.

SAUERBRATEN   German dish of a joint of beef previously marinated with vinegar and other ingredients and then braised.

SHALLOT   Grows in clumps like garlic; milder than onions – they are not spring onions. We have a variety of shallot available known as a golden shallot.✢

SHIITAKE MUSHROOMS   Highly prized in Japanese and Chinese cooking, they need to be soaked before use and the tough stem discarded.✦

SILVER TREE FUNGUS   One of the most versatile of the Chinese dried fungi, crunchy and not too enormous after soaking. Can be dropped into soups or sautéed. *See also* cloud-ear fungus.

STAR ANISE   Powerful Asian spice with an aniseed flavour; a little goes a long way. Available in all Asian markets.

SZECHUAN PEPPERCORN   Another powerful Asian spice available in Asian

---

✢ We can now buy pinkish-grey shallots as well as golden shallots. The pinkish-grey ones are milder in flavour than the golden ones. The situation is confused by shallots being sold as 'eschallots' in New South Wales.

✦ Both fresh and dried shiitake mushrooms are available. The dried ones are more highly regarded by Asian cooks.

markets. The peppercorns are often roasted and then crushed to release more of their aroma.

TRUFFLE   Naturally occurring French and Italian fungus that commands exorbitant prices. I have never tasted a fresh truffle but have tasted first-cooking truffles. They are canned and processed at a lower temperature and for a shorter time than the truffles we obtain in Australia. The difference in flavour and texture is considerable. Canned truffle juice, however, does have lots of flavour.✢

WASABI   Japanese green horseradish, sold in tins as a green powder. It must be mixed to a paste with a little water and is very strong. Indispensable with sushi and sashimi (Japanese raw fish).✦

✢ I have written more about truffle juice and truffles on page 186. The very valuable French black truffle, *Tuber melanosporum*, and the even more valuable white truffle found in Piedmont in Italy, *Tuber magnotum*, are gastronomic luxuries and most of us will taste them rarely, if at all. I have described my adventures with *Tuber melanosporum* in *Cooking & Travelling in South-West France*.

✦ This root vegetable is related to horseradish and is grated to accompany raw fish in Japanese cuisine. It has a wonderfully pungent flavour and is a clear bright green. It is now being grown experimentally in Tasmania and New Zealand. The powder in tins is in fact mustard powder mixed with dried horseradish and coloured green. It was not until I visited Japan in 1996 that I tasted the real thing. Many Japanese buy the fake stuff, too, as the real product remains very expensive.

Select bibliography

Barca, Margaret, *Making Your Own Cheese and Other Dairy Products*, Melbourne, Nelson, 1978.

Brown, Marion, *Pickles and Preserves*, New York, Avenel Books, 1955.

Burchett, Mary, *Through My Kitchen Door*, Melbourne, Georgian House, 1960.

Chapel, Alain, *La Cuisine c'est beaucoup plus que des recettes*, Paris, Robert Laffont, 1980.

Conran, Caroline (ed.), *The Nouvelle Cuisine of Jean and Pierre Troisgros*, London, Macmillan, 1980.

Cribb, A. B. and J. W., *Wild Food in Australia*, Sydney, Collins, 1974.

Dahlen, Martha, and Phillips, Karen, *A Guide to Chinese Market Vegetables*, Hong Kong, South Morning Post, 1980.

—— *A Further Guide to Chinese Market Vegetables*, Hong Kong, South Morning Post, 1981.

David, Elizabeth, *French Country Cooking*, Harmondsworth, Penguin, 1959.

—— *Mediterranean Food*, 2nd rev. edn, Harmondsworth, Penguin, 1965.

—— *Summer Cooking*, rev. edn, Harmondsworth, Penguin, 1965.

—— *French Provincial Cooking*, 2nd rev. edn, London, Michael Joseph, 1965.

—— *Italian Food*, Harmondsworth, Penguin, 1969.

—— *Spices, Salt and Aromatics in the English Kitchen*, Penguin, 1970.

Grigson, Jane, *Food with the Famous*, Harmondsworth, Penguin, 1973.

—— *Good Things*, Harmondsworth, Penguin, 1973.

—— *Vegetable Book*, New York, Atheneum, 1979.

—— *Fruit Book*, Harmondsworth, Penguin, 1983.

Holuigue, Diane, *The French Kitchen*, Sydney, Methuen, 1983.

Kamman, Madeleine, *When French Women Cook*, New York, Atheneum, 1982.

Kuo, Irene, *The Key to Chinese Cooking*, Melbourne, Nelson, 1977.

Larkcom, Joy, *The Salad Garden*, Sydney, Doubleday, 1984.

Olney, Richard, *The French Menu Cookbook*, Glasgow, Collins, 1975.

—— *Simple French Food*, New York, Atheneum, 1980.

Penton, Anne, *Customs and Cookery in the Périgord and Quercy*, Newton Abbot, David & Charles, 1973.

Sing, Phia, *Traditional Recipes of Laos*, ed. Alan and Jennifer Davidson, London, Prospect Books, 1981.

Time-Life International, *The Good Cook Series: Offal* and other titles, 1981.

Tsuji, Shizuo, *Japanese Cooking: A Simple Art*, Tokyo/New York, Kodansha International, 1980.

Index

257

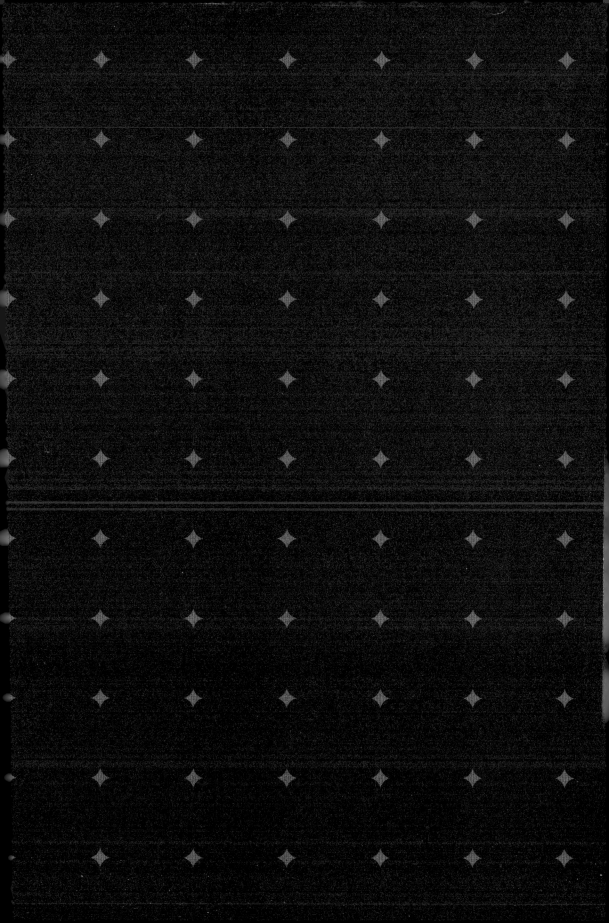

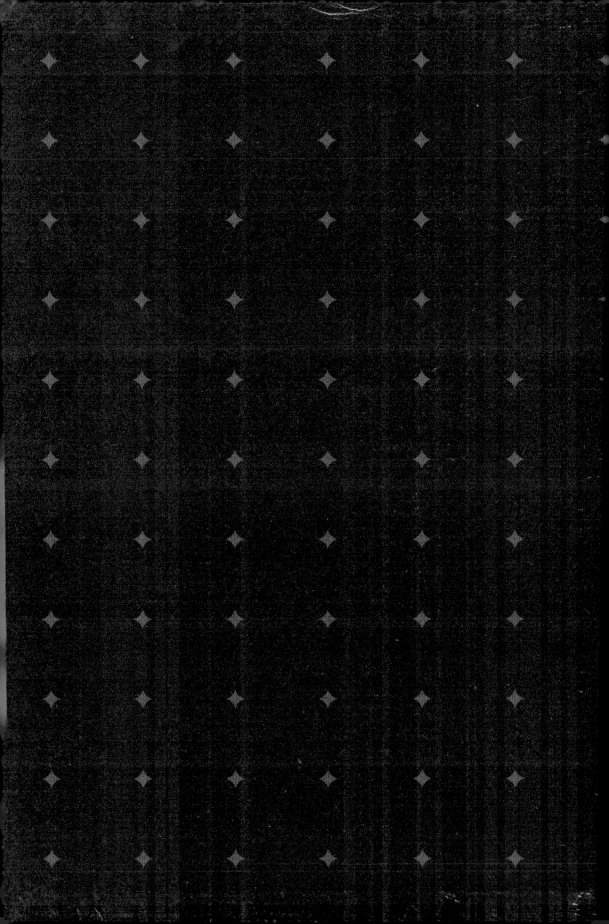